FIREFIGHTING

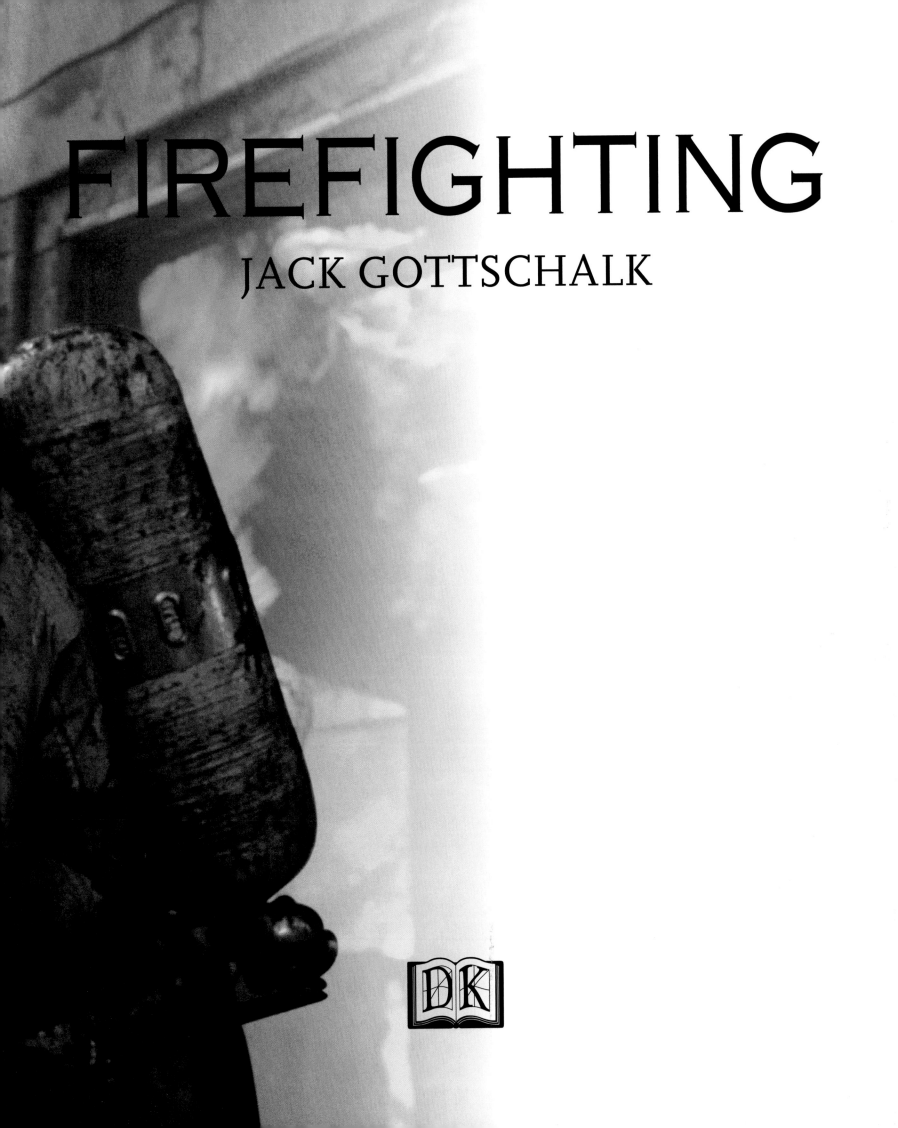

FIREFIGHTING

JACK GOTTSCHALK

DK

LONDON, NEW YORK, MUNICH,
MELBOURNE, and DELHI

Project Editor and Contributing Writer Barbara Berger
Senior Art Editor Michelle Baxter
Creative Director Tina Vaughan
Project Director Valerie Buckingham
Jacket Art Director Dirk Kaufman
Publisher Chuck Lang
Production Manager Chris Avgherinos
Contributing Writers Jennifer Williams, Jill Hamilton,
Madeline Farbman, Lucas Mansell, and Nancy Burke
Contributing Designers Matt Llewellyn, Vince Vendetti,
Gus Yoo, Megan Clayton, and Mandy Earey
DTP Designer Milos Orlovic
Picture Researcher Tracy Armstead
Research Assistant Lisa Cupido
Design Assistant Rynjin Song

The author, Jack Gottschalk would like to dedicate this book
to Mom and Misty.

First American Edition, 2002
00 01 02 03 04 05 10 9 8 7 6 5 4 3 2 1

Published in the United States
by DK Publishing, Inc.
375 Hudson Street
New York, New York 10014

DK Publishing offers special discounts for bulk purchases for sales
promotions or premiums. Specific, large-quantity needs can be met
with special editions, including personalized covers, excerpts of
existing guides, and corporate imprints. For more information,
contact Special Markets Department, DK Publishing, Inc.,
375 Hudson Street, New York, NY 10014 Fax: 212-689-5254.

Library of Congress Cataloging-in-Publication Data

Gottschalk, Jack
    Firefighting / Jack Gottschalk
        p. cm.
    ISBN 0-7894-8909-0
    1. Fire extinction. 2. Fires. I. Title: Firefighting. II. Title.

TH9148 .G68 2002
628.9'25--dc21

A CIP catalog record for this book is available from the British Library
UK ISBN 0 7513 4888 0

Reproduced by Colourscan, Singapore
Printed in the United States by
R. R. Donnelley & Sons, Willard, Ohio

see our complete product line at
www.dk.com

CONTENTS

INTRODUCTION

FIRES ARE AS OLD AS THE EARTH ITSELF. They had long burned out of control over immense areas, but when early man first sniffed the air and smelled smoke, the opening page in the history of fire was written.

Both the problems and benefits of fire quickly became evident, and that was particularly true when the cave dwellers became house dwellers. Wooden walls and grass roofs, combined with ever-present cooking and heating fires, were a bad combination. A high wind, a spark, an overturned pot with hot fats, were the recipe for murderous fires. While it can be assumed that some early "firefighter" threw water on the flames, it can be equally assumed that, in most cases, the effort was unsuccessful.

LEATHER FIRE BUCKET
Usually kept filled with sand, which was used initially, then refilled with water. Every home and shop in the Middle Ages was required to have one.

As civilization expanded, fire became an increasing concern because of the obvious threat to life and property. Interestingly, while most of the fires of early civilization were caused by accidents or nature (particularly lightning), the first urban fires of historical importance were probably the products of arson. Though in rural terms, arson has long been around in the form of slash-and-burn agriculture.

URBAN RENEWAL BY FIRE

Historians today believe that when Lugdunum (now Lyons, France) was a Roman colonial capital in AD 59, it did not meet desired appearances and thus, was deliberately set ablaze. The fact that Roman soldiers did nothing to stop the flames is of particular note given the interest of the Romans in fire prevention and control.

PIKE
Modern-day descendant of the ancient pike used to tear down the walls of burning structures, often to create firebreaks. This is the "hook" of hook-and-ladder companies.

Very early in its history, Rome had established a rudimentary fire code and a firefighting organization (called a *vigile*) comprised of soldiers and slaves. Buckets of water, handheld syringes (giant water squirters) for water delivery, pikes to tear down walls, and short ladders were the firefighting tools. Whatever lessons were learned by the Romans about fighting fires (or setting them) as a result of the flames at Lugdunum, only five, short years later were applied to Rome itself.

BUST OF NERO, c. AD 54–68
Legendary emperor and fiddle-player (in reality, he sang, as the fiddle had not yet been invented), Nero used fire to rearrange Rome more to his liking.

Rome had suffered many large fires before the huge one of AD 64 that burned for days and probably killed hundreds. It also resulted in major changes to the city's map; changes that exactly fit the desires of Emperor Nero.

GREAT FIRE OF LONDON, 1666
This 19th-century engraving depicts the ravaging inferno known as the Great Fire of London. A total of 436 acres (176 ha) within and without the city walls were reduced to ashes. At the time, many of the structures were of wood with thatched roofs and no efforts were made to secure combustible materials from fire. For many years the scars remained, and debtor's prisons were packed by those financially ruined by the blaze. Many modern systems, such as insurance and regular firefighting brigades, came about as a result.

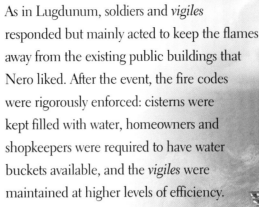

As in Lugdunum, soldiers and *vigiles* responded but mainly acted to keep the flames away from the existing public buildings that Nero liked. After the event, the fire codes were rigorously enforced: cisterns were kept filled with water, homeowners and shopkeepers were required to have water buckets available, and the *vigiles* were maintained at higher levels of efficiency.

BELLS, FIREWALLS, AND GUNPOWDER

As civilization plunged into the Dark Ages and then lurched forward into the Renaissance, smoke rose from hundreds of villages and cities because centralized, organized firefighting was largely as absent as centralized, organized rule.

There was little done to prevent or stop the flames. Except for the continued use of the tools already developed by the Romans, the best ideas came from William the Conqueror and Richard I in England. William ordered that bells be sounded in case of fire, an act that gave the bell a permanent place in firefighting annals. Likewise, Richard I decreed that fire-resistant walls be built (fire walls) to impede the spread of fire.

During this general time frame in England, London virtually burned to the ground in 798, 982, and 1212. York and Carlisle did, too, as did Nantes, France, and Venice, Italy in 1106, Dresden, Germany in 1491, Oslo, Norway in 1624, Copenhagen, Denmark in 1728, and Stockholm, Sweden in 1751. Oslo was so ravaged that it was totally razed and moved 20 miles to its present site. Constantinople, Turkey was almost constantly on fire, with conflagrations taking place in 1750, 1756, 1761, 1763, 1765, 1767, 1782, and 1784.

Despite the prominence of these conflagrations, the fire that marked what is considered to be the first in modern history occurred in London, England in 1666.

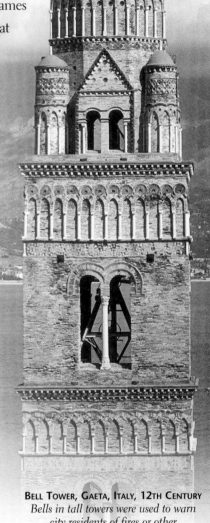

BELL TOWER, GAETA, ITALY, 12TH CENTURY
Bells in tall towers were used to warn city residents of fires or other emergencies. If a fire broke out, a citizen would run to the tower and start ringing the bell to alert others to the danger.

It is memorable for the facts that the flames killed the rats, which spread the Black Plague, and it witnessed the first use of gunpowder to create firebreaks. In addition, insurance companies now came into existence to provide financial protection from future fires and to help prevent and fight fires for those who could afford the insurance.

London's firefighters did have some extra tools in addition to those that had been used by the Roman *vigiles*. Individual, hollowed-out logs were kept filled with water that could be accessed by drilling holes into them. In later years, they would be outfitted with precut holes and plugged until needed with removable "fireplugs," while in Colonial America networks of hollow logs would even be used as piping. The Londoners' handheld syringes were also much larger and were hauled to fire scenes, where they were then filled by bucket brigades.

HOLLOW LOG
Used as early "piping" in Colonial America, the wooden water mains would be drilled into and breached by the fire brigade. When finished, plugs would be inserted into the holes.

LEATHER HOSES, INSURANCE, AND FIRE MARKS

Gradually, other technological developments occurred. A few years after the Great Fire of London, leather hoses went into use as replacements for water buckets. Hoses allowed firefighters to fight fires aggressively inside buildings for the first time. Philadelphia, in 1803, was the first American city to use leather fire hoses.

Meanwhile, English-made fire engines and the need for fire prevention rapidly became part of the North American scene. By 1709, most of the larger cities in the English colonies in America had imported pumpers that, as in England, were pulled by hand to a fire and, once there, required manual labor in order to operate the pump mechanism. It was a very labor-intensive operation.

Water-main distribution systems were widely in use by 1800, and the first underground pipes were functioning in many cities by 1810. Fire insurance, which initially came prominently onto the scene after the Great Fire of London, rapidly took hold in Colonial America. Benjamin Franklin was a founder of one of the first Colonial insurance companies, starting a firm in Philadelphia in 1752. In both Great Britain and America, the insurance companies, having obvious financial motives, provided help in fire department organization, fire safety and prevention, and improved technology.

Indeed, the insurance carrier interest in Great Britain led to the creation of the Edinburgh Fire Brigade, which was headed by James Braidwood and who set the British firefighting standard in terms of training and organization. After his death in 1861, Braidwood was succeeded by Eyre Massey Shaw, who held office until 1891 and was chiefly responsible for creating the London Fire Brigade.

HAND-DRAWN, MANUAL PUMPER
Hand-drawn pumpers required many men to transport and operate. Pumper units were separate from hook-and-ladder companies, which did rescue and clearing work and the pulling down of burning structures. Hand-drawn pumpers were used in Holland as early as the mid-17th century. They were replaced in the West by horse-drawn pumpers in the 1820s.

In both Great Britain and Colonial America, the fire mark was tied to insurance. The mark was a metal plate bearing the name of an insurance company and was attached to the front of a building covered by that carrier. Fire patrols, financed by the insurance companies, would respond to and fight only those fires in buildings on which their company provided coverage.

Despite better technology, major urban fires were common well into the nineteenth century, mostly because of wooden construction. New York City burned in 1776, 1835, and 1845. The 1835 conflagration (which destroyed several banks and was one cause of the 1837 financial crisis) was also notable because fire hydrants, invented by a New York fireman named George Smith, were used as replacements for the hollow-log plugs. In 1848, hydrants were installed in London. Another important firefighting tool, the soda-acid fire extinguisher, was added to the suppression arsenal around 1837.

On both sides of the Atlantic, wherever major fires took place during the first half of the nineteenth century, including

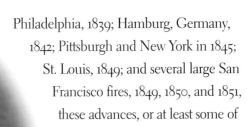

CAPTAIN EYRE MASSEY SHAW
Chief organizer of the London Fire Brigade. He succeeded James Braidwood as head in 1861 and was an outspoken public proponent of fire safety.

Philadelphia, 1839; Hamburg, Germany, 1842; Pittsburgh and New York in 1845; St. Louis, 1849; and several large San Francisco fires, 1849, 1850, and 1851, these advances, or at least some of them, proved their value.

Even the ancient problem of "response delay," long reliant on the bell tower or word of mouth, was being addressed. In 1851, the corner firebox, based on a telegraph system, was functioning in most American cities and within a few years it was operational in Great Britain as well.

CONFLAGRATIONS AND WARS

More comprehensive training, better alarm systems, sprinklers, fire-resistant construction, larger and heavier horse-drawn hose carts, steam pumpers, and ladder trucks (which carried extension ladders for both rescue and water distribution on upper floors), were major additions to firefighting efforts as the nineteenth century gave way to the twentieth.

Despite these improvements, the fires that did take place were often far more devastating. The Tooley Street fire in London during 1861 (in which James Braidwood died) was one of those. Others included the New York City Draft Riot fires of 1863; the blazes of Atlanta, Georgia, Richmond, Virginia, and Columbia, South Carolina, during the Civil War; and of Portland, Maine, in July 1865. By the 1870s, fire equipment was too big

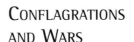

FIRE HYDRANT
In 1802, the first order for modern-style, cast-iron hydrants was placed by the city of Philadelphia with a cannon maker. They have changed little since then.

FIRE MARKS
Though useful as advertising for the fire-insurance company, the primary purpose of these fire marks was to denote which properties were under the protection of which company. Should a property lack a fire mark, it would be allowed to burn by that company's firemen unless the owner wanted to quickly hire the services of a fire brigade. Once a formal postal system was introduced in the mid-1800s and every structure was issued an identifying address, the fire marks were no longer needed and became strictly a promotional item.

Designs were often related to the insurer's location, history, and/or services. Some would even note whether the structure had been rebuilt at the insurer's expense.

WESTMINSTER, LONDON, 1717–1906
Design first used by the House of Tudor.

LONDON ASSURANCE, C. 1720
Heavy, tin design depicting Britannia.

UNION INS., C.1808
"Restored" meant the insurer had paid for rebuilding.

PHILADELPHIA, 1752
B. Franklin's firm would not insure homes near trees.

MUTUAL ASSURANCE COMPANY, 1784
First to insure homes with nearby trees.

1901 LaFrance Horse-drawn Steam Pumper
These more-powerful steam pumpers replaced the hand-drawn, manually operated pumpers in the early 1800s. Both designs were imported into the U.S. from Europe, where they originated. LaFrance was an early American firefighting equipment manufacturer, based in New York, and is still in business today.

and too heavy (steam pumpers could weigh as much as 16,000 pounds, 5,972 kg) to be hand-pulled. Horses were widely employed and gained quick, public adoration. The negative aspects of horses were that they drank gallons of water and ate oats. Also, the words "clean up" took on a new meaning for firefighters.

Legendary fires raged, such as in Chicago in 1871 and Boston a year later. In the latter, the conflagration was the first major blaze to be heralded by a box signal

and also resulted in the first Boston fireboat, purchased in 1873. London's first modern fireboat entered service in 1900.

While fires continued to plague cities in North America—Seattle, 1889; Jacksonville, 1901; Baltimore and Toronto in 1904; San Francisco, 1906; and Atlanta, 1917—advances in equipment also occurred: water towers (vehicles with a long hose pipe and an elevated nozzle to work with hook-and-ladder crews during upper-floor rescue attempts), better hoses, and the beginnings of mechanized vehicles.

Steam-powered Pumper
These pumpers were often highly decorated devices that reflected the pride of the operators. Once on-scene, the mounted steam engine would pump water from the available source and be directed onto the fire via hoses, which arrived separately.

But as history shows, accidents and nature constantly challenge resources. In December 1917, a ship collision caused massive damage in Halifax. San Francisco in 1906 and Tokyo in 1923 suffered gigantic fires on the heels of devastating earthquakes. Meanwhile, by the mid-1920s the horse had been retired in America and Great Britain, replaced by even heavier trucks and engines, powered first by gasoline and later by diesel fuel. Specialized units to fight chemical fires were developed and more protection, such as oxygen tanks, was provided to firefighters.

World War II gave birth to some of the most horrendous fires in history; "firestorms" (coined in 1945 as a result of the bombings) that ravaged London, Dresden, Cologne, and Tokyo.

SELF-CONTAINED BREATHING APPARATUS
As early as 1824 devices were used to aid breathing in smoke-filled areas. Eventually, these became the modern SCBA pictured. Many firemen and rescued owe their lives to this invention.

FIREBOAT
Fire is one of the worst disasters that can happen on a ship. It soon became apparent that every harbor needed specialized vessels capable of fighting a shipboard fire. Some vessels are primarily pumpers, while others, usually smaller and speedier, are more suited for rescue work.

AIRPORT FIRE TRUCK
A common sight at airports the world over, these "crash" trucks are specially designed to deal with the chemicals and fuel common to aircraft. They also have equipment particular to aircraft rescue.

SUPER PUMPERS, SNORKELS, QUINTS, AND QUADS

By the mid-1960s, the super pumper, which was capable of simultaneously pumping water from several hydrants at a rate of 8,000 gallons (30 kl) per minute, was being used in several large U.S. cities. In 1958, the "snorkel" (a truck equipped with a hydraulic lifting arm topped with a platform and a high-pressure hose) was introduced in Chicago and proved extremely useful in both rescue and fire suppression, especially for upper floors. The crash truck, which was specially designed to fight aircraft fires, made its appearance at airports in virtually every major country.

The desire for equipment that could serve multiple purposes (such as combining pumper truck and ladder truck functions) was first satisfied by a British design that went into service in 1934. By the 1960s, fire-vehicle design efforts in both Great Britain and the United States had resulted in the "quad" (a combination ladder and pumper truck) and the "quint," (equipped with hose, deck gun, aerial ladder, some ground ladders, and light rescue equipment). These designs reduced the number of vehicles that had to be purchased and maintained in many departments (large and small) while also conserving human resources.

HAZMAT (hazardous materials) vehicles also made their appearance in recognition of the increasing numbers of incidents involving chemicals and other dangerous materials that were being faced by both firefighters and the general public.

Personal equipment designed to provide increased protection for firefighters was also improved. Better and often specialized protective clothing, the advent of the Personal Alert Safety System (PASS), an infrared light capable of penetrating dense smoke, and much-improved radio communications were some of the major advances. Finally, as a result of the huge 1991 Oakland, California fire, a modern management concept, the Incident Command System, was introduced into the U.S. as a method of command and control at major fire and disaster scenes.

PERSONAL ALERT SAFETY SYSTEM
The PASS device emits a signal when the wearer fails to move after a given period. This lets other firefighters know that the fireman has stopped moving and may need help.

THERMAL VISION SYSTEM
Designed for use within smoke-filled and collapsed areas, these devices allow the user to see the body heat of trapped or buried victims. Also, these can be used to locate hidden fires burning within walls or ceilings. High-tech equipment such as this represents the latest in a long history of firefighting gear.

Writing about fire history is a particularly challenging task because of the desire not to omit fires that were an important part of it. Of course, cities like London, New Orleans, Chicago, San Francisco, Tokyo, Toronto, Boston, Baltimore, and hosts of others were victims of conflagrations. But smaller infernos have had their casualties as well, killing many and causing massive destruction when striking theaters, factories, circuses, forests, hotels, and, of course, homes. Names such as Iroquois Theater, Triangle Shirtwaist, Cocoanut Grove, MGM Grand, Our Lady of the Angels, *General Slocum*, *Morro Castle*, and *Noronic*, as well as strange-sounding forest sites such as Peshtigo and Tillamook, are all part of the fire-history lexicon.

These fires and many others less infamous have killed thousands, with many of the victims being the firefighters themselves. The Albert Embankment and Smithfield Market fires of London; the West 23rd Street fire in New York; the Hackensack fire in New Jersey; the Worcester, Massachusetts fire;

SEPTEMBER 11 AT THE WORLD TRADE CENTER
Despite truly enormous first-responder losses, New York City firemen bravely continued their efforts to fight the flames and conduct search-and-rescue operations within the enormous wreckage of the aftermath of the World Trade Center attack. Many of them lost coworkers, friends, and family that day.

and, most recently, the World Trade Center, where 343 firefighters died along with thousands of innocent civilians, police officers, and other first responders, is a very small list of places where firefighters have perished. From Lugdunum and London to San Francisco and Halifax, from Dresden and Tokyo to the World Trade Center and tomorrow, the one cardinal lesson of a fire is that it is always destructive and often deadly.

FEMALE FIREFIGHTER IN TRAINING
The first-known female firefighter was African-American Molly Williams in 1818 in New York City. From that point on, women have been part of volunteer companies alongside men, wartime fire brigades when civilian men were scarce, and since 1974, as professionals when Americans Judith Livers and Sue Mertens became the world's first urban women firefighters.

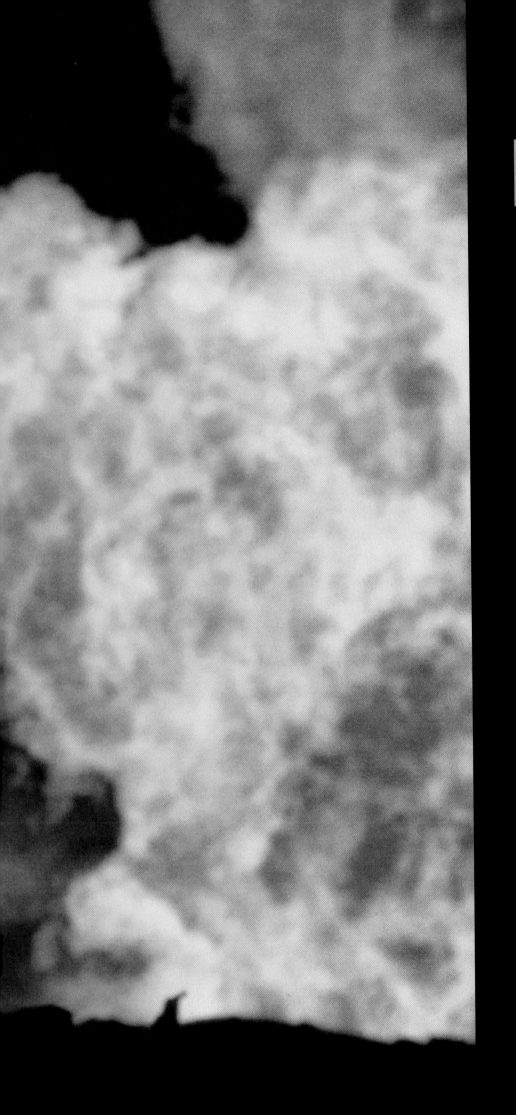

PART ONE

THE GREAT FIRES

GREAT FIRE OF LONDON
——LONDON, ENGLAND, 1666——

THE CITY BURNS DOWN TO THE THAMES
This late 17th-century hand-colored lithograph depicts a blazing inferno burning London down to the waterfront, where flammable products stored on quays and in wharves fueled the flames.

WHEN THE ROMANS LEFT LONDON in the early fifth century after their 400-year occupation of the city, knowledge of Roman fire brigades and pump technology was quickly forgotten and fire once again became a severe problem in London. The constant battle was fought with incremental developments over the next millennium: in the ninth century, a bell rung to mark the hour for extinguishing fires became known as the *curfew*—from the Norman *couevre feu* (cover the fire), an iron bowl placed over hot embers—and 12th-century building codes that encouraged the use of brick and stone.

After a devastating fire burned down London Bridge and the surrounding area in 1212, killing 3,000 people, severe punishment was meted out to those who caused fires: arsonists were burned alive; smithies and other tradesmen working with open fires—including bakers—were heavily fined if they did not keep their wooden walls plastered and their fires doused at night. Once the brick trade began to flourish in the 1500s, wooden buildings were slowly replaced with brick—stone was still too expensive for most. Yet none of these advances prepared London for 1666, when the first great fire in modern history destroyed almost the entire city. The impact of the Great Fire of London forever transformed urban life—the way we construct buildings and the way we fight fires.

In 1666, London was under siege from another enemy, Black Death (bubonic plague), which had been killing people in great numbers for almost a year. The plague was brought to the city by rats that arrived aboard ships docked along the Thames. Both the populace and the government were unprepared for disaster, expending energy instead on fighting the plague.

ELEMENTS OF DISASTER

The Great Fire began as a small fire in the early morning hours of Sunday, September 2, 1666, in a bakery and house on Pudding Lane. The owner, Thomas Farynor, who was Baker to the King, was awakened by his apprentice as smoke from a neglected oven began to permeate the household. The preceding summer had been unusually hot and dry. There was,

according to observers, a strong wind from the east. It blew the blaze from the bakery roof to a great swathe of houses, aided by the crowded, narrow streets; pitch or thatch-covered roofs; and interior fireloads that consisted of tallow, pitch, rushes, wooden furniture, and textiles. The fire then spread to wharves on the Thames, igniting stores of oil, tallow, and hemp, as well as bales of wood, hay, and coal stacked on the piers.

Available resources and equipment could not match the formidable task of fighting the fire. There was much pandemonium before the firefighting actually began. After the slow start, volunteers fought the blaze along with London residents and the military. The best that could be done was to evacuate homes and shops and then to get water onto

the fast-moving fire whenever and wherever possible. The latter was a truly daunting experience. The fire equipment had to be hauled, from wherever it was housed, by hand—requiring anywhere from five to ten men. Placement of the sites where the equipment was housed had not been based on any plan linked to high-risk areas.

And then, once the equipment arrived at the scene, the real work began, then as now. The equipment used in the Great Fire was not very effective. Pumps with nozzles were not yet in use in London in 1666—although they were being used in Amsterdam at this time. There were ordinances for parishes to stockpile buckets, axes, and squirts (giant syringes that squirted about a gallon of water into the flames), but many of these were in disrepair. Ladders were short and unsafe. If there were any rescues attempted from the rare house with upper floors, the ladders were inadequate.

And, being made of wood, they often became part of the fire.

DIGGING FOR WATER

Water had to be carried to the fire in buckets, much the same way that it had been during the fire of Rome. Firefighters no longer had to rely on open cisterns located around the city—at the time of the fire, London was served by a water distribution system that had been constructed during the first years of the century. Cast-iron pipe had not yet been developed. Water mains were made from logs that were hollowed out and then buried in the ground. When needed for firefighting, the pipe was exposed and a hole

FIGHTING THE FIRE FROM AFAR
Londoners attempt to extinguish flames with squirts—the giant syringes did not have much range and the firefighters were unable to get very close to the fire. St. Paul's is visible in the background (although the artist portrayed the reconstructed version of the cathedral, it was not built until after the fire). This illustration was featured in Repository of Arts, *an 1809 magazine published by German-born London lithographer and print-shop owner Rudolf Ackermann.*

FIRE TURNS DAY INTO NIGHT
A 19th-century engraving shows flames swirling around buildings gutted by fire or pulled down to create firebreaks. The estimated damage at the time was a staggering $15 million (£10 million).

was bored into it. Water was then pumped from the hole. Once the fire was out, the log was plugged up. This was not always a practical system: It was difficult to drill into cobblestone streets. In the dark of night the wooden pipe was often cut at the wrong spot, causing leaks. If the water pressure was too low, there would not be enough water to fight the fire. Once the water was acquired from the pipe it was poured into squirts or leather buckets. Bucket chains of 100 or more people conveyed the water to the fire.

TOTAL DESTRUCTION

The fire roared on for four days. Although Londoners made valiant efforts, water did not extinguish the flames. Houses that stood in the path of the fire were ripped down by order of the

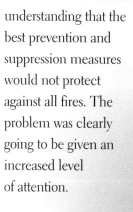

WOODEN WATER PIPE
Large hollowed-out logs, such as this one, were used to supply water in medieval Europe and Colonial America. Holes drilled to access water for a fire are evident on the left and top right of the log.

reigning king, Charles II, in order to create firebreaks—but the progress was too slow to check the spread of the flames. Authorities resorted to the use of gunpowder to open ever-larger areas. It was the first time in history that explosives were employed to fight the spread of fire. Today, demolition remains one of the final options available to stop the movement of fire, although its use is very rare principally because the planning and construction of modern cities has reduced wide-area burning.

Despite the work of demolition crews, the fire came under control only after the wind dropped and the hot embers were no longer being carried over the firebreaks. The resulting destruction of buildings was without parallel in fire history up to that date. It was estimated that some 100,000 were made homeless by the fire that ravaged four-fifths of London—almost 500 acres (200 ha) containing 13,200 houses, 88 churches, 44 guildhalls, and thousands of smaller structures were burned to the ground. Yet given the immense geographic area

involved, only six deaths were reported, although there were probably many injured. When compared to the loss of life in other major fires—even up to the present day—this low number is truly astounding; the fire prevention practices implemented over the previous ten centuries, although modest, were a major factor.

REBIRTH

And then the city began to rebuild, a task that required some seven years. Despite the destruction caused by the London fire, there were many positive effects that would have a significant impact on firefighting in both England and Colonial America. An immediate benefit was that the plague-carrying rats died in the flames. It was acknowledged that more had to be accomplished in terms of protecting what was then a modern and growing city from the dangers of fire, both in terms of prevention and suppression. Further, there was the social and economic understanding that the best prevention and suppression measures would not protect against all fires. The problem was clearly going to be given an increased level of attention.

SAMUEL PEPYS (1633–1703), *famed English diarist and naval administrator, lived near the Tower of London. After his maid woke him with news that London was burning, Pepys raced to the top of the Tower and witnessed "one entire arch of fire . . . above a mile long." Horrified, he rushed off to brief the king, writing in his diary that "the King commanded me to go to my Lord Mayor . . . and command him to spare no houses." Pulling down houses to make fire-breaks was unsuccessful; gunpowder crews were called in. At some point, Pepys went home to bury his valuables (money, wine, and Parmesan cheese) in a hole in his yard.*

Thatched and pitch-covered roofs were replaced by tile or slate. Any remaining wooden buildings rapidly gave way to brick and stone. The water system was upgraded as well.

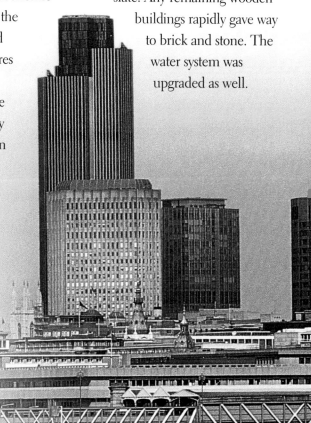

Wooden mains were outfitted with pre-cut holes and removable plugs (called "fire-plugs") that extended above the ground for easy identification—precursors to the fire hydrant. Over 1,600 leather buckets were distributed to home and shop owners, to be used in bucket brigades, in the event of fire. Finally, when fire insurance companies were formed shortly after the fire to pay future losses, they also began to undertake a major role, as a means of reducing their risk, in pushing for new fire-related construction laws and their enforcement, as well as financing paid company fire brigades.

SIR CHRISTOPHER WREN – *REBUILDER OF LONDON*

ASTRONOMER, GEOMETRICIAN, *urban planner, inventor, and great, prolific, English architect Christopher Wren (1632–1723) singlehandedly designed and oversaw construction of almost 50 new churches after the Great Fire. His greatest masterpiece was the redesign of St. Paul's Cathedral, which had been almost completely destroyed in the fire—its stones supposedly exploded with the heat, and molten lead from the roof ran onto the streets. The burned structure, known as Old St. Paul's, dated back to 1087, and had experienced fire before in 1561. Nine days after the Great Fire, Wren presented the royal commission with his plan to reconstruct the entire city with streets arranged in star-shaped radiations; it was rejected, as was his plan for a gold stone and clear glass St. Paul's. His third design for the cathedral was accepted in 1675. The new building was completed in 1710, and Wren, at 87, was the first English architect to see his design for a cathedral completed.*

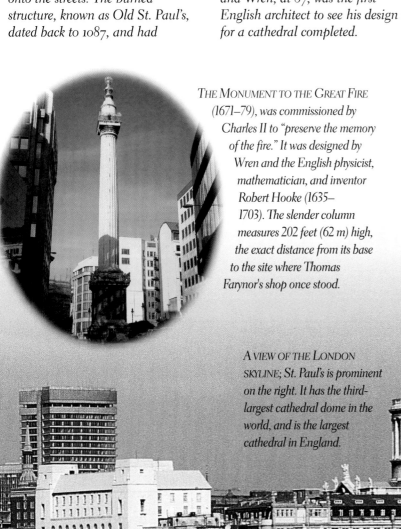

THE MONUMENT TO THE GREAT FIRE *(1671–79), was commissioned by Charles II to "preserve the memory of the fire." It was designed by Wren and the English physicist, mathematician, and inventor Robert Hooke (1635–1703). The slender column measures 202 feet (62 m) high, the exact distance from its base to the site where Thomas Farynor's shop once stood.*

SIR CHRISTOPHER WREN, *seen here in a 19th-century engraving, wanted to build an open-colonnaded piazza in front of St. Paul's; these plans were not realized until 1962, when the cathedral was reconstructed after damage from WWII bombing.*

A VIEW OF THE LONDON SKYLINE; *St. Paul's is prominent on the right. It has the third-largest cathedral dome in the world, and is the largest cathedral in England.*

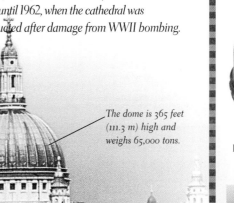

The dome is 365 feet (111.3 m) high and weighs 65,000 tons.

BURNING OF ROME
ROME, ITALY, AD 64

THE ROMANS WERE ONE OF THE EARLIEST CULTURES to develop highly sophisticated fire prevention techniques, including the development of the water pump in the second century; and the organization of the *vigiles*—a paid, military fire department. By AD 26 there were almost 7,000 *vigiles* outfitted with pumps, ladders, and hooked poles protecting Rome and strongly enforcing fire codes. Rome also had a highly complex water system that moved water throughout the city via a system of aqueducts, cisterns, and ceramic pipes.

Despite this advanced technology and the Roman government's high level of awareness about the perils of fire, Rome itself was the scene of several notable fires. The conflagration of AD 64, however, stands alone as a monument in the history of fire.

The fire began on July 19: there is debate as to whether it was an accident or a deliberate act. Fire regulations existed, but were often ignored and cooking fires burned in close proximity to highly flammable items such as wood, cloth, or animal fat. A hot summer wind helped push the flames down Rome's winding, narrow streets and alleyways.

The number of deaths attributed to the fire is unknown but was estimated in the hundreds given the density of the city's population. The fact that most of the buildings (with the exception of temples, patrician residences, and public buildings) were made of wood, would also contribute to fatalities. The fire was voracious, consuming shops, homes, stables and all of their contents. The army, augmented by slaves—the latter presumably being more expendable than soldiers in the firefighting endeavor—did respond, but mainly to keep fire away from existing public buildings.

Contemporary historians noted that the fire burned on and off for over one week. The result was the complete or significant destruction of 70 percent of the city.

The fire reignited several times. Although that could have been the result of fire-fighter error, it is also possible that human intervention kept the flames alive. After eight days, it finally burned out. Nero found a scapegoat in the Christians, and executed several of them. Whether or not the fire was accidental, the result was

NERO FIDDLES WHILE ROME BURNS
This 18th-century engraving illustrates the popular myth about Nero fiddling—this legend has never been confirmed, and fiddles were not invented until the 1500s.

the same—a new city arose from the ruins. Before the first ember had cooled, Nero's government began to put existing plans into effect for parks, modern buildings, and new streets. Improved fire-safety codes were implemented as well.

FIRE REPORT

⚜ CAUSES
• Accidentally started; some historians believe Nero set the fire, or allowed it to burn so that he could redesign Rome.

⚜ FIRE FACTS
• Roman army mainly fought to keep fires from burning public buildings, not homes.

• Ten of Rome's 14 districts— 70 percent of city—destroyed.

• Nero blamed Christians for starting the fire.

⚜ LOSSES
• Unknown; many were likely killed or injured, as population thought to be near one million.

⚜ DEVELOPMENTS
• Building heights were limited and constructed with higher percentage of stone.

• More cisterns filled with water and strategically placed.

• Citizens required to keep buckets at the ready, *vigiles* better organized.

• Streets were broadened to make access easier.

ROMAN CITIZENS IN DISTRESS
An unknown 18th-century artist imagines the burning of Rome.

FIRES OF ISTANBUL
—— ISTANBUL, TURKEY, 700 BC–AD 1930s ——

THE HISTORY AND DEVELOPMENT OF ISTANBUL is intertwined with the numerous fires that literally scorched its very existence. Known as Byzantium from 667 BC to AD 330, the strategically sited and economically important city was conquered in ancient times by Greeks, Macedonians, and Romans. In AD 330 the Roman emperor Constantine took Byzantium, renamed it Constantinople, and made it the capital of the Byzantine empire. Over the next 11 centuries the city was invaded by the Persians, Avars, Bulgars, and Russians. With invasion came fire, as in the famed Sack of Constantinople in 1204, which torched the city. The city finally fell to the Ottomans in 1453 and became Istanbul.

In 1589, fire engulfed Istanbul, burning 38,000 homes and shops. The city was rebuilt, with wood, and almost burned to the ground in 1633. There were no less than 109 major blazes between 1633 and 1839. Some historians believe that Istanbul's culture, based on ancient Ottoman nomadic tradition, explains why houses were always reconstructed with wood—a more temporary building material —instead of stone, which was reserved for public structures and monuments.

THE FIRE OF 1660
Turkish illuminated manuscript from 17th century depicts men attempting to pull down houses during an Istanbul fire.

In addition to wooden houses, another cause for recurring fire was the city's layout. Istanbul had grown without planning. Streets were extremely narrow, with many dead ends, making firefighting difficult. Finally, constant political and social unrest prevented the development of cohesive fire safety plans.

The Industrial Revolution did not reach Istanbul until the late 1800s, and earlier attempts to modernize did not fully address fire planning. Between 1839 and 1906, the number of extensive fires totaled 229. Even after the disastrous fires of the late 1700s, nothing was done to solve the problem of wooden homes and crowded streets. Indeed, more and more monuments were erected and placed amid the already dense and haphazard street layout. It would not be until the 1870s that a real effort was made to improve the street layout to permit easy firefighter access, and modern fire and building codes enacted. These steps were taken in the wake of an 1870 fire that burned down some of the foreign consulates along with some 3,000 other buildings. Political pressure, much of it from the international community, was a motivating factor.

Economic upheaval in the 1900s, and World War I, occupation, and revolution in the early twentieth century, kept the city from achieving the same municipal standards that had been attained in New York, London, Paris, Rome, and other cosmopolitan centers. Fires continued to rage throughout Istanbul through the first three decades of the twentieth century.

FIRE REPORT

⚜ CAUSES
• Wooden construction and narrow streets hampered firefighting efforts.

• Invaders over the centuries burned the city while looting and pillaging.

• Political and economic upheaval delayed the formation of fire safety and prevention plans.

⚜ FIRE FACTS
• Over 300 fires took place in Istanbul from 1633–1906.

• Firemen carried water hand pumps on a dais to fires until at least 1930.

⚜ LOSSES
• Unknown, but deaths and injuries must number in the thousands.

• Billions of dollars' worth of real estate, art, and valuables destroyed over the centuries.

⚜ DEVELOPMENTS
• Gradual improvements in street layouts and signage.

• Fewer buildings reconstructed with wood.

TURKISH FIREMEN
Turkish firemen carry a water hand pump on a dais, in this 19th-century illustration.

FIREMEN CARRY HAND PUMP, ISTANBUL, 1925
The dais-carried hand pump was used in Istanbul until at least the late 1920s; while not powerful, they were easier to maneuver along the narrow streets than trucks.

GREAT CHICAGO FIRE

CHICAGO, USA, 1871

THE SUMMER OF 1871 in the Midwest was extremely hot, with virtually no rainfall after July 3. The cisterns and rudimentary water-distribution system were both almost dry. Incorporated as a city in 1837, Chicago was only a few decades removed from being a frontier town, and was constructed mostly of the kind of wooden buildings and sidewalks that were leading factors in fires throughout the U.S.

FIRE IN THE SKY
The Great Chicago Fire sends flames leaping into the night, as portrayed in a dramatic 19th-century lithograph by Currier & Ives.

Fires, both large and small, had been burning around the city since the end of September. One, which started on the night of October 7 on Van Buren Street, had been particularly difficult to bring under control. It sapped the energies of the city's firefighters, who stayed up all night to battle the blaze. It also destroyed some equipment (including hoses, which were already in short supply) that would be sorely missed when the big one started. The Great Chicago Fire started in Patrick and Catherine O'Leary's barn on the corner of DeKoven and Jefferson Streets, at about 9:00 PM

on October 8. Official reports state that the fire was first noticed by Daniel Sullivan, an acquaintance of the O'Learys, who was sitting on the sidewalk across the street.

Soon after Sullivan's sighting, a fire watchman in one of the city's towers saw the flames. He was unable to determine the exact spot, and sent out a signal to an alarm box over a mile from where the blaze was located. Realizing his mistake, he then contacted the telegraph operator who had sent his original alarm; the operator refused to retransmit the signal to another box. In addition, fire alarm boxes were located approximately two blocks in either direction from the barn, yet no one turned in signals from those boxes. Due to the signaling mixup, firefighters arrived more than 15 minutes after the fire had started. Engine No. 5 was the first company at the scene,

RIVER OF FLAME
Chicago River's busy port is consumed by fire, as illustrated in this 19th-century hand-colored woodcut. The blaze consumed buildings all the way to the waterfront. It burned over bridges, and sent sparks flying into the river, igniting oil slicks and setting fire to many vessels. A fireman on a horse-drawn pumper is depicted at bottom center; at bottom left, firemen with a trumpet and pike.

but its engine temporarily stalled, adding yet more delay. Within minutes, the fire began to travel northeast, pushed by a sudden high wind from the prairie. Soon, firefighters were overwhelmed

by the out-of-control flames. The available hose lines were inadequate and the hydrants were too few and too far away. Many of the fire department's pumpers were abandoned as the flames roared across the city, and with them the hope that pumping water from Lake Michigan would halt or slow the flames literally melted away. Firefighters and more equipment were rushed to the city by train from points all over the Midwest including Cincinnati. Finally, soldiers were brought in, not only to keep order, but to fight the fire and blow up buildings, creating firebreaks around the flames.

CURIOSITY TURNS TO PANIC

Thousands of Chicagoans, who believed their offices or residences to be "fireproof" (as many were advertised by real estate companies), were soon fleeing in disbelief as their buildings succumbed. Fire pursued them even on the ground as the wooden sidewalks burned beneath their feet.

MRS. O'LEARY – WAS HER COW TO BLAME?

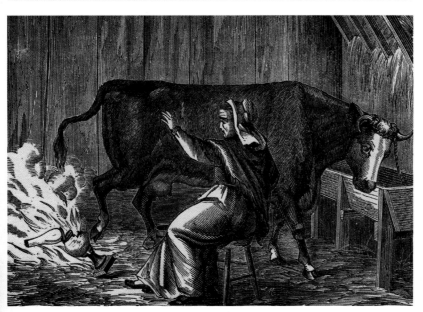

BEFORE THE FLAMES DIED, the Chicago Evening Journal *of October 9 reported that a cow Mrs. O'Leary had been milking kicked over a kerosene lamp, igniting some hay. In reality, the O'Learys were never accused of starting the fire — by all accounts they were asleep — and it seems that Mrs. O'Leary would have made a greater effort to call for help and extinguish the fire if she had been in the barn at the time. The cause of the fire is still a matter of debate today, although the cow legend persists. The Chicago Fire Academy was built in 1961 on the site of the O'Leary home; a Maltese cross marks the spot where the barn once stood.*

The *Chicago Tribune* building was said to be "fireproof" until its interior burned to ash, the girders melted, and the structure collapsed. The courthouse tower was destroyed as well. Its huge bell burned from its moorings and plunged into the flames.

CAUSES AND CONSEQUENCES

The famous Mrs. O'Leary, in whose wooden barn the fire started, did indeed have a cow,

SMOKING RUINS
This view of the ruins after the Great Fire was taken from the site of the former city hall (which was gutted in the fire) looking north on Clark Street, the street in the center of the photograph. The fire razed the entire cityscape in the camera's range, and beyond—an effect that eerily replicates the look of cities bombed during World War II. In the middle of Clark Street and in the foreground, several figures are visible within the ruins.

named Daisy. Whether or not the animal survived the fire is unknown, but by evening, the newspapers had already blamed the cow for starting the blaze. The actual cause of the fire was never determined. Although there was never any suspicion of arson, some recent theories speculate that one of the O'Learys' friends—possibly Sullivan—who had been in the barn earlier that night, accidentally started the fire. Others surmise that a spark from the chimney was blown into the barn by the wind, and landed on a bale of hay.

Chicago burned for two days; a rainstorm on Tuesday morning quenched the flames, which had left almost four square miles (10 sq km) of the city in smoking ruin. The fire killed some 300 people; burned out over 18,000 buildings of all types; and left at least 100,000 homeless, a number that represented almost one-third of the city's population. The burned-out ruins smoldered for several weeks. The fire, which devoured everything in its path, proved not only that delay in fire response was deadly, but that the term "fireproof" was not one in

which people could take significant comfort. It became clear from that time onward that "fire-resistant" was a much more accurate term.

A few days after the conflagration, Chicago mayor Joseph Medill and the U.S. Army Corps of Engineers announced immediate plans for rebuilding, including a new levee, market, and grand plaza. Although the ground was frozen, by December over 200 brick and stone buildings were under construction. Fire debris was used as landfill to create parks

along Lake Michigan. The fire department was reorganized on a military model for greater efficiency. Two Chicagoans made important contributions to fire safety with their inventions: the firehouse pole (Fire Captain David Kenyon, 1878), and the portable fire-escape ladder (Daniel McCree, 1890). And, as a result of the fire, new methods of building —including the use of reinforced concrete—were investigated for their applicability in the fireproofing of buildings.

FIRE REFUGEES

The fire burned 100,000 people out of their homes. The scene on the street was one of unmatched chaos. Tradesmen and bankers, prostitutes and society ladies, lost children and immigrants—all fled with whatever possessions they could carry. There were some reports of looting and drunkenness (many tavern owners rolled their barrels into the streets), although stories of violence were greatly exaggerated, as were accounts of wagon drivers who sought to take advantage of victims by charging inordinate amounts to cart their household valuables. Makeshift refugee camps were erected along Lake Michigan and the Chicago River.

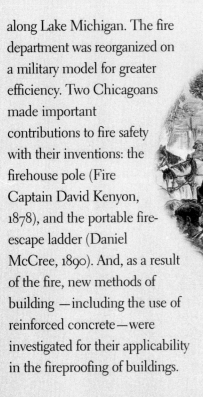

FIRE REPORT

CAUSES
• Legend blames fire on Mrs. O'Leary's cow kicking over a lamp in a barn, but probably a human accident or chimney spark igniting a hay bale.

OTHER CAUSES
• Watchman's incorrect location signal misdirected firefighters, causing delay.

FIRE FACTS
• Soldiers brought in to make firebreaks by exploding buildings in the fire's path.

• Many supposedly fireproof buildings destroyed.

• Great deal of firefighting equipment lost in fire, making fighting it even more difficult.

LOSSES
• Close to 300 people killed, 100,000 made homeless.

• Almost four square miles (10 sq km) laid to waste; 18,000 buildings and homes were destroyed.

• $200 million ($2.3 billion today) in damages; most costly disaster in U.S. history until 2001 World Trade Center attack.

DEVELOPMENTS
• Fire department reorganized military-style, with battalions.

• New city plan implemented, with brick and stone buildings.

• Firehouse pole and portable fire-escape ladder invented.

• Advances in construction of fireproof structures.

RELATED FIRES

• Pittsburgh, PA, 1845: Thousands left homeless by conflagration.

• Seattle, WA, 1889: Factory fire exploded 20 tons of ammunition.

• Toronto, Ont., 1904: Fire in warehouse fanned by strong winds raged for hours.

GREAT FIRE OF 1835

NEW YORK CITY, USA 1835

FREEZING TEMPERATURES were the last thing New York City's firefighters needed on December 16, 1835. They were exhausted from battling large fires that had broken out two nights earlier. When a new fire started in a warehouse at 25 Merchant Street, the tired men had to pull the hand-drawn pumpers and ladder trucks to battle the flames. The freezing temperature froze the water in the hoses and the wind quickly spread the flames throughout the financial district.

The Hudson and East Rivers were frozen solid, as were the street wells, and the firefighters had to break through the ice to get water for their pumps.

The water froze again once it was in the hoses, making it difficult to maintain a stream of water to douse the flames. Leather hoses had become common in the 1820s. They allowed firefighters to pump water from a safe distance or carry hose into a structure to fight the fire at the source. The advent of the hose also allowed for relay pumping, whereby a number of pumpers could be connected to transport water over some distance. Hose reels were required along with pumpers and ladder trucks at the scene of the fire. Although hoses were a crucial tool in the New York conflagration, they could not be used to their utmost advantage. In addition to the freezing water in the hoses, the intense cold also made it difficult for firefighters to hold the nozzle.

The blaze was so enormous that it could be seen from 90 miles (145 km) away. Reinforcements arrived from Philadelphia, but the fire burned for two days. It finally was brought under control by exploding gunpowder to create firebreaks that halted the fire's spread. The fire had consumed

17 city blocks in the heart of the city's downtown. Shops, counting houses, storehouses, and several large banks on or near Wall Street were among some 700 buildings destroyed. The cause of the fire was determined to be gas escaping from a broken line and igniting from coals in a nearby stove.

The concentration of damage in the financial district is thought to have contributed to the economic downturn that gripped New York and the nation in 1837. Immediately after the fire, merchants returned to their demolished businesses to search for the metal company safes that contained crucial records and agreements. The $20 million ($378 million today) in damages ruined many small insurance companies, which generally operated without reserve funds. The fire prompted the insurance industry to restructure, making provisions for such large disasters. Another important development from the fire was the implementation of the modern New York City water system and the building of the Croton Aqueduct, brought about because firefighters were unable to tap into the frozen street wells—which, even in working order, supplied little water.

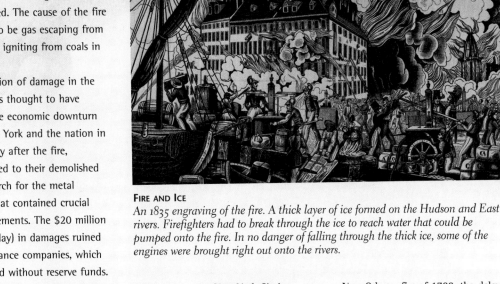

FIRE AND ICE
An 1835 engraving of the fire. A thick layer of ice formed on the Hudson and East rivers. Firefighters had to break through the ice to reach water that could be pumped onto the fire. In no danger of falling through the thick ice, some of the engines were brought right out onto the rivers.

Within two years, New York City's downtown revived. New buildings were constructed and business returned and expanded. The legacy of the fire is visible today in the grand structures erected in those 17 charred blocks.

TEN YEARS LATER

In 1845, New York City faced another great conflagration. In the early hours of July 19, the watchman in the city hall bell tower fell asleep on the job and failed to sound the alarm bells when a fire broke out. A factory was already burning furiously by the time the first firefighters arrived. As in the New Orleans fire of 1788, the delay in sounding the alarm had disastrous results. The fire spread, eventually reaching a building in which explosives were stored. The resulting detonation blew down masonry structures and sent shards of glass across the city. Hundreds were badly injured and 30 people died. Over 300 buildings were destroyed as well.

The damage from this fire would have been less had the fire department received earlier notification. The telegraphic alarm box filled this need shortly after. Invented in 1851, the new technology consisted of street-corner boxes that were connected by telegraph to the fire department. However, alarm boxes were not used in New York City until 1870, when 346 boxes were installed around lower Manhattan, below 14th Street. These devices were gradually added throughout the city and are still in use today, providing immediate notification to the fire department of the site of a fire.

SMOKE AMONG THE RUINS
A 19th-century painting by Nicolino Calyo shows the ruins of New York City. Energetic civilians pitched in to help the firefighters battle the blaze, not a few of them merchants hoping to save their shops and goods.

FIRE REPORT

CAUSES
• 1835 fire began in a warehouse when gas escaped from a broken line, igniting coals in a stove.

• Strong winds spread flames throughout Wall Street.

FIRE FACTS
• Fires on recent nights had left firefighters exhausted, slowing response.

• Water froze in hoses and firefighters had to stomp on them to break ice and maintain water flow.

• Fire could be seen from 90 miles (145 km) away.

LOSSES
• Only 2 deaths reported.

• Fire burned 50 acres (20 ha) of land—17 city blocks.

• Some 700 buildings destroyed.

• Fire caused $20 million ($378 million today) in damages.

• Fire was a blow to smaller insurance companies that lacked funds necessary to continue business.

DEVELOPMENTS
• City and state goverments required insurance companies to maintain reserve funds.

• Fire was catalyst for development of modern New York City water system, culminating in completion of Croton Aqueduct in 1841.

• Fire-alarm boxes finally installed in 1870.

GREAT ST. LOUIS FIRE
ST. LOUIS, USA, 1849

ST. LOUIS HAD BECOME A MAJOR CITY by 1849 and was firmly established as the gateway to the great American West. Overpopulated at about 45,000 people for its available infrastructure, St. Louis was crowded and unhealthy. Conditions were reflected in a cholera outbreak, which was taking over 300 lives a week.

The arrival of Mississippi steamboats brought an increased risk of fire from the huge stocks of combustible supplies.

FIRE CAPTAIN THOMAS TARGEE
Killed while setting a keg of gunpowder to help create a firebreak, Captain Targee died bravely, but the plan ultimately saved the remainder of the city of St. Louis.

Grain, cotton, and tobacco, as well as wood for the steamships' boilers, were all stored on the wharves.

As an added danger, the all-volunteer fire brigades had a habit of racing with one another to get "first-water" (so named because insurance firms paid a bonus to the first brigade to arrive). This practice often entailed hiring "plug-uglies," thugs paid to keep all fire brigades but their own from a water main. It was a situation ripe for disaster.

On the night of May 17, 1849, *The White Cloud* steamship caught fire while moored at the wharf near present-day Franklin Street. Soon, 23 steamships were wreathed in flames. With the fire brigades ineffective in the face of all the waterfront combustibles, the flames soon spread into downtown: a maze of shoddy, wooden shacks, narrow, twisting streets, and stuffed warehouses. The inferno was unstoppable by normal means. Finally, gunpowder was used to level six buildings around the fire, creating a firebreak.

FLAMES SOARED OVER BURNING STEAMSHIPS
An 1849 Currier & Ives color lithograph depicts the enormous fire that engulfed the St. Louis riverfront.

In all, 430 houses, three newspaper offices and banks, the post office, and the entire waterfront, including warehouses and virtually every vessel, became cinders. Total damage amounted to $2.7 million ($62 million today). Incredibly, only three lives were lost.

In the aftermath, troops had to be called in to restore order, and the cholera continued unabated until October. Over the next two years, the damaged sections were rebuilt, but with an emphasis on modernity, order, and safety.

There has always been a suspicion that the fire was incendiary (arson) in origin, but it has never been proved.

INFERNO ON THE WATER
After setting the steamboats nearest it ablaze, The White Cloud broke away from its moorings and floated downstream, igniting any ship in its path. A quarter of a mile down it returned to shore, touching off the conflagration in the city proper.

BOSTON FIRE
— BOSTON, USA, 1872 —

NINETEENTH-CENTURY BOSTON was a tinderbox waiting for a spark. Its network of narrow streets crowded homes, shops, and people into a small area, all lit by gas lights. The buildings were tall, with much exposed timber; many incorporated a new architectural style from France, the mansard roof. This building design created a large space above the top floor of the structure, through which fire could move easily. No structures in the city were large or strong enough to act as a bulwark against the spread of fire.

Boston's fire chief, John Stanhope Damrell, was concerned about these conditions. He argued that the Boston fire department was dangerously unprepared for a major fire, but the city ignored his requests for more equipment. The underwriters who insured the city apparently shared Damrell's concern. Shortly before the fire, they sought to cancel their coverage, feeling the risks were too great.

The Boston Fire began in a four-story building housing textile and clothing merchants. Around 7:30 PM on Saturday, November 9, an alarm was received from Box 52 at the corner of Sumner and Livingston Streets. It was the first time a city-wide conflagration was heralded by an alarm-box signal. But the slow mobilization of the city's firefighters allowed the fire's rapid spread through the city.

The Boston fire department faced several obstacles that slowed their response. An outbreak of distemper had left only 10 fire department horses in commission, and many of the heavy pumpers and ladder trucks had to be pulled by hand. Although Boston was one of the first cities to construct a water-distribution system, these pipes had fallen into disrepair, leaving firefighters without easily accessible water. Steam pumps ran low on fuel, and firefighters broke up boxes and other scrap wood. However, the effort was aided by citizens who pitched in to save their city.

The fire was brought under control mid-morning on Sunday, November 10. Firefighters had arrived from as far as 100 miles (161 km) away, and firebreaks were created with explosives. The fire had covered a huge area, destroying 776 buildings, but only 13 people perished. Within a year, construction had begun on a "Better Boston," with wider streets and safer buildings.

JOHN STANHOPE DAMRELL
Portrayed in an 18th-century painting, Boston fire department chief Damrell had petitioned the city for a new engine, hydrants, and water pipes. Having been sent to Chicago following that city's great fire the previous year, Damrell compiled a report listing Boston's many shortcomings. His prediction of Boston's vulnerability proved correct in 1872.

CITY IN RUINS
A contemporary newspaper engraving of the view from Washington Street shows the charred remains of downtown Boston. After much of the financial district was destroyed, the city began to look outward. Although this area remains the heart of the city, Boston has expanded far beyond its original borders.

FIRE REPORT

CAUSES
• Began for unknown reasons in a textile building.

OTHER CAUSES
• Wind spread the fire through the narrow streets.

FIRE FACTS
• Many people anticipated a conflagration—even the city's insurers had wanted to cease coverage for Boston.

• Distemper outbreak had left only 10 fire department horses available, so many pumps and hoses were hand drawn.

LOSSES
• 13 people were killed.

• 776 buildings on 65 acres (26 ha) of land destroyed.

• $75 million in damage ($1.1 billion today).

DEVELOPMENTS
• Boston fire-commissioner board created.

• New buildings provide increased safety precautions.

• Fire Chief Damrell founded National Association of Fire Engineers to disseminate information to other fire departments about new techniques and equipment.

IROQUOIS THEATRE
─── CHICAGO, USA, 1903 ───

SOME OF THE MOST TRAGIC fires in fire history have occurred in theaters, where the potential for deaths caused by flame, smoke, and panic is great. Even without the added concern of possible code violations such as overcrowding or blocked exits, most theaters have cavernous interiors filled with air, which fires could feed on; large amounts of fireload (flammable materials) in terms of carpets, seats, curtains, and scenery; and a captive audience that can very easily panic at the first sight of flame or wisp of smoke.

By 1903, fire precautions were standard (and sometimes legally required) in many American and European theaters. Most building ordinances for theaters called for the installation of fire-alarm boxes, sprinklers, house firemen positioned by the stage, extinguishers, fire hoses, pike poles to pull down burning curtains or scenery, and clearly marked and well-lit exits. In addition, electrical wiring was to be covered with fire-resistant casing, not only to prevent fire, but to protect the lights if a fire occurred. All of these safety measures except one (there was an in-house fireman equipped with Kilfyres, a powdered chemical extinguisher) were missing from Chicago's new luxurious Iroquois Theatre on the afternoon of Wednesday, December 30, 1903.

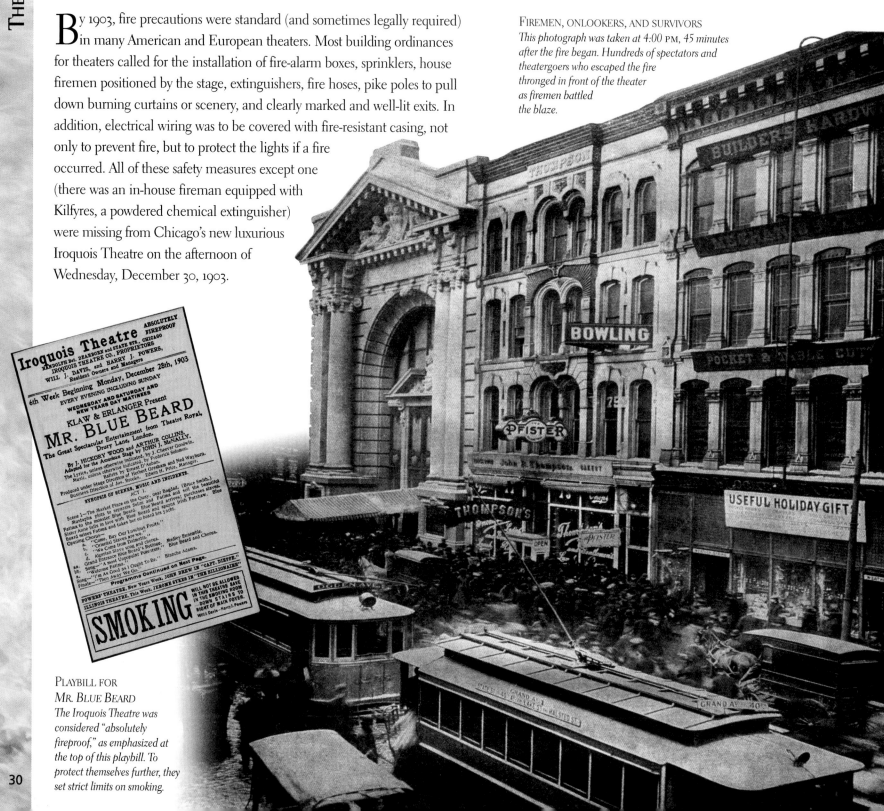

FIREMEN, ONLOOKERS, AND SURVIVORS
This photograph was taken at 4:00 PM, 45 minutes after the fire began. Hundreds of spectators and theatergoers who escaped the fire thronged in front of the theater as firemen battled the blaze.

PLAYBILL FOR
MR. BLUE BEARD
The Iroquois Theatre was considered "absolutely fireproof," as emphasized at the top of this playbill. To protect themselves further, they set strict limits on smoking.

The only other preventative fire measure in the theater, which had opened only five weeks earlier, was an asbestos curtain above the stage: in the event of a stage fire, it was supposed to be lowered to separate the audience from the fire.

The six-story Iroquois was "a palace of marble and plate glass, plush with mahogany and gilding," and, as stated on the playbill, "absolutely fireproof." At the matinee on December 30, over 1,900 people (mostly women and children during the school vacation) packed the theater to see the popular vaudeville actor Eddie Foy and his 500-member troupe perform in the musical comedy *Mr. Blue Beard*. The theater had only 1,724 seats, so over 200 people stood in the back row and aisles.

INVESTIGATORS INSPECT A LOCKED GATE AT ONE OF THE EXITS
The theater had 27 exits, but only three were available on December 30. Most of the exit doors in the downstairs portion of the theater were locked or covered with iron gates. Those that were unlocked were latched shut with a small lever that was not easily operable.

A DANGEROUS COMBINATION

The show's many set changes were accomplished with moveable canvas backdrops decorated with flammable oil paint, hung high above the stage near the hot lights.

As Act II started at 3:15 PM, a stage-hand in the rafters watched helplessly as one of the canvas backdrops brushed against a floodlight and began to burn; it was several inches out of his reach. The house fireman rushed up to the catwalk and tried to put out the fire by sprinkling it with Kilfyres. The chemical powder works by suffocating flames on a solid surface, but was ineffective in dousing the midair blaze. The fire spread to the ropes and other back-drops; an exploding light showered sparks onto the curtains. Foy ran to stage center, yelling for the asbestos curtain to be lowered, and for the audience to remain seated. The curtain either got caught on a light fixture or jammed halfway down in its wooden tracks (these would have been flammable, too). Some witnesses reported that it was in fact a burning scenery curtain that had been pulled down, others claimed that the theater never even installed an asbestos curtain.

EDDIE FOY TROUPE - *ONSTAGE FIRE AND ESCAPE*

EDDIE FOY *was one of the most popular stage comedians of the early 1900s. In December 1903, his 500-member troupe opened the musical* Mr. Blue Beard *at the posh new Iroquois Theatre. The fire began during the December 30 matinee, as the dancers began promenading the stage at the start of Act II. Foy came from backstage, shouting for the asbestos curtain to be dropped as burning scenery began to fall.*

The curtain became stuck, and Foy pleaded with the audience to stay calm and seated so that they would not harm themselves in the rush to leave. He then told the performers to exit through the backstage door into the alley behind the theater, not knowing that their doing so would create a deadly backdraft. Foy, and all but one performer, escaped.

FOY OFTEN DRESSED IN DRAG *as part of his comedy routine. The native New Yorker began his career as a variety artist in the Wild West, and by the 1920s he achieved the status of Broadway icon when he put his children in the musical act he billed as Eddie and the Seven Little Foys.*

This star marks the spot on stage directly below the floodlight that caused the fire.

THE SCENE ON STAGE *just before the fire started. One showgirl testified that "I first saw just a little bit of flame . . . just above the lamp that was reflecting on the moonlight girls. . . . going down stage I saw the flame getting larger. . . . we sang one verse of 'The Pale Moonlight' song and then Mr. Foy came out and spoke to the audience."*

FIRE REPORT

☙ CAUSES

• Flammable canvas scenery ignited by hot stage light.

☙ FIRE FACTS

• Worst theater fire in U.S. history.

• Huge fireball erupted into theater when fleeing actors opened backstage door, creating a backdraft.

• Because there was no firebox, fire department did not get call until 13 minutes after fire started.

☙ LOSSES

• 602 people killed; many survivors were disabled by fire.

☙ DEVELOPMENTS

• All theaters must have operational fire alarms, steel fire curtains, sprinkler systems, outward-opening "panic" doors, and sufficient firefighting equipment.

• Theaters must be constructed with broad aisles and well-lit and unobstructed, unlocked exits.

• Uniformed ushers must be posted at exits, and trained in fire drills.

RELATED FIRES

• Bolshoi Theatre, Moscow 1805, 1853: second-largest theater in 19th-century Europe. Completely destroyed by fire in 1805; reopened in 1825. In 1853 gutted by a three-day-long fire. Rebuilt in 1856.

• Gran Teatro La Fenice, Venice, Italy, 1836, 1996: Built in 1792 after being burned out from previous site, "La Fenice" (the phoenix) was burned again and rebuilt in 1836. Burned down during a 1996 renovation and reopened in 1999.

• Karamay, China, 1994: Theater burned down when curtain caught fire during a school pageant, killing 300 children and their teachers.

BACKDRAFT FIREBALL

When the doors to the street from backstage were opened by escaping actors, it was if they had let in a monster. The cold air rushed in and created a bellowslike effect that shot tongues of fire out across the audience.

The interior of the theater, including the exit doors, was covered with plush fabric. The wooden seats were upholstered with hemp, and the floors carpeted. Within seconds the entire fireload spontaneously combusted, forcing hundreds of panicked audience members to run from their seats. The theater had 27 exits, but on that day only three were accessible and they had inward-opening doors (others were locked or latched). The new theater was supposed to have fire escapes that would allow people exiting from the balcony easy access to the street, but they were not yet installed and many people jumped to their death. Hundreds more were crushed, suffocated, or burned as they clogged the balconies' only exit corridor inside the theater, which led to the locked doors. The people who were able to reach the lobby got trapped while trying to run down the grand marble staircase, and soon became entangled in a sea of bodies. Because of the

A VIEW OF THE BURNED INTERIOR
The fireball that destroyed the theater was described by survivors as a "great, rolling sheet of flame." The flues in the roof that could have drawn the fire and smoke upward were closed or boarded up.

lack of a firebox, the call for help was delayed for 13 minutes, so although the firemen arrived only 2 minutes after the call was received, it was to an eerily quiet blaze; 572 had already died. The final death toll was 602.

A subsequent inquest with testimony from hundreds of witnesses revealed a pattern of almost unbelievable corruption and carelessness that made national headlines. The trial uncovered a bribery scheme between theater owners and city inspectors, many of whom were indicted (including Mayor Carter Harrison) but never tried. The Iroquois was not heavily damaged, and reopened a year later as the Colonial Theatre. The original façade was restored in 1998 as the entrance to the new Ford Theater.

The Iroquois fire led to sweeping fire prevention reform in the industry: The new codes not only dictated improved equipment and building requirements, but also the hiring of uniformed ushers trained in fire drills.

A NEW FIREBOX INSTALLED
A group of survivors demonstrate a new firebox, which was installed at the Iroquois Theatre at a ceremony held on December 30, 1949.

LONDON THEATER FIRES
LONDON, ENGLAND, 1613–1856

UNTIL THE ADVENT of electricity in the late 1800s, theaters relied on gas or kerosene lamps to light stages and seating areas, greatly increasing the threat of fire. From the early 1600s to the 1850s, many European theaters experienced cycles of fire and rebuilding. London—the theater capital of Europe with an enduring stage tradition dating back to the Middle Ages—witnessed countless theater fires, and was the birthplace of many of the fire prevention developments practiced today.

THE GLOBE THEATRE

Perhaps the world's most famous theater, the original Globe was built on the banks of the Thames in 1599. The circular structure was the venue for plays by London's leading playwrights, including William Shakespeare. At a 1613 production of *Henry VIII*, a prop cannon shot out a blank that set the thatched roof on fire. The Globe burned to the ground; the 3,000 audience members miraculously escaped without harm. It reopened one year later, only to be razed by the Puritans during the English Civil War in 1644. American actor and director Sam Wanamaker founded and built the new Globe Theatre in the 1990s.

DRURY LANE THEATRE

Built in 1663 by the dramatist Thomas Killigrew, the Drury Lane is the oldest theater in London still in operation. After a major fire in 1672, it was rebuilt by the great London architect Sir Christopher Wren. The Drury prospered until 1809, when another cycle of fire and rebuilding closed it for two years.

COVENT GARDEN THEATRE

Now known as the Royal Opera House, the Covent Garden Theatre opened in 1732 on the east side of Covent Garden. The theater was destroyed by fire in 1808 and again in 1856. The current building dates back to 1858, and is the premiere London theater for ballet and opera.

THE NEW GLOBE THEATRE

The new Globe is almost an exact replica of the original: a 20-sided timber and plaster polygon, open to the skies above the stage pit. There are no microphones, sets, or special lights. It is the first building since the Great Fire of London (1666) allowed to have a thatched roof (it is fire treated). The new structure has both indoor and roof sprinklers and a layer of fireproofing installed between the thatch and the roof frame.

THE DRURY LANE THEATRE BURNS, 1809
Although the Drury was the first theater to install a fire-safety curtain (c. 1794), it burned down again in 1809 (shown above in a painting of the same year). The theater's present-day incarnation was built in 1811.

ACTORS BEG AS COVENT GARDEN THEATRE BURNS, 1808
The 1808 fire at Covent Garden may have been the catalyst for a 19th-century London fire code that called for blankets soaked with water to be kept just offstage to smother fires (the phrase "wet blanket," which now refers to a person who dampens others' enthusiasm, may have come from this practice).

FIRE REPORT

☙ CAUSES
•Usually started by live flame from props (like sound-effect cannons) or lamps coming in contact with highly flammable materials such as thatching, curtains, scenery, or wood.

☙ LOSSES
• Minimal loss of life.

☙ DEVELOPMENTS
•Many basic fire safety measures used by theaters today were initiated by firemen and theater owners over a 250-year period of trial-and-error tactics to eliminate recurrent theater fires.

• First fire curtain was installed in the Drury Lane Theatre around 1794.

• A 19-century London fire code called for blankets soaked with water to be kept offstage to smother fires.

• Captain Eyre Massey Shaw, pioneering captain of the London Fire Brigade, did a survey of London theaters in 1880 in an attempt to curtail number of fatal theater fires, and introduced first system of street alarm posts.

RELATED FIRES

• The Olympic Theatre, Westminster, 1849.

• Alhambra Theatre, 1883: Prince of Wales (King Edward VII), an amateur fireman, was nearly killed by a falling wall while fighting the fire.

• Savoy Theatre, 1990: Built in 1881 as a showcase for Gilbert and Sullivan, one of world's first public buildings to be lit by electric incandescent light. Although safer than fuel lamps, electrical systems are equally dangerous when flawed. An electrical fire gutted the Savoy in 1990. No one was injured, and theater reopened in 1993.

BROOKLYN THEATRE
BROOKLYN, USA, 1876

THE BROOKLYN THEATRE OPENED IN 1871, a luxurious renovation of the former Park Theatre, in the Brooklyn Heights section of what was then the third-largest city in the United States. The theater was managed by a pioneering woman in the theater industry, Sarah Conway, the first manager to establish a permanent company in one of the largest cities in America. On December 5, 1876, the Brooklyn Theatre was showcasing one of the most popular actresses of the time, Kate Claxton, in the hit play *The Two Orphans.*

Over 1,000 people packed the sold-out theater. At the start of the last act, a piece of canvas scenery brushed against one of the kerosene stage lamps and began to burn. The stagehands believed the small fire was controllable, and futilely tried to pull off the burning section without lowering the canvas, so as not to disrupt the performance or endanger the actors. Claxton was onstage as the fire began, and continued to act until the flames grew out of control. The curtain was lowered (there was no evidence of a fire curtain) as the stage manager came out to speak to the audience, urging them to exit in an orderly fashion. Claxton escaped without harm.

The audience members in the orchestra were able to evacuate from the main exit. There was more of a panic in the first balcony, known as the dress circle or second gallery, but most injuries there occurred from people trampled in the rush to escape. The top balcony, or gallery, where the most inexpensive tickets were sold, was extremely overcrowded with 400 people, and had only one exit to the stairs leading down and out, a doorless passageway approximately 12 feet (3.7 m) wide. Ten minutes after the first spark, smoke began to fill the auditorium and the stage had quickly turned into an inferno, fed by the kerosene and gas lamps, canvas, ropes, and wooden stage structures. As the lights went out and the flames roared, people began tripping over one another and the narrow passageway became a wall of bodies

that blocked the exodus. Witnesses reported that the flames were so great and loud that it was impossible to hear a conversation a block away; firefighters, who arrived at the scene quickly, fought valiantly to put out the raging fire. After one-and-a-half hours, the balconies and the back wall had collapsed, leaving only the façade intact. The deaths from the first major theater fire in America officially numbered 275, but the real toll is probably closer to 300.

KATE CLAXTON, IN A 19TH-CENTURY TRADE CARD CIGARETTE ADVERTISEMENT
Claxton was a minor Broadway actress until 1874, when she landed the lead of the blind heroine in The Two Orphans, a play set during the French Revolution. The role made her famous, and she was the headliner at the Brooklyn Theatre production when the theater burned to the ground. After the fire, Claxton went on tour. On April 11 she checked into the Southern Hotel in St. Louis. At 2:00 AM, the hotel caught fire; Claxton covered herself in wet towels and rolled downstairs. Over 40 people died. The press went wild, claiming she was a fire jinx, but the publicity helped her career, garnering fan loyalty and media attention.

FIRE REPORT

CAUSES
• When a kerosene lamp ignited a backdrop, stagehands did not make strong efforts to fight the fire, not wanting to disrupt the play.

FIRE FACTS
• Firemen arrived quickly, but the theater was destroyed in one and a half hours.

• Unclaimed victims of the fire were buried in a common grave in Brooklyn's famous Greenwood Cemetery.

LOSSES
• It is believed that at least 300 lives were lost.

BROOKLYN THEATRE FIRE
A contemporary sketch of the fire from the Washington Street entrance of the Brooklyn Theatre depicts a 19th-century pumper fire engine in the lower-right corner.

RINGTHEATRE
—— VIENNA, AUSTRIA, 1881 ——

GERMAN-BORN FRENCH COMPOSER Jacques Offenbach died the year before his unfinished opera, *Les Contes d'Hoffman (The Tales of Hoffman)* had its Austrian premier at the Ringtheatre in Vienna, on December 7, 1881. The next night's performance would prove to be fateful. One of the most disastrous fires in Europe burned down the theater and killed over 400 people. The fire prompted the formation of a Viennese volunteer rescue society the next day, and dramatically transformed the field of theater construction, engineering, and fire

safety. The issue of fire prevention was already a matter of grave concern in the late 1800s; in 1881 alone, a fire destroyed a theater in Nice, France, and the National Theater of Prague. In Prussia, the Ringtheatre fire and other theater blazes resulted in the publication of national fire codes in 1889, regulating the construction of entrances, building materials, and even fabrics used on stage. The use of reinforced concrete in auditorium construction became standard in Prussia. In Hungary, the State Opera House installed metallic stage hydraulics,

an iron fire curtain, and a sprinkler system. The Ringtheatre fire was also prominent in the design of what is now the Mahen Theatre, constructed in 1882 in Brno, Czech Republic. The number of exits and staircases was increased and their dimensions enlarged. More importantly, the theater was electrified—the second theater after the London's Savoy was electrified in 1881. Thomas Alva Edison's assistant, Francis Jehl, oversaw the installation of the lighting system.

Firemen hold a life net, a device developed in the early 18th century as buildings became increasingly taller. Early versions were made of webbed netting. Later, canvas was used. Today, gigantic air-filled "pillows" are used, but usually as a last resort.

FIRE REPORT

✦ CAUSES
• Unknown, probably kerosene.

✦ FIRE FACTS
• Offenbach opera that premiered at the Ringtheatre the night of the fire, *Les Contes d'Hoffman,* was viewed as an unlucky work to perform.

✦ LOSSES
• 400 were killed.

✦ DEVELOPMENTS
• Most influential fire in Central Europe in the late 19th century, prompting sweeping fire reform. Improvements included:

• *Formation of a Viennese volunteer rescue society;*
• *Use of reinforced concrete in construction;*
• *Numerous and wide exits and staircases;*
• *Metal stage hydraulics; iron fire curtains;*
• *Electric lighting systems.*

JACQUES OFFENBACH (1819–1880)
In the superstitious world of theater, his Les Contes d'Hoffman *was considered "bad luck" after the fire—a view reinforced by a fire that burned down the Paris Opera Comique during an 1887 performance. The piece was only performed once more until after 1910, but is now performed all over the world and considered a masterpiece.*

JUMPING TO SAFETY
An etching from the 1881 Illustrated London News shows a woman leaping into the firefighters' life net from the Ringtheatre balcony. Life nets were not always successful at saving lives, especially when people jumped from great heights—the force of their fall often broke the nets, or they would miss the net altogether.

MGM GRAND
—— LAS VEGAS, USA, 1980 ——

FIREMAN ASSISTS HOTEL GUESTS IN CLIMB DOWN FIRETRUCK LADDER
Some of the guests staying on lower floors at the MGM Grand were able to escape via ladder extensions on fire department ladder trucks.

The MGM Grand in Las Vegas was the world's largest hotel when it opened in 1973, with a tower containing over 2,000 rooms and a ground-floor casino big enough to contain a football field. Before construction was completed, the owners won a dispute with the local fire marshals: A Clark County building official ruled that they did not have to install a $192,000 sprinkler system in the casino. Eight years later, this would have cataclysmic consequences when a fire tore through the casino and the MGM became a giant chimney. It was the second worst hotel fire in U.S. history.

The fire began in the Deli, a restaurant in the unsprinklered casino decorated with cloth, plastic, vinyl seating, plywood veneer, and wall-to-wall carpeting. According to the Clark County Fire Department investigation, it was caused by an electrical ground fault. A soffit, or false cupboard, that housed the compressor for a refrigerated pastry display case contained improperly installed wires: The wires were not grounded, only partially insulated, and the constant vibration of the compressor caused them to chafe against each other. The compressor also emitted an almost continuous stream of warm air into the soffit that caused a buildup of heat in the wires. These processes, over a six-year period, caused the wires to galvanize (create a self-generated current), erode, and finally, on November 21, 1980, to short-circuit.

It did not take long for the soffit to ignite as the wires heated up to become glowing metal. The small fire smoldered, undetected, for several hours (the unsprinklered Deli also lacked heat and smoke detectors). At 7:05 AM, an employee who entered the Deli saw the flames and notified the security office. His efforts to contain the blaze with an extinguisher were thwarted by air pressure and smoke, and he fled for safety, leaving the doors open.

FLASHOVER AND SMOKE
The fire consumed the flammable furnishings in the Deli, and broke through the ceiling into the plenum, the 1,300,000 square-foot air return system that ran above the entire length of the first-floor ceiling. At 7:20 AM, fire roared through the open Deli doors into the casino, where it was greatly accelerated not only by the decorations (including "crystal" chandeliers and mirrors made of plastic) but also by the cellulose fiber acoustic tiles and the glue (an estimated 12 tons) that affixed the tiles to the ceiling.

Flashover then occurred, creating a fireball that traveled 336 feet (112 m) in 25 seconds and blew out the front doors. The casino was entirely aflame within six minutes. Smoke began to recycle and collect at the plenum.

Approximately 5,000 people were in the hotel, but because of the hour, the casino was mostly empty. Clark County firefighters quickly arrived after receiving the initial call at 7:17 AM. The first firemen to arrive were not aware of the amassed smoke that was beginning to ascend through every available vertical opening into the high-rise portion of the building. Smoke easily penetrated the hotel's air systems through the plenum, seeping through unsealed vents. It also shot up through seismic joints (vertical gaps that allow the building to move in an earthquake), stairwells and elevator shafts.

HELICOPTER PILOTS RESCUE HUNDREDS

RESCUE HELICOPTERS LIFT PEOPLE to safety from the MGM Grand roof. Some of the most dramatic rescue missions at the MGM were undertaken by helicopter pilots, who saved hundreds of people from the smoke-covered hotel roof during three peril-filled hours. Pilot Ray Poss, owner of a charter helicopter business and part-time pilot for the Las Vegas Police Search and Rescue squad, teamed up that morning with a police pilot, Harry Christopher, and a pilot from the Valley Hospital, Paul Kinsey. The three men flew their choppers through the blinding, poisonous black smoke over and over, rescuing almost 20 people per trip.

Excessive heat and flame from the 2800°F (1538°C) inferno penetrated the poorly sealed elevators and caused some of the cables to melt and snap. Two cars dropped, leaving the elevator shafts to act as giant funnels of smoke.

The fire also burned "protective" plywood coverings off of the smoke-proof stairwell doors, allowing smoke to enter. The hotel only had a manual, local alarm system (not connected to the fire department), which, when sounded by security, was supposed to set off bells and a

FIREMEN INSPECT THE WRECKAGE
This dramatic photograph was taken on the afternoon of November 21 after the fire was extinguished. The fire's intense heat—over 2800°F (1538°C) melted the ceiling in the casino.

public address system. This alarm never sounded. Many people were trapped in the dark smoky hallways and stairwells (stairwell doors locked automatically and prevented reentry). Others were trapped in their rooms. Dramatic rescues ensued—firefighters and paramedics raced into the building to help people escape, helicopters lifted people off of the rooftop, and construction workers renovating the hotel assisted guests out onto scaffolding. There were 85 fatalities: 14 victims were killed in the casino fire; almost 70 died from smoke

inhalation and carbon monoxide poisoning in the tower; several people jumped. Over 700 were injured. Investigators believe that the loss of life would have been minimal if sprinklers had been installed in the casino.

MGM GRAND LEGACY

There were no criminal convictions in the landmark MGM Grand fire case, but a personal injury suit led by Wendell Gauthier, a noted liability lawyer, won plaintiffs a $208 million settlement.

FIRE REPORT

⚜ CAUSES

• Electrical fire started by an improperly installed refrigerator compressor connected to ungrounded, uninsulated wires.

• Fire accelerated by huge air-return system, casino's lack of sprinkler system, and combustible furnishings—especially glued-on ceiling tiles.

BURNED CEILING TILES AND PLASTIC CHANDELIER

⚜ FIRE FACTS

• Second-worst hotel fire in U.S. history after the Winecoff.

• It took six years for electrical wires to produce enough heat to cause a fire.

• Exposed vertical openings created a chimney effect.

⚜ LOSSES

• 85 died, mostly from carbon monoxide poisoning and smoke inhalation in the tower.

⚜ DEVELOPMENTS

• Fire was a catalyst of U.S. Hotel and Motel Fire Safety Act of 1990.

• State and local improvements in communications, ventilation, lighting systems, fire apparatus, and reopenable fire doors.

RELATED FIRES

• Newhall House, Milwaukee, Wisconsin, 1883: One of first big hotel fires in U.S.; 71 died.

• Duc de Brabant, Brussels, Belgium, 1977: 302 died.

• Stouffer's Inn, Harrison, New York, 1980: arson fire kills 26.

The hotel was remodeled with highly advanced fire safety systems and reopened in 1981; it became a Bally hotel in 1986.

The MGM fire, and a 1986 fire at the Dupont Plaza in San Juan, Puerto Rico, were benchmarks in the battle against hotel fires in the U.S. They spurred the enactment of the Hotel and Motel Fire Safety Act of 1990 (PL101-391), a law that promotes fire safety in public lodgings by using the "federal travel dollar" as an incentive for hotels and motels to install fire-safety systems. The law requires federal employees to stay in public accommodations that comply with the legislation provisions, and bans federally funded meetings from noncomplying properties. PL101-391 stipulates that smoke detectors and automatic sprinklers must be installed in every room; buildings three stories or less are not required to install sprinklers.

A number of state and local laws were put into effect nationwide after these devastating fires. Many hotels today have high-tech communication systems, with alarms and speakers in rooms. High-rise buildings are constructed with emergency barriers to prevent smoke from "stacking" or moving up through ventilation and other vertical systems. Corridors are equipped with fire extinguishers, alarms, and emergency lighting. Stairwells are constructed with fire doors that prevent the spread of fire and smoke, but do not automatically lock. Stairwells are also outfitted with smoke detectors, sprinklers, and emergency phones. When a fire alarm is triggered, most modern high-rise elevators are programmed to automatically return to the ground floor, where they shut down and remain available for firefighters to use if necessary.

WINECOFF HOTEL
——— ATLANTA, USA, 1946 ———

AMERICA'S DEADLIEST HOTEL FIRE occurred at an Atlanta establishment advertised as "fireproof." The brick facade of the Winecoff Hotel, built in 1915 on the corner of Peachtree and Ellis Streets, was fireproof. But the building itself was highly unsafe. At 15 stories, the Winecoff was Atlanta's tallest hotel, yet it lacked sprinklers and fire escapes: When Atlanta revised its fire codes in 1943, the city attorney exempted all preexisting buildings, to avoid burdening landlords with costly remodeling fees.

There was only one staircase located in the center of the building; it was spiral and had no fire doors, which allowed smoke and flame to easily penetrate the upper floors. On the evening of December 7, 1946, the Winecoff was filled to capacity—many of the 280 guests were teenagers attending a State legislative youth assembly. There were also resident veterans and tourists in town for holiday shopping.

The fire began at 3:15 AM on the third floor and quickly traveled up the spiral staircase and along the corridors. Firemen arrived on the scene within minutes, but were unable to save those guests who were overcome by the acrid smoke. Many died of asphyxiation or carbon monoxide poisoning in their rooms, or near windows with no means of escape.

By the time the fire was exinguished at 6:00 AM, there were 119 fatalities. It was officially declared as an accidental fire started by a dropped cigarette, but one theory is it may have been arson perpetrated by a petty criminal.

Within days of the fire, codes to improve fire safety in older public buildings and hotels were enacted by Georgia's legislature, and in other states across the U.S.

ROARING FLAMES AT THE FIRE'S PEAK
Firemen's ladders were not tall enough to reach the higher floors so dozens jumped to their deaths to escape the fire and smoke. Even those who landed in firemen's life nets were at risk—several were killed or seriously injured upon impact. Others dangled precariously from sheet ropes tied to windows, climbing down to safety or falling.

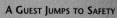

A GUEST JUMPS TO SAFETY
This Pulitzer–prize winning photograph was taken by Arnold Handy, a 26-year-old grad student and amateur photographer who was the first lensman at the scene. The woman pictured, Daisy McCumber, broke many bones but survived the fall.

FIRE REPORT

CAUSES
• Official cause, a dropped cigarette; now thought than an arsonist set the fire.

FIRE FACTS
• No sprinklers or fire escapes due to a fire code exemption for old buildings in Atlanta.

• A single spiral staircase acted as a tunnel for fire and smoke.

• At the time, it was the most fatal—and most famous— hotel fire in world history.

LOSSES
• 119 died, many more injured.

DEVELOPMENTS
• Sweeping fire safety reform in Atlanta and across the U.S. for hotels and existing buildings.

DUPONT PLAZA
— SAN JUAN, PUERTO RICO, 1986 —

AT 3:00 PM ON December 31, 1986, guests on holiday at the Dupont Plaza hotel and casino in San Juan were anticipating New Year's Eve festivities. By 3:12 pm, 97 guests had died in a devastating fire, that—along with the MGM Grand fire six years earlier—was the catalyst for the 1990

STAIRWAY ESCAPE
Emergency workers help a girl who was able to escape from a fifth floor balcony. Over 400 guest rooms were affected by smoke.

U.S. Hotel and Motel Fire Safety Act. On the day of the fire, the hotel's management was in the midst of a labor dispute with striking union workers. To keep strikers from breaking into the hotel, the managers had locked the casino exit that led directly outdoors. Several angry workers did get inside, though, into the lower level ballroom complex. At 3:00 pm they set fire to a huge stack of corrugated cartons in the South Ballroom containing particleboard hotel dressers and sofa beds filled with urethane foam. The fire consumed this substantial fireload in minutes, gaining fuel from polyester fabric glued to the walls and 50 wooden chairs stored in the room.

Flames and smoke roared through an opening in the laminate partition separating the South Ballroom from the North Ballroom. Seven minutes after the fire began, smoke started to emerge through a door in the North Ballroom, into a glass-walled foyer, and up an open staircase leading to the main lobby and casino, where guests first became aware that there was a fire in the hotel. Only three minutes after this

first sighting of smoke, flashover occurred in the South Ballroom. The intense heat and pressure of the blast broke the glass walls between the foyer and ballrooms, fanning the fire. Within 40 seconds, a searing, toxic smoke front filled the lobby and casino, blocking the main exit; the outdoor casino exit had been locked—there was no escape. Two minutes later a flame front blew through the glass west wall of the casino. The 20-story hotel was nonsprinklered and its localized manual fire alarm system was broken. There was no fire-evacuation plan or employee training. Within 12 minutes, 97 had died.

Wendell Gauthier, lead lawyer in the MGM Grand case, won a suit brought by 2,000 Dupont victims against 200 defendants—one of the largest awards made to personal injury victims: $230 million. This victory, coupled with the Hotel and Motel Fire Safety Act, brought new levels of safety to U.S. hotels.

ROOF RESCUE
As smoke climbed through ventilation ducts, stairways, and open windows, many guests ran to the roof, where they were rescued by U.S. Coast Guard helicopters.

DUPONT PLAZA
san juan

FIRE REPORT

⚜ CAUSES
• Arson: three striking union workers torched a highly flammable pile of furniture.

⚜ FIRE FACTS
• Fire grew to fatal proportions only 12 mintues after it began.

• Dupont Plaza did not have a sprinkler system, working fire alarm, or evacuation plan.

• Management locked one of two exits in the casino to prevent strikers from entering.

⚜ LOSSES
• 97 died, many more injured.

⚜ DEVELOPMENTS
• A catalyst, along with the MGM Grand Fire, to the U.S. Hotel and Motel Fire Safety Act.

• Unprecented personal injury settlement of $230 million awarded to victims.

THE GENERAL SLOCUM
NEW YORK CITY, USA, 1904

THE TRAGEDY ABOARD THE EXCURSION STEAMER *GENERAL SLOCUM*, although not nearly as famous as the sinking of the *Titanic* on April 15, 1912, was just as memorable. It occurred much closer to home, in the warm waters of New York City's East River. At 9:20 AM, on June 15, 1904, the 264-foot (80 m) paddlewheel vessel *General Slocum* slid away from a 3rd Street pier in downtown Manhattan. Sixty minutes later, more than 1,000 people, half of them under the age of 20, would be dead.

THE STARK REMAINS
Little more than one of the paddlewheels and two of its three stacks is visible in this photo, as the steamer sinks into the East River.

Gen! Slocum

RESCUE ATTEMPTS
Tugs, rowboats, and even sailboats were among the hundred or more vessels that joined in the frantic effort to get passengers off the burning General Slocum. *The Scot artist Sir William Russell Flint (1880–1969), hired by the* Illustrated London News *just a year before the* Slocum *fire, painted this watercolor for publication in the paper.*

In the aftermath of the tragedy, tough new reforms in maritime standards were instigated, but for nearly a century the burning and sinking of the *General Slocum* claimed the dubious distinction of being the worst domestic disaster to befall New York City. In addition, it decimated the largest ethnic German community in the United States—a prosperous, bustling Lower East Side neighborhood once called the Weiss Garten.

The *General Slocum* was chartered by St. Mark's Lutheran Church for its 17th annual Sunday School outing, which was to have taken about 1,200 members of the largely German-speaking congregation to Locust Grove, a popular picnic spot on Long Island's north shore. Named after a Civil War officer who had gone on to Congress, the *Slocum* was considered one of the largest and grandest excursion steamers in New York. Three decks high and made entirely of wood except for her three stacks and hull, the boat slid away from Lower Manhattan with all the usual fanfare: pennants flying from bow to stern, the band playing, paddles churning, and puffs of black smoke rising from the stacks. Because it was a workday, most of the passengers were women and children. It was a sunny, cloudless day with a cool breeze blowing off the East River. As the *Slocum* reached the treacherous whirlpools of Hell Gate, near the shoreline of Astoria, thick clouds of smoke began to boil from the bows.

THE SPREAD OF THE BLAZE

The exact cause and location of the fire has never been ascertained, although it is believed that a steward, smoking in a cabin containing barrels of oil, oil lamps, and an assortment of other highly combustible materials, accidentally set off the blaze. When a deckhand smelled the fire and opened the door to the cabin, the rush of oxygen caused a backdraft that shot him across the deck, which was set on fire. Creating its own wind as it moved along the wide waters of the river, the boat continued to burn furiously. The crew attempted to fight the fire, but it was beyond control. Fire hoses had rotted and were

CAPTAIN WILLIAM VAN SCHAICK

FOR YEARS *before it burned and sank in the East River, the* General Slocum *had been prone to accidents. The ship collided with other vessels on at least four other occasions and had run aground six times. Captain William H. Van Schaick had crashed the ship into piers and hit tugboats, but because none of these accidents were particularly serious, officials looked the other way. In the weeks before the fatal fire aboard the* Slocum, *however, it was rumored that the 61-year-old captain, who was nearing retirement age, might be relieved of his duties.*

IN THE AFTERMATH *of the* Slocum *affair, Van Schaick was charged with manslaughter and criminal negligence for not holding fire drills, not training the crew properly, and not maintaining fire apparatus. He was sentenced to 10 years of hard labor in Sing Sing, the infamous penitentiary in upstate New York. But Van Schaick's perverse luck didn't run out, even though he'd been blinded and crippled by the accident. After serving a few years of his sentence, Van Schaick was pardoned by President William Howard Taft at Christmas, 1912. To the end of his days Van Schaick maintained that he had done everything possible to save lives aboard the* General Slocum.

unusable, and even had they worked, the pumps that would have fed them didn't function. Inexplicably, the captain continued to steer the boat full speed ahead, instead of attempting to beach the *Slocum* on the Astoria shore or drop anchor so that nearby vessels could provide rescue. Instead, Captain William H. Van Schaick seemed determined to beach the *Slocum* upriver on North Brother Island, over two miles away. As he plowed into a brisk wind, waves of oil-fed flames fanned over hundreds of passengers on deck. Horrified crowds witnessed the scene from the shore, unable to help the screaming passengers as they leapt into the East River, their clothes on fire, only to drown in the swift currents as their clothing, and even their life preservers, became waterlogged. Few New Yorkers knew how to swim in 1904. Many passengers were caught in the huge paddlewheels on both the starboard and port sides of the vessel and were crushed to death, while others were pitched into the

burning core of the ship's hull. More than a hundred small vessels and a dozen tugboats rushed to the scene to pick victims off the burning steamer and out of the water, but only a

RECOVERY EFFORTS
In the days after the fire, divers recovered the bodies of casualties from the sunken wreck of the steamboat. In addition to the recovery vessel shown at the right, rowboats can be seen surrounding the paddlewheel—in all likelihood, carrying friends and family of the missing and deceased.

FIREFIGHTING EFFORTS
Water was sprayed on the smoking skeleton of the General Slocum *from fireboats before the steamer sank below the surface of the East River in Hell Gate. All but the paddlewheels, hull, and stacks were wood and burned quickly as the* Slocum *continued down the East River at full speed.*

RAISING OF THE WRECK
Little was left of the General Slocum when the burned-out hull was sold. Once the diving had been completed, the wreck was raised from the East River and towed to one of New York City's piers.

few hundred were saved. More than 1,000 died. Some of the rescue boats, in fact, caught fire as they came alongside the *Slocum*.

FEDERAL INVESTIGATION

An inquest, ordered by President Theodore Roosevelt, showed that the *General Slocum*, which had burned all the way down to the waterline, had been in grave violation of the most basic safeguards. The flammable materials, such as the barrels of oil and other combustible materials, were not properly stowed. Cheap fire hoses and life jackets were rotten or ripped, lifeboats were not seaworthy, and officials had ignored the captain's record of previous accidents. Also, in a bid to save money, the boat's owners had hired an inexperienced crew, none of whom had experience with fire drills. The boat itself had not been inspected in years. The captain, first mate, officers of the steamboat company, and a steamboat inspector were indicted, but only the captain was convicted. Meanwhile the

boat's operators, possibly the greatest offenders in the *Slocum* tragedy, were least affected by it. According to the law, their liability was limited to the value of the vessel. The burned out hulk was raised and sold for $1,800.

Following the *General Slocum* fire, Congress tightened the requirements for firefighting and lifesaving provisions on passenger ships. In the wake of the tragedy, hundreds of ships were given safety inspections, and many were found to have the same violations as the *General Slocum* had.

THE SLOCUM MONUMENT
Joseph Bermel's monument to the many women and children who perished was unveiled on the anniversary of the tragedy, July 15, 1905.

IN MEMORIAM

GREAT HOBOKEN PIER FIRE

HOBOKEN, USA, 1900

SALVAGE OF THE *SAALE*

The Saale, *the first of the four North German Lloyd ships to catch fire and the most extensively damaged, lies by Ellis Island after the fires were extinguished. The heat was so intense that the paint peeled off the ship, leaving large white spots. The portholes, too small to permit escape by adults, are visible at the third level above the water. Here, the* Saale *is seen next to the derrick of the salvage company that repaired the* Main *and the* Bremen *as well.*

ON THE AFTERNOON of Saturday, June 30, 1900, a fire broke out at Pier 3 in Hoboken, New Jersey. Whether the cause was baled cotton that had caught fire by accident—or arson—no one knows for sure. Nor is it possible to establish the total number of people who lost their lives that day. Hundreds drowned in the Hudson River; scores were incinerated in the steel hulls of burning ships; and many others died in passenger liners, as they attempted to escape through portholes that were too small for adults to fit through. Weather conditions were hot and dry. The sky was cloudless and the wind was blowing from the southwest—factors that would affect the swift progress of the fire as it swept from pier to pier and ship to ship.

On the day of the fire, visitors crowded the North German Lloyd Steamship Company piers, where four of its ships were docked on the Hudson. The largest, the *Kaiser Wilhelm der Grosse,* was moored on the south side of Pier 1. The biggest and fastest ship in the world at the time, she was the first of the famous four-stacked liners and was famous for her luxury and profitability. Moored on the north side of Pier 1 was the sleek new steamer *Main*, a one-stack ship with four large cranes for loading cargo. Built in 1886, the *Saale* was used primarily for cargo. She was moored on the south side of Pier 2. The *Bremen*, one of the first in a class of German-built ships that weighed over 10,000 tons, was docked on the north side of Pier 2.

At approximately 3:55 PM, a watchman noticed smoke coming from Pier 3, where about 700 bales of cotton and a cargo of whiskey barrels were being stored. It took him several minutes to reach a telephone, but by 4:01 PM, the headquarters of the Hoboken Fire Department, which was only two blocks away, had logged his report. The fire spread quickly because of the strong breeze and the flammability of the pier sheds, which were made of wood. Of the three 600–900-foot (183–274 m) long piers, only Pier 1 had a steel frame. The flames jumped quickly from the piers onto the ships. Some witnesses reported that the whole area was ablaze within only 10 to 20 minutes.

Workers and visitors were forced toward the river, where they jumped into the water, or onto lighters (flat-bottomed barges used for loading and unloading cargo). Some tried to escape from the burning piers by running through the fires toward Hoboken, while others frantically entered the two ships on Pier 2—the *Saale* and the *Bremen*—despite efforts of the crews to stop them from coming aboard. The *Saale* was the first ship to catch fire and drift away from the pier, and those trapped behind the small portholes had no escape. Meanwhile tugboats and other harbor boats were on their way to put out the fires and rescue people who were either already in the water or hanging over the sides of the great ships.

Next, the *Bremen* caught fire and drifted from the pier. Both the *Bremen* and the *Saale* were

SALVAGE TUGS—SAVING OR STEALING?

WHILE MOST TUGBOAT CREWS acted out of purely altruistic sentiments to save the human victims of these tragedies, there were others who flocked to shipwrecks and pier fires with other, less noble purposes in mind. Floating barges of cotton or coal, or even barrels of whisky, were attractive prizes for these crews, who often bypassed drowning victims in favor of making a quick profit.

THE DESTRUCTION OF THE PIERS
The smoke cloud from the Hoboken pier fire could be seen for miles around. The remains of the North German Lloyd piers can be seen in this picture; the dark building near the center was one of the pier buildings that fell into the water. The Campbell's Stores, at left, has just burst into flames.

burning out of control. The *Kaiser Wilhelm der Grosse*, the flagship of the Northern German Lloyd, was carrying the greatest number of tourists and would have been the next to catch fire, but she was saved—without any casualties—thanks to her well-trained, disciplined crew, and the many tugboats that came to tow her away from the burning pier and other burning ships. Compared to the damage of the other three ships, the *Kaiser*

Wilhelm de Grosse escaped with only minor damage to the ship itself: a fire in the bow caused by a burning coal barge; 200 square feet (19 sq m) of paint burned off; glass broken by the heat; and some wooden objects stored on the deck, such as the lifeboats, burned. The *Main*, which had been moored the farthest north on the north side of Pier 1, was the next to catch fire. Breaking away from the pier, the ship eventually foundered on the

Weehawken Flats. The *Bremen* was also towed to Weehawken Flats while it was still burning, to keep it clear of the *Kaiser*, and the *Main* and *Bremen* could be seen, burning, side by side. Some of the ships continued to burn for a few more days.

In the end, between 326 and 400 people had lost their lives to the fire. If all of the boats had maintained a sufficient level of steam to be able to leave their moorings without assistance from tugboats—as all boats are required to do now—the fires would not have spread as quickly as they did, nor caused as many casualties. The lack of fireproof covers for the baled cotton and the wooden docks and pier buildings led to the quick spread of the fire and, most probably, the deaths of hundreds of people, including many longshoremen who were working on the piers that day.

THE LAST STAND
A hose is directed at the one corner still remaining of Campbell's Stores, which had been built at a cost of $1.5 million. The rest of the building, along with the large Hoboken warehouse, was burned down.

FIRE REPORT

CAUSES
• A carelessly thrown cigarette or spark from a tool or machinery, or arson.

FIRE FACTS
• Largest fire loss in the U.S. during 1900.

• In 10–20 minutes North German Lloyd Piers were ablaze.

LOSSES
• 326–400 dead.

• $5 million in property loss.

• Losses included 3 North German Lloyd piers and 1 Thingvalla Line pier, Campbell's Stores, and Hoboken Warehouse.

• 4 liners burned; 3 seriously damaged.

• 27 barges, work boats, and harbor craft lost.

DEVELOPMENTS
• Fireproof covers required for baled cotton stored on docks.

• New fire-prevention techniques, concrete and steel used to build piers.

• Portholes widened to provide usable fire exits.

45

MORRO CASTLE
— ASBURY PARK, USA, 1934 —

THIRTY YEARS AFTER the *Slocum* tragedy, fire on the high seas was in the news once again. On September 8, 1934, the *Morro Castle*, reputed to be one of the era's most luxurious and popular passenger ships, was returning to New York from a cruise to Havana, Cuba, when a devastating fire broke out on the Promenade Deck. Sometime between 2:15 AM and 2:40 AM, a steward discovered the fire in an empty writing-room locker.

Unlike the Slocum, the *Morro Castle* had a fire-alarm system, fire doors, and a full complement of required fire-protection equipment, but 137 people lost their lives nevertheless, and the ship itself was reduced to a burned-out hulk. Later investigations showed that the crew was not adequately trained in the use of firefighting devices or in managing passengers in an emergency. Indeed, it was reported that members of the crew, including the chief engineer, fled the burning ship in the first lifeboat, leaving many passengers to swim for their lives in the open ocean (there were not enough lifeboats for all of the passengers).

The *Morro Castle* had been built to conform to all the latest safety standards, including fireproof bulkheads, but it contained any number of highly flammable trappings that were customary in most ships at the time. Ultimately, the effect of combustible furnishings in cabins and public spaces outweighed the advantages of fireproof partitions, fire doors, and the like, enabling the blaze to sweep unchecked through the ship. Some passengers were burned to death in their cabins; some managed to escape in the remaining lifeboats; some floated in the turbulent waves until 11:00 AM the following morning, waiting for rescue boats; and a few actually swam to the shores of New Jersey, eight miles (13 km) from the ship.

In the hours before the blaze, the *Morro Castle* had already escaped a hurricane and was reeling from the unexpected death of the ship's captain. First Mate William F. Warms took command of the ship after Captain Robert R. Willmott was found dead, presumably from a heart attack, in his cabin at about 7:00 PM on September 7. Eight hours later, the *Morro Castle* was on fire. As the inferno grew, Warms sailed the vessel into a wind off the starboard quarter of the ship, which fanned and fed the spreading flames. For reasons that remain a mystery to this day, Warms delayed in sending an SOS and rallying the crew. By late morning, rescue boats—including those of the U.S. Coast Guard—arrived on the scene, but by then 137 people had died. The smoldering hulk of the ship eventually drifted ashore, settling behind Asbury Park, New Jersey's Convention Hall, where it was viewed by curious tourists.

GEORGE WHITE ROGERS, ARSONIST?
The ship's Chief Radio Operator, George Rogers, was hailed as a hero for staying on the ship long enough to send the SOS—while "almost in a coma." However, his heroism aboard the Morro Castle *was later reexamined when he was convicted of several violent murders. Some theorize that he might also have murdered Captain Willmott and set the ship on fire to cover his tracks.*

BEACHED CRUISE SHIP
The smoking remains of the Morro Castle *were viewed from the shores of Asbury Park, New Jersey, by hundreds of tourists in the days after the fire.*

PHILIPPINE FERRY FIRES
PHILIPPINES, 1987–2002

THE PHILIPPINE ECONOMY has long been dependent on sea transport. Passenger ferries are the main form of transportation in the Philippines' more than 7,000 islands, and overcrowding and accidents are common. Gross infringements of maritime regulations have also contributed to the number of passenger ferries that collide, catch fire, and sink every year in the Philippines. Most of these tragedies share a common feature: the number of survivors and fatalities always greatly exceed the number of passengers recorded on the manifest.

THE DONA PAZ

While overloading is not the major cause of most ferry disasters, excess loads greatly affect a vessel's stability, increasing the chances of capsizing. Many passengers buy their tickets onboard, which means their names do not appear on the ship's manifest. Consequently, it is impossible to tell exactly how many passengers are on a ferry at any

given time. This was the case of the *Dona Paz*, a 2,215-ton passenger ferry that collided with the *Victor*—a tanker carrying 8,300 barrels of oil in its holds. Survivors of the *Dona Paz* said so many people were jammed onboard that up to four passengers shared individual berths, and hundreds of others were sitting on the floors of the three-deck ship when it collided with the *Victor*.

The collision occurred at 10:00 PM on Sunday, December 20, 1987, in the Tablas Straits, about 100 miles (161 km) south of Manila. One passenger described "a jerk and an explosion," before fire broke out and rapidly engulfed the ship. Both vessels sank. Merchant ships plucked fewer than 30 survivors, most of them suffering from

burns as a result of a sea of blazing oil. It was the worst accident in Philippine maritime history and, arguably, one of the most catastrophic of the 20th century.

The *Dona Paz*, which had the capacity to carry about 1,500 passengers, was in all likelihood carrying at least three times that number—if not more. Over 4,500 people may have died on the *Dona Paz* .

On April 11, 2002 there was another deadly fire aboard a Philippine ferry. The *Maria Carmela* was carrying 290 passengers when a blaze broke out in the cargo hold. Over 200 people were rescued by passing fishing boats and the Coast Guard, but at least 23 people were reported dead. Dozens of others are presumed to have drowned.

DONA PAZ
Originally named the Himeyuri, the ferry was sold to Sulpicio lines in 1975 and renamed the Dom Sulpicio. After a fire in 1975, the boat was rebuilt and given its third and ill-fated name—Dona Paz, meaning "Lady Peace."

MARIA CARMELA
The fire aboard this ferry is thought to have started when a cigarette butt was tossed into a sack of copra (coconut byproduct) in one of several trucks parked in the cargo hold of the vessel. The captain claimed that the fire was an act of arson because the Maria Carmela had long transported copra without any untoward incidents.

A smaller ferry tries to put out the fire on the Maria Carmela.

FIRE REPORT

CAUSES
• Collisions, overloading, carelessly discarded cigarettes, and perhaps arson in the case of the *Maria Carmela*.

LOSSES
• 4,000 to 4,500 fatalities on *Dona Paz*.

• The maritime death toll in the Philippines between 1993–2002 alone has been estimated at 10,000 lives, with 169 ships lost.

FIRE FACTS
• *Dona Paz* was the world's worst peacetime shipping disaster.

DEVELOPMENTS
• Strict enforcement of maritime codes regarding overloading and operation of vessels

• Measures taken to reduce number of illegal passengers and dangerous crowding on ferries by color-coding tickets, based on destination, so when passengers disembark from a vessel, only the equivalent number will be allowed to go onboard

SAN FRANCISCO EARTHQUAKE

SAN FRANCISCO, USA, 1906

OF THE MANY FIRES that had ravaged San Francisco in previous years, all would pale before the one that took place on April 18, 1906. It was the most devastating fire ever to savage an American city. It began with an earthquake, one of the most significant in recorded history, which released 12,000 times the destructive force of an atom bomb. By the time the fire burned itself out, three days later, an estimated 3,000 people were dead and 250,000 citizens were left homeless. San Francisco, which had enjoyed a building boom since the Gold Rush of 1849, was the ninth-largest city in the U.S. Now, about 75 percent of San Francisco—an area of some four square miles (10 sq km), covering almost 3,000 acres (1,200 ha)—was destroyed.

RESCUED FROM THE FIRE.
This dramatic, panoramic painting by William Alexander Coulter (1849-1936) depicts the blazing shoreline between Fort Mason and the foot of Lombard Street, where more than 30,000 San Franciscans were rescued by a flotilla of vessels that carried them to safety in nearby Sausalito.

Undaunted, San Franciscans began cleaning up and rebuilding their city while the rubble was still warm. Ten days after the fire, streetcars started to run again and by 1909 the city was virtually rebuilt: over 20,000 new buildings now stood where 28,000 had gone up in flames just three years earlier. San Francisco had experienced other big quakes—over two dozen of them, in fact—dating from 1836. But, as big as some of the previous quakes had been, and as quickly as San Franciscans had recovered from each of them, no one was prepared for the events of April 18, 1906, when the city was literally shaken to its foundations.

On that day, at 5:12 AM, a foreshock was felt throughout the San Francisco Bay area. About 20 to 25 seconds later the great earthquake broke loose, rupturing the northernmost 290 miles (470 km) of the San Andreas Fault. The rupture itself ripped through the ground at about 5,800 miles an hour (9,300 kmh). Violent shocks and shaking lasted for less than a minute, but the earthquake, registering a 7.9 on today's Richter scale, was felt from southern Oregon to south of Los Angeles and inland as far as central Nevada. In San Francisco, near the epicenter, a low rumble could be heard. Seconds later, the ground heaved.

Concrete-and-steel buildings shook violently and then collapsed. The three main lines that fed San Francisco's water-distribution system cracked, and then the gas mains broke. Fire from a dozen sources, including the ruptured gas lines, broke out immediately and almost all at once. There was no telephone or telegraph service, the entire streetcar system had come to a standstill, and sewage, combined with water, was spewing from broken pipes throughout the city.

Vibrations from the quake had liquefied the ground under the Valencia Street Hotel, which had been built on landfill. The hotel sank a full story, thereby breaking a water main and taking the lives of nearly 200 people.

Thousands fled into the streets, where they were injured or killed by falling debris. Even the great

SAN FRANCISCO IN FLAMES.
Four square miles (10 sq km) — 520 city blocks — were on fire. Billowing clouds and columns of smoke could be seen from one hundred miles (161 km) away, while the roar of the fire, the crash of falling walls, and continuous explosions made San Francisco a living hell. Financial buildings along Market and Mission Streets were ignited one after another, while the so-called Ham and Eggs fire that destroyed the Hayes Valley neighborhood was started by someone who foolishly began preparations for breakfast, not realizing that the chimney was already badly damaged.

tenor Enrico Caruso, who had sung *Carmen* the previous evening at San Francisco's Grand Opera House, was seen fleeing from the luxurious Palace Hotel in nothing but his nightshirt.

South of Market Street more than 40 fires smoldered and eventually merged with fires farther north on Hayes Street, creating a firestorm that roared through the city. Many of the concrete and brick buildings in downtown San Francisco—including the Call Building, which was one of the first skyscrapers in the U.S.—had been thought to be fire-resistant until they succumbed to flames that day.

The fire department responded to the many alarms as quickly as possible—but with increasingly limited resources. Without access to water, the city's 600 firefighters were severely handicapped.

The speed of the fire, the condition of the city's streets—made impassible by fallen debris and rubble—as well as the sheer number of stranded, stunned, and injured residents crowding the streets, made the firefighters' job all the more difficult.

FROM BEER TO DYNAMITE

A local legend has it that when a fire threatened to burn a canvas tarp covering valuable police records, firefighters doused the flames with beer. They worked tirelessly in the Mission and Harbor districts, which had been particularly hard hit. When fire began to sweep over the piers connecting the city to valuable shipments of food and other vital supplies, firefighters pumped water from San Francisco Bay to quench the flames. Meanwhile, city workers labored to repair the cracked water mains. And when the decision was made to create firebreaks by dynamiting buildings in the fire's path, firefighters threw themselves into the job, working side by side with policemen and the army troops that had been placed at the city's disposal. The dynamiting lasted for days, but the

fire took on a life of its own and either jumped over the breaks or came up from the rear.

As it became apparent that fire would sweep the entire city, thousands of refugees either

headed for nearby hills or took advantage of free transportation (furnished by the Southern Pacific Railroad) and left the city altogether. At least 100,000 homeless citizens camped in

ON PATROL
Troops from the Presidio walk east along Market Street after the earthquake. Part of their mission was to protect private and public property as well as to assist police and firefighters. Smoke is billowing out of the tall Call Building—one of America's first skyscrapers.

FREDERICK N. FUNSTON, BRIGADIER GENERAL, U.S. ARMY

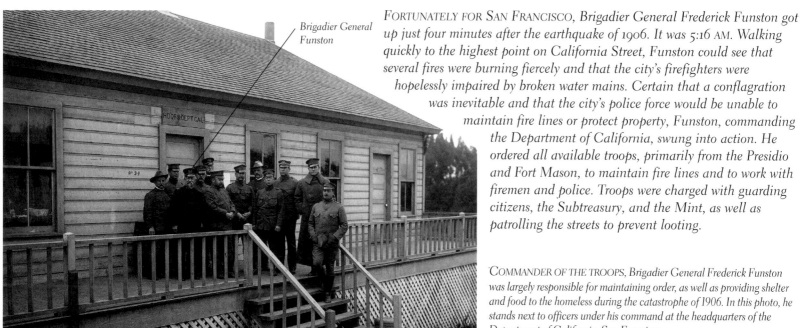

Brigadier General Funston

FORTUNATELY FOR SAN FRANCISCO, *Brigadier General Frederick Funston got up just four minutes after the earthquake of 1906. It was 5:16 AM. Walking quickly to the highest point on California Street, Funston could see that several fires were burning fiercely and that the city's firefighters were hopelessly impaired by broken water mains. Certain that a conflagration was inevitable and that the city's police force would be unable to maintain fire lines or protect property, Funston, commanding the Department of California, swung into action. He ordered all available troops, primarily from the Presidio and Fort Mason, to maintain fire lines and to work with firemen and police. Troops were charged with guarding citizens, the Subtreasury, and the Mint, as well as patrolling the streets to prevent looting.*

COMMANDER OF THE TROOPS, *Brigadier General Frederick Funston was largely responsible for maintaining order, as well as providing shelter and food to the homeless during the catastrophe of 1906. In this photo, he stands next to officers under his command at the headquarters of the Department of California, San Francisco.*

One or two outer walls were all that was left of many of these financial buildings when the fire—and the firefighting efforts—had ended

One of the few buildings that remained, albeit burned out and gutted within, among a ghostly stand of chimneys

CHIMNEYS TOWER ABOVE THE RUBBLE
Almost 30,000 buildings, including mansions on Nob Hill, City Hall, and San Francisco's Grand Opera House, were destroyed in 1906.

public parks and graveyards, where they watched in horror as buildings burned around them. People simply packed as many possessions as they could into trunks and fled their homes, dragging the trunks over the cobblestoned city streets. Others, whose homes had miraculously survived but who no longer had any other source of income, took in boarders.

When there was no more fuel to feed the flames, they extinguished themselves, leaving a broad swath of desolation through the heart of the city. Although martial law was never imposed, over 4,000 troops served during the emergency and oversaw relief efforts. Civil authorities took over the responsibility on July 1, 1906, and the army withdrew.

In the wake of this disaster, city planners incorporated land-based saltwater pumps to access water from the bay if necessary in the future.

HOMES DESTROYED
Victorian houses on Howard Street lean dangerously to the side in this hand-colored contemporary photograph. The earthquake broke foundations, cracked walls, and compromised the structure of hundreds, if not thousands, of homes all over San Francisco.

FIRE REPORT

⚡ CAUSES
• Broken gas mains, due to an earthquake.

⚡ FIRE FACTS
• Broken water mains hampered firefighting efforts.

• Dynamite was used to create firebreaks.

• The fire of 1906 went out on its own after 3 days.

⚡ LOSSES
• Over 3,000 deaths.

• 225,000 people (out of 400,000) left homeless

• 28,000 buildings destroyed

• $400 million in property damage ($7.8 billion in today's dollars).

⚡ DEVELOPMENTS
• City planners improved the fire department's water supply infrastructure and designed earthquake-proof and fireproof buildings

• U.S. cities designed water distribution systems to include subsystems for firefighting use. Buffalo, New York, and Rochester, New York, were the first cities to adopt this design.

RELATED FIRES

• Agadir, Morocco, 1960. Approximately 12,000 to 17,000 people died around midnight on February 29, 1960, when a 5.7-magnitude earthquake set off a tidal wave and a fire in Agadir, Morocco. Much of the city was leveled and half of its inhabitants were buried alive in about 15 seconds. Most of the houses had been built of stone and clay tile or poor-quality cement.

GREAT KANTO EARTHQUAKE
SOUTHEASTERN JAPAN, 1923

THE EARTHQUAKE THAT SHATTERED TOKYO AND THE PORT CITY OF YOKOHAMA on September 1, 1923, was, as in the case of San Francisco, the precursor to fire. The magnitude 7.9 quake struck at around noon, just as the citizens of Tokyo and Yokohama were lighting fires in gas or coal-burning stoves to make their midday meals. Within moments of the quake fires sprang up everywhere—88 in Yokohama alone. Although the wind was not blowing as fiercely in

Yokohama as it was in Tokyo, where gusts became the chief obstacle to firefighting, the wind-fed firestorms swept through the city's paper and wood structures and quickly engulfed them in a fire that would last for two days. A particularly pernicious addition to the conflagration was made by one of the government's large arsenals, which blew up, burst into flame, and killed everyone near it. The water-distribution system, although modern by Western standards, failed when the mains were shattered by the first tremors, and was of no use to firefighters. In the ensuing panic, no effort was made to repair them.

The number of deaths in the area where the quake hit hardest—about ten square miles (26 sq km)—was appalling. The worst casualties involved people who were trapped in collapsed buildings or who had fled en masse to areas that were later overtaken by fires. Perhaps the most tragic example of this phenomenon occurred in Honjo, a district of Tokyo, where about 30,000 people had gathered in a huge, military, clothing depot to escape the fires. With brisk gusts fanning flames in every direction, the crowd was eventually engulfed in a huge blaze that fed on the possessions they had fled with—clothing, bedrolls, and furniture. No one survived.

The worst damage was in Yokohama, Japan's premier commercial port. By nightfall on September 1, Yokohama harbor was full of refugees, who had boarded a staggering assortment of ships and vessels in order to escape the spreading conflagration on land. From the harbor they could see a rim of fire all around Tokyo Bay. They could hear the fire, as well. A survivor recalled that it sounded like heavy surf, punctuated with frequent crashes of thunder. Farther inland, enormous pink-colored clouds hovered in the sky over the burning city of Tokyo. The refugees in the harbor, however, were not aware that oil from destroyed refineries in the area had been

seeping into the water. The next morning it caught fire. The flaming oil spread quickly over the surface of the harbor, setting off a massive panic to get the ships out to open sea before they were engulfed. The number of people who perished in the harbor that day is unknown, although estimates soar into the thousands.

Official estimates of the total number of fatalities in Yokohama and Tokyo approach 150,000, while injuries were reported to be in the millions. Roughly 65 percent of Tokyo was destroyed.

The Great Kanto disaster continued to have widespread ramifications in Japan. The local Korean community was blamed for the catastrophe and a wave of brutal reprisals ensued. Today, some blame the Japanese government for promoting anti-Korean policies in order to keep the public from focusing on the lack of relief measures for victims of the earthquake and fires.

STILL ON FIRE
In the aftermath of the 7.9-magnitude earthquake, crowds of people gathered in Tokyo to watch buildings burn. There was nothing they could do. The first tremors had destroyed the city's water mains, leaving firefighters defenseless. The blaze itself grew at an incredible rate, making it all the more impossible to contain or control.

A CITY IN RUINS.
The victims of the earthquake and fire of 1923 had little to come home to. Almost 65 percent of Tokyo burned down and hundreds of thousands were left homeless. Largely constructed of paper and wood, traditional Japanese structures provided the blaze with abundant fuel.

FIRE REPORT

⚜ CAUSES
• Coal or charcoal stoves toppled by the earthquake ignited the contents of traditional Japanese wood-and-paper houses.

⚜ OTHER CAUSES
• Improperly stored chemicals and fuel and an explosion at a munitions factory helped fuel the flames.

⚜ FIRE FACTS
• Tokyo (1923) and San Francisco (1906), both caused by earthquakes, were the largest peacetime urban fires in history.

• Broken water mains made conventional firefighting impossible.

⚜ LOSSES
• Over 150,000 fatalities; 40,000 missing.

• The city and port of Yokohama were destroyed, as well as 65% of Tokyo.

⚜ DEVELOPMENTS
• Ushered in the modern age of earthquake engineering.

• Building code changes for the reconstruction of Tokyo and Yokohama included restrictions on height, building materials, and architectural design.

PREPARED FOR THE WORST
A young Japanese schoolgirl in protective headgear crouches under her desk in an earthquake drill.

BIG BURN
— IDAHO, USA, 1910 —

ON AUGUST 20–21, 1910 a massive forest fire devastated 3 million acres (1.2 million ha) of timberland and killed 85 people in Montana and Idaho. The Big Burn of 1910 remains a milestone in firefighting history for more than just the environmental damage and human casualties it caused. It was a literal trial by fire for the newly created United States Forest Service, and the lessons learned from the Big Burn influenced government forest-fighting policy into the 21st century.

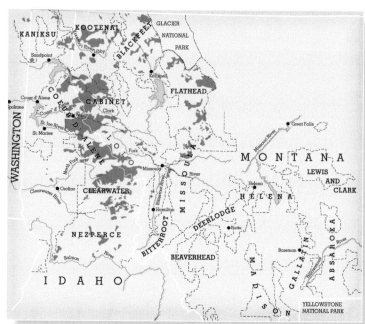

THE FIRE ZONE
This map shows the extent of the 1910 fires, which affected about 500 square miles (1,300 sq km) in eastern Idaho and western Montana. The blaze ranged south to the Snake River and north to the Canadian border.

The run-up to the Big Burn began in June when scattered fires took hold along the Montana–Idaho border. Lightning was probably the main cause of the initial fires. Sparks from coal and wood-burning railroad locomotives may have played a part, too, as well as vagrants' campfires. By late July the scattered fires began to combine, helped by dry weather. Forest fires were common in this mountainous, forested region, but that August the fires reached a scale and intensity unmatched in the memory of the area's oldest residents.

FIRE'S RAVAGES
Residents of Wallace, Idaho, who had been evacuated before August 20, survey the damage to their town upon their return.

A FATEFUL DECISION

Confronted with the biggest crisis of its short history, the Forest Service faced a stark choice: whether to do nothing and hope that the fires would burn themselves out, or to attempt to actively contain the blazes. In the end, the desire to preserve as much valuable timber as possible led Secretary of Agriculture James Wilson to choose the latter. "Without hesitation, I called upon the forest officers to stop the fires," Wilson later wrote, ". . . every source of help was called in."

Those sources soon included about 4,000 firefighters, including locally recruited civilians and soldiers rushed to the area. Camps were set up and firebreaks dug. But it wasn't enough.

On the night of August 20 high winds swept over the Bitterroot Mountains, merging the countless individual fires into an inferno that reached speeds of 70 miles per hour (113 kmph), sweeping away everything in its path. By morning the smoke was so thick that the sun couldn't be seen in Billings, Montana, some 500 miles (800 km) away from the fire zone.

MEN DRIVEN MAD

Rescue trains managed to carry most of the region's citizens out of the fire's path, but for the crews, the fight against fire turned into a struggle for survival as the wall of flame raced forward on the night of August 20–21. Some found refuge in streams or old mineshafts. Others tried in vain to outrun the blaze. A few men shot themselves to avoid burning to death.

On August 23 rain and snow began to fall and the fire finally started to recede. The exhausted survivors—many of whom had been terribly injured, some even driven insane—staggered down from the smoldering mountains. The Big Burn was over, but the debate over how to prevent and fight forest fires in the future was just beginning. The tragedy of the Big Burn turned debate over forest-fire policy into heated public controversy.

The U.S. Forest Service had been created in 1905 as part of the Department of Agriculture. Its first director, Gifford Pinchot, saw the Service as guardian of the nation's forests in the public interest. Timberland owners from heavily forested states (and the politicians they supported), however, believed the service's primary task was to keep their future profits from going up in smoke. Also, some of Pinchot's deputies promoted the then-radical idea that occasional fires were natural and necessary for healthy, expanding forests.

EDWARD PULASKI - HERO AND INVENTOR

ONE OF THE HEROES OF THE BIG BURN *was 40-year old Forest Service ranger Edward Pulaski. When he and his men met the fire on the divide between the St. Joe River and the Coeur d'Alene, he knew firefighting would not be an option. He decided to hide from the fire and wait for it to pass.*

Forest Service ranger Pulaski

FROM HIS DAYS AS A PROSPECTOR, Pulaski remembered that two old mine tunnels were nearby, and he led as many of his men as could rally into one of them (right). All but six of them survived a hellish night underground. Pulaski himself passed out. When the ground cooled enough to allow the survivors to escape, one of his men shouted "Come outside, boys; the boss is dead." "Like hell he is," Pulaski replied.

IN 1913, PULASKI INVENTED the firefighting tool that bears his name. The pulaski combines an ax for chopping with a "grubhoe" for digging. It remains standard equipment for Forest Service fire crews.

A firefighter surveys the entrance to the 75-foot-deep (23 m) hole near Wallace, in which Pulaski and his men sheltered on the night of August 20–21, 1910.

FIRE REPORT

✲ CAUSES
• Lightning combined with drought and high winds—classic forest-fire conditions.

✲ OTHER CAUSES
• Sparks from locomotive smokestacks.

• Vagrants' campfires.

✲ FIRE FACTS
• Involved 4,000 firefighters.

• First use of the telephone to send a forest-fire alarm.

✲ LOSSES
• 85 people killed (78 firefighters and 7 civilians); hundreds injured.

• 3 million acres (1.2 million ha) of forest with 8 million board feet (2.4 million m) of lumber destroyed.

✲ DEVELOPMENTS
• U.S. Forest Service policy shifted from passive emphasis on conservation of forest resources to actively fighting forest fires.

SMOKEY BEAR
For over 50 years Smokey Bear has been the symbol of forest fire prevention in the U.S.

RELATED FIRES

• Peshtigo, Wisconsin, 1871: 1,200 deaths, 4 million acres (1.6 million ha) in the worst forest fire in U.S. history.

• Minnesota and Washington, 1919: Over 1,000 people die in a series of forest fires.

• Oregon, 1933: Tillamook Burn wipes out 250,000 acres (101,000 ha) of timberland.

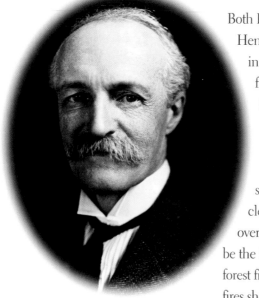

GIFFORD PINCHOT
(1865–1946) Born in Connecticut, Pinchot studied forestry in Europe and became America's first professional forester in 1898. He was ousted from his post as first chief of the U.S. Forest Service by President William Howard Taft shortly before the Big Burn of 1910. An ardent conservationist, he later served as governor of Pennsylvania.

Both Pinchot and his successor Henry Graves believed strongly in fighting forest fires, but the fledgling Forest Service was too small, underfunded, and ill-equipped to be very effective in that role.

The Big Burn made the service's weakness terribly clear. It also ended the debate over whether the service should be the front-line defense against forest fires—and also whether some fires should be allowed to burn. For the next 60 years every forest fire would be fought aggressively. This policy set the stage for the fire conditions that are now faced by firefighters. Fuels have built up in forests across the country, making fires larger and more dangerous.

FIRE-WATCHING
Various forms of air surveillance of fires have been tried to limit forest fires and protect property. The oldest and simplest remains one of the most reliable: the lookout. Volunteer or government fire wardens staff each tower, scanning the area for trouble throughout the wildfire season.

FORESTS IN RUIN
Scorched and denuded of greenery, skeletal gigantic tree trunks tower over the scene or lie on the ground like matchsticks. Battered by high winds on August 20, many trees had toppled even before the flames reached them.

YELLOWSTONE NATIONAL PARK

WYOMING, USA, 1988

THE 1970S SAW THE FOREST SERVICE and the management of U.S. National Parks return to the idea of letting some naturally occurring fires burn unchecked. For many years that policy seemed to work well, especially in Yellowstone, the nation's oldest national park. Between 1972 and 1987 235 "let-burn" fires occurred in the park. None destroyed more than 7,600 acres (3,100 ha); the average fire claimed only 240 acres (100 ha). Then came a season of fires that renewed the old debate about "lighting vs. fighting."

FOUR MONTHS OF FIRE

On July 11, 1988, a small fire began at Clover Creek. Analysts decided it posed no danger. Then classic "blow-up" conditions

HELP FROM ABOVE
Over 100 planes flew over Yellowstone National Park, dropping tons of fire retardants and water, as part of an effort to contain the forest fire in September 1988.

developed—dry weather, high winds, and the presence of other fires nearby. Eventually, the small Clover fire multiplied into 56 separate fires. Some 10,000 firefighters, supported by 117 aircraft, had to be called in. Although the containment effort kept flames from reaching some of Yellowstone's most-visited areas, like the "Old Faithful" geyser, the fires continued to burn until they were put out by the snows that began to fall in September. Just as

the forest fires were started by natural forces, they were finally extinguished that way as well.

The Clover fire could have been easily put out in its early stages, but "let-burn" advocates charged that the fire had spread so rapidly because old-growth underbrush hadn't been allowed to burn off in the pre-1972 era. They also cited an amazing revival of plant and animal species—including stands of lodgepole pine, a tree whose cones are opened by fire's heat—in the burned-over land. So like fire itself, the "fight vs. light" debate rages on.

IN THE WAKE OF "FIERY '88"
No lives were lost in the 1988 Yellowstone fires, but there was considerable damage to government and private property—like the burned-out car shown here—in the park and nearby communities.

STRIKING A BALANCE
A truck drives out of a smoke cloud created by the Shoshone Fire of 1988 in Yellowstone National Park. Yellowstone hopes to preserve the process of natural fire in the park while minimizing adverse effects on visitors and neighbors.

FIRE REPORT

🔥 CAUSES

•Lightning—the cause of most "naturally occurring" forest fires—sparked the initial blaze at Clover Creek.

🔥 FIRE FACTS

• 10,000 firefighters engaged.

• 117 aircraft used.

• 56 separate fires.

🔥 LOSSES

• 1.4 million acres (570,000 ha) in Yellowstone Park and adjoining federal land.

• The firefighting effort cost the federal government $120 million.

• At least 350 animals known to be fatally burned.

FOLLOWING PAGES:
FIRE IN THE PINES
A wildfire whips through a ponderosa pine forest in Mescalero, New Mexico during November of 1995. The Southwest has been subject to devastating wildfires in recent years because of drought compounding the effect of years of quelling all fires as quickly as possible.

OAKLAND HILLS BRUSH FIRE
OAKLAND, USA, 1991

ON OCTOBER 20, 1991, a small brushfire started in the hills above the cities of Oakland and Berkeley, California. The drought that year had affected the entire western U.S., but California had been especially hard hit, and numerous wildfires broke out across the state. Unseasonably high temperatures, low humidity, and winds gusting to 50 miles per hour (80 kmph) enabled small fires to spread quickly and grow to enormous size. This was the case in Oakland, where fire, fanned by high winds, spread rapidly to neighborhoods within the wooded hillsides, destroying almost 3,500 homes and taking the lives of 25 people—including a firefighter and a police officer. Labeled the worst urban disaster in U.S. history, the conflagration caused about $1.5-$2 billion dollars in direct damage and burned over 1,500 acres (600 ha).

A FIRESTORM IS CREATED
The Oakland hills fire spread so quickly because it was supplied with a large store of fuel for maximum growth—lots of bone-dry vegetation in close proximity to houses, many of which were constructed with untreated wood shingles and unprotected wood decks.

Strong, hot winds sent fires leaping from roof to roof, reducing 790 homes to ash in the first hour of the conflagration.

Eucalyptus and Monterey pine ignited like torches and shot burning embers into roof gutters filled with dry, dead pine needles, while residents did what they could to save their homes with water from garden hoses. But there was nothing they could do to keep the fire from jumping wildly from one house to the next. Soon the blaze became uncontainable, as strong winds created a firestorm, the magnitude of which was increased by the fire's intake of oxygen. In the first hour alone it engulfed 790 homes.

As the fire progressed, numerous agencies were summoned to control it, but dense black smoke covered most of the area, masking fire lines and spot fires—making reconnaissance extremely difficult. Without a handle on the extent of the fire, where it was moving, or where new hot spots were developing, firefighters were unable to stop the fire's advance. They were further hampered by narrow roads and steep, uneven terrain. Fortunately, the wind died down to about 5 miles an hour (8 kph) that evening, finally giving firefighters an opportunity to contain the devastating blaze.

AERIAL VIEW OF THE DESTRUCTION
One house and a partially standing home were all that remained of the Broadway Terrace section of Oakland after the fire on October 20, 1991.

NEIGHBORHOODS IN PERIL
The fire that swept up the densely populated, heavily wooded hills above the cities of Oakland and Berkeley was unstoppable. Virtually nothing could be done to save homes in the path of the fire.

FIRE REPORT

CAUSES
• Brush fires, started by low humidity and unseasonably high temperatures.

OTHER CAUSES
• High winds and proximity of houses to dense, flammable vegetation.

FIRE FACTS
• Worst urban fire in California history.

• Poor visibility from dense smoke, steep terrain, narrow roads, and non-standard hydrant openings thwarted firefighting efforts.

LOSSES
• 25 deaths; 150 injuries.

• 3,500 homes destroyed, 1,520 acres (615 ha) burned.

• $1.5–2 billion in damage.

DEVELOPMENTS
• Fire-resistant building codes.

• Homeowners mandated to clear vegetation.

• Neighborhood access to fire-fighting equipment and water.

• Firefighters given forest fire training and equipment, such as thermal imaging devices and portable hydrant systems.

BLACK CHRISTMAS
— NEW SOUTH WALES, AUSTRALIA, 2001 —

THE "BLACK CHRISTMAS" FIRE of December–January 2001 caused no human deaths and few serious injuries, but the blaze was one of the worst ecological catastrophes in the history of Australia. Striking at the height of summer in the Southern Hemisphere, flames ravaged a million acres (405,000 ha) of the southwestern Australian state of New South Wales, killing an unknown but certainly huge number of wildlife and nearly invading Sydney, Australia's largest city. Making the devastation even more appalling was the fact that, while lightning caused many of the more than 100 separate fires that made up the blaze, the rest were the result of deliberate arson.

BACKYARD BATTLES

By December 25—Christmas Day—scores of fires raged in Sydney's suburbs. After four days of struggle by thousands of firefighters and homeowners, cooling temperatures slowed the fires' spread. The blaze flared up again on New Year's Day, coming within 11 miles (18 km) of central Sydney. Not until heavy rains began to fall on January 15 was the government able to declare the crisis over.

HOLDING THE LINE
One of more than 15,000 firefighters and civilian volunteers wets down a containment line near Fairy Bower, north of Sydney. Despite their efforts, 170 houses were destroyed.

Fixed-wing and helicopter "waterbombers" from Australia, New Zealand, Canada, and the U.S. dropped millions of gallons of water and fire-retardant compounds (seen here) on the bushfires.

THE BUSHFIRES BEGIN

In December 2001 New South Wales suffered from the deadly trio of weather conditions—drought, low humidity, and high winds—that usually precede forest fires, or bushfires as they are called in Australia. The first of the Black Christmas fires began on December 24 in the Blue Mountains, part of a national park about 70 miles (110 km) west of Sydney. Winds gusting to 50 miles per hour (80 kmph) swept the fires toward Sydney's outskirts, consuming acre after acre of drought-parched gum and eucalyptus trees along the way. Firefighters even resorted to pumping water from swimming pools to help beat back the flames.

DARKNESS AT NOON
A young boy fishes as the pall of smoke that gave the Black Christmas fire its name drifts toward the city's famed Opera House. Smoke from the bushfires was visible to ships more than 1,000 miles (1,600 km) offshore.

CAUSES

• Lightning probably started the first fires in the Blue Mountains, but New South Wales authorities believe half the fires in the Sydney suburbs were the work of arsonists.

• In January 2002, 24 people, half of them under 18, and one only nine years of age, were arrested in connection with the fires

FIRE FACTS

• 15,000 firefighters.

• 800 vehicles.

• 55 aircraft.

• $100 million spent on firefighting.

DEVELOPMENTS

• In response to the Black Christmas fires, the Australian federal government announced a program to create a nationwide, coordinated firefighting strategy.

• New penalties for arson.

LOSSES

• 1.6 million acres (650,000 ha) of forest and farmland destroyed.

• 170 homes lost.

• More than $35 million in property damage.

• Massive depletion of species and animal habitats.

• Sydney Zoo lost its entire colony of 400 funnel web spiders. They were used to create antivenim for the city.

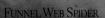

FUNNEL WEB SPIDER

TRIANGLE SHIRTWAIST FACTORY

NEW YORK CITY, USA 1911

IN LATE SUMMER OF 1911, THE OUTSIDE of the Asch Building at the corner of Washington Place and Greene Street would have looked like any other Lower East Side loft. A new addition to Manhattan's overcrowded, poor, immigrant neighborhood, the eleven-year-old building would seem to have lacked only a fire escape.

A more careful examination would have revealed broken windows at the eighth, ninth, and tenth floors, along with some scorch marks. The mounts for where a fire escape had existed would have been visible behind the building. The fire escape itself had collapsed under the weight of massing people. The ladders connecting each level of the fire escape had never been installed. The interior, once it had been cleared of burned furniture and charred human remains, would have been usable soon after the fire. Overall, the building would have seemed as good as new. Ironically, it had been certified as "fireproof," but that hadn't helped the most recent 146 occupants. Of those, 50 had jumped 100 feet (30 m) to the sidewalk below in a panicked attempt to escape a raging inferno. The then-current ideas of what "fireproof" meant pertained only to the structure itself.

At 4:40 PM, on March 25, 1911, everyone was preparing to leave. The girls, many aged 16–23, and the few male employees, had worked their 12-hour shifts just like they had the other days of the week, and they were only waiting to hear the end-of-the-day bell to release them from

work. Instead, on the eighth floor, what they heard was "Fire!"

A TINDERBOX

From one end to the other of each floor, blouses hung down from wires stretched above. Next to each sewing station, boxes were filled with cloth, thread, lace, and lint.

TRIANGLE FIRE, BY SELF-TAUGHT PRIMITIVE ARTIST VICTOR JOSEPH GATTO, C. 1935
The artist witnessed the fire as a teenager. To the left, two firemen attempt to catch a falling victim as horrified bystanders look on. Two others stack bodies on the sidewalk. To the right, steam pumpers have arrived, but their water only reaches as high as the seventh floor. In the far-right back, men are at the top of the ladders, several floors too low to help those trapped inside.

SHOCKED SPECTATORS JAM THE STREETS
Hundreds watched helplessly as victims threw themselves in desperation or were pushed by those behind from the Triangle Shirtwaist Company. In center background can be seen the horse-drawn pumpers. The fire had an enormous impact on workplace rights and safety.

Workstations were packed together with barely room to move. On the same floor, cans of machine oil were stored to make sure the equipment could be kept running with as little downtime as possible. All was designed to maximize the number of workers per floor and the sewing efficiency, with no thought for human comfort or safety.

Once ignited, the blaze swept through the floor in what was described as a "whirlpool" of fire. It lasted only 30 minutes. Within that brief time, which must have seemed like an eternity to the occupants of the eighth, ninth, and tenth floors, 146 people died of suffocation, burns, or injuries sustained in 100-foot (30 m) falls. Perhaps worst of all, the doors leading to the internal fire escape, the only exit once the external escape had collapsed, were locked.

Firefighters came within minutes of the alarm. The nearest company was number 72, only six blocks away. When they arrived, they had to dodge what they thought were bolts of cloth being hurtled from the windows. As they came closer, they saw that the "bolts of cloth" were instead people. Desperate to escape, and with no other way out, the workers' instinctual fear of fire had driven them to escape in any way possible—including the scant chance of surviving such a fall.

WOULD-BE RESCUERS

More pumper companies soon arrived, only to discover that the water from their hoses would only reach as high as the seventh floor. Hook-and-ladder men grabbed their ladders and found that they only reached to between the sixth and seventh floors. People jumped, attempting to grab the ladders, only to miss and fall to the street below. Firefighters, police, and bystanders attempted to catch the jumpers in special jump-nets and even sheets, all to no avail. The jumpers either missed, or simply tore through the material, their velocities too high to safely stop.

Many of those jumpers were smoldering or on fire and trailed smoke and flame as they fell.

NOWHERE TO RUN

As the fire spread within, the elevator doors opened, releasing fresh air up the elevator shaft, which resulted in a backdraft. People then rushed the elevator, which could only hold ten. Inside the elevator itself, bodies could be heard landing on the roof as people threw themselves onto the car, vainly trying to escape.

TRIANGLE SHIRTWAIST FIRE OF 1911
With their equipment unable to reach the fire on the upper floors or perform rescues there, firefighters were left with containing the blaze on the lower floors. Though short in duration, many described this fire as the worst they had ever seen.

FACTORY OWNERS

MAX BLANCK AND ISAAC HARRIS, *owners of the Triangle Shirtwaist Co., were involved in as many as seven previous factory fires. Three days after the fire, they placed a Help Wanted ad for a new location—the public was outraged. Charged, but eventually acquitted of manslaughter, the two collected on a very large fire-insurance policy.*

Others headed to one of the two fire escapes. The exterior escape quickly became overloaded as the drop ladders connecting each level had never been installed. It pulled free of the building and crashed into the alley. At the interior fire escape, hapless victims found themselves trapped against the fireproof doors, locked to prevent anyone from stealing and making an exit. Those who ran to the stairway fared no better. They were crushed by the mob stampeding against the inward-opening doors.

Those on the tenth floor had an easier time. About 150 were able to gain access to the roof and from there to the adjacent New York University Law School (now part of NYU, the Asch Building is today known as the Brown Building, at 23-29 Washington Place). The NYU building was 12 feet (4 m) higher, but with the aid of the students, the Triangle employees were able to make their escape.

Three men on the eighth floor managed to make a human bridge over an alley to the next building. A few people managed to cross before the men lost their grip. All three of the men and those on them died.

VOLATILE AFTERMATH

In only 30 minutes, one of the worst fires in New York City history was over. What remained were three floors filled with charred

COLLAPSED FIRE ESCAPE
With the drop ladders connecting the various levels of the fire escape left uninstalled, those who rushed to what they thought was safety instead found themselves trapped. With those behind crowding on, and no one able to move off of the platforms, the fire-escape began to melt from the heat within the building. Pulling free of its mounting, it collapsed, killing all who were on it.

remains. Many veteran firefighters and police described it as the worst they had ever seen. The building had been declared fireproof, despite the fact that the doors opened inward rather than outward, despite the fact that the external fire escape had never been completed, despite the fact that the interior fire escape was kept locked to protect against theft, and despite the fact that around 700 people were working on three, cramped floors of a single building. In truth, the building suffered little damage, and it was now understood that the term "fireproof" pertained more to

LITTLE TO BE DONE
As in the aftermath of any battle, the pumpers and hook-and-ladder engines create a somber scene. Even today, fighting fires and making rescues in tall buildings is extremely difficult.

FIRE REPORT

🔥 CAUSES
• Probably a discarded cigarette.

🔥 FIRE FACTS
• Blaze lasted only 30 minutes.

• Fire escapes were locked or incomplete.

• Firefighters' ladders only reached the sixth floor.

• Water from the steam pumpers only went as high as the seventh floor.

• Jump-nets proved useless at such heights.

🔥 LOSSES
• 146 people killed, approximately 50 from jumping while attempting to escape the fire.

🔥 DEVELOPMENTS
• 36 new workplace health and safety statutes enacted.

• Smoking forbidden around combustibles.

• Exits must be clearly marked.

• Exits may not be locked while employees are present.

• Bureau of Fire Investigation established in New York City with the power to enforce new regulations.

• Automatic sprinklers required in commercial establishments with more than 25 employees.

CHARRED INTERIOR
Little remained after the fire had raged through the top three floors of the Asch Building. Packed with cloth and finished shirts as well as machine oil and wooden workstations for sewing, the fire burned very rapidly, consuming everything and everyone within. The occupants rushed from one supposed exit to another, only to find the doors locked or blocked, leaving them trapped with the flames.

the building's structure than to the safety of any occupants.

One result of the fire was the recommendation by the investigative committee for the establishment of better safety standards, such as clearly marked exits, regularly scheduled drills and fire alarms, outward-opening doors, external fire escapes, the installation of automatic sprinklers, and restrictions on smoking—all of which we now take for granted.

Indeed, had these recommendations already been in place, far fewer lives would have been taken. If even the last suggestion of automated sprinklers had been implemented, it is likely no lives at all would have been lost. Invented in 1862 by Connecticutt piano maker Henry Parmalee, automatic sprinklers have proven to be one of the most efficient life-saving and fire-suppression inventions ever. No multiple deaths have ever occurred in a building equipped with automated sprinklers.

Another outcome of this tragic and horrific fire was the renewal of efforts to improve workplace safety and workplace rights. Labor unions, political groups, and religious communities, at least for a while, banded together to demand drastic changes.

The Bureau of Fire Investigation was established later that year and was given the power to enforce the new fire regulations. Eventually a state commission was created and 36 new statutes to establish work health and safety were passed.

Max Blanck and Isaac Harris, the owners of the Triangle Shirtwaist Company, were indicted on April 11, 1911. The trial was held eight months later and, after 18 days, on December 27, the two were acquitted of any responsibility. In spite of the evidence, their brilliant attorney,

INVESTIGATORS EXAMINE THE REMAINS
The exact cause of the fire was never determined, though it has long been thought that a worker's discarded cigarette had ignited the murderous blaze. As a result, sweeping changes in occupational health and safety laws were mandated.

Max Steuer, had managed to plant doubt in the minds of the jurors as to whether or not Max Blanck and Isaac Harris had specific knowledge of the doors to the factory being locked during work hours. Over the next three years, 23 individual civil suits were settled out of court on March 11, 1913, for the remarkable sum of only 75 dollars per death (approximately $1,340 in today's money).

RELATED FIRES

• Kader Toy Factory, Thailand, 1993: 188 deaths.

• Zhimao Electronics Factory, China, 1999: 16 killed, 8 seriously injured.

• Chowdhury Knitwear and Garments Ltd, Bangladesh, 2000: 47 dead, 8 of them children.

EQUITABLE BUILDING

NEW YORK CITY, USA, 1912

THE FIRE AT THE EQUITABLE BUILDING IN DOWNTOWN MANHATTAN on January 9, 1912 was one of the worst fires in the history of New York City and yet, at the same time, was one of the most eerily spectacular.

The weather was bitterly cold and windy that January morning, when a small blaze broke out in the basement of the Equitable Life Assurance Society Building at 120 Broadway. Building employees first discovered the fire at about 5:15 AM but, rather than calling in the alarm immediately, they attempted to put it out on their own. The first alarm was not called in until 5:34 AM, when two police officers patrolling the area caught sight of the fire. Within minutes the clanging of fire engines could be heard outside the Equitable. Deputy Chief Binns arrived with the first wave of firefighters and immediately ordered a second, and then a third alarm. By now the fire had made its way into an elevator shaft and was voraciously eating its way through the core of the building. In two hours, only the walls would be left standing.

THE EQUITABLE BUILDING IN THE EARLY STAGES OF THE FIRE
The blaze began in the basement of the building near the kitchen and storage area attached to the Savarin, a café located on the ground floor of the Equitable. An elevator shaft may have acted as a flue through which the fire could quickly spread to the upper floors of the building.

MANNING THE LINES
Firefighters doused the burning Equitable Building with sprays of water that seemed to freeze in the air. Within an hour, for a block in both directions, Broadway was a lake of ice that was six or more inches (15 cm) deep.

AFTER THE FIRE
The Equitable Building looms over Broadway between Pine and Cedar Streets. The fire, which had burned from the inside out, gutted the building. At one point during the conflagration the walls were literally held together with ice.

EERILY BEAUTIFUL
The ruined Equitable was transformed into a thing of strange beauty by mantles of ice. On the night of the fire, the ice-sheathed building "glistened like an iceberg," according to some witnesses.

UNEXPECTED IMPEDIMENT

The second alarm, which had been ordered only ten minutes after the fire was first reported, brought Chief Kenlon from bed–despite a fractured foot. In the bitter cold, with a stiff wind whipping down Broadway, firefighters were up against formidable odds. Water from stiffening hoses quickly transformed the area into a sea of ice, making it difficult to move equipment or ladders onto the building. The firefighters themselves were weighed down under coats of ice that had to be hacked off periodically. Icicles formed in their mustaches and gaining a foothold anywhere was unimaginably difficult. Meanwhile the fire–now an inferno contained within a hardened case of ice– continued to consume the Equitable Building from within.

When Chief Kenlon arrived on the scene at about 6:00 AM, along with Fire Commissioner Johnson, the decision was made to order the fourth and fifth alarms.

CHIEF JOHN KENLON AND THE BIRTH OF RESCUE COMPANY 1

CHIEF KENLON *realized that a special team was needed with expertise in extracting victims. Firefighters had had to use hacksaws—for want of more specialized tools—to rescue people trapped behind windows reinforced with two-inch (1 cm) steel bars. Worst, they had virtually no breathing apparatus to protect them from heavy smoke.*

FROZEN TO THE GROUND, the icy conditions made firefighting all the more challenging, because the water pumped to extinguish the fire quickly turned to ice on engines, trucks, and fire hoses, rooting them to the frozen streets and creating an impromptu and hazardous "skating rink."

COATED IN ICE, and with the mercury dipping well below freezing and a wind stiffening into a 60-mile (97 km)-an-hour gale, Chief Kenlon led the desperate resistance. Spray from the fire hoses froze and hung from eyebrows, hair, and mustaches.

Almost simultaneously another decision was made to call in reinforcements from the Brooklyn Fire Department—a first in the history of New York City's Fire Department: Kenlon had correctly assessed the severity of the blaze when he pronounced it "a tough one, sure."

In the very first stages of the fire, three men, who were probably building employees, had fled to the roof. Now they were stranded there. Chief Kenlon gave orders to have them brought down, but the extension ladders fell short and a lifeline burned and snapped. Then the roof collapsed and all three plunged into the inferno.

Reports that others were still in the building prompted Battalion Chief William J. Walsh to step forward. With 14 other volunteers he entered the building—and was never seen

again. Walsh, who was a revered veteran of the New York fire service, is believed to have died somewhere between the 3rd and 4th floors of the Equitable.

That evening, crowds gathered to watch the spectacular play of flame within walls of ice. The fire was finally extinguished by 11:00 on the following evening, January 10. Loss of life was relatively limited because the Equitable blaze had started well before work hours.

In two relentless and exhausting days, firefighters distinguished themselves again and again in dramatic acts of bravery, not the least of which was the rescue of William Giblin, President of the Mercantile Safe Deposit Company, from a vault—where he had fled to escape the smoke and fire.

THE RUINS

In 1919 a new, 36-story Equitable Building rose 540 feet (165 m) above street level on the same site the old building had occupied. Covering an entire city block measuring 49,000 square feet (4,552 sq m), the new Equitable Building cost $11,500,000. The land itself was worth $14,000,000.

IMPERIAL FOOD PROCESSING PLANT

HAMLET, NORTH CAROLINA, 1991

ON SEPTEMBER 3, 1991, at about 8:15 AM, hydraulic oil from a ruptured line ignited only a few feet away from a natural gas-fueled cooker at Imperial Food Processing Plant in Hamlet, North Carolina. Ignition resulted in rapidly spreading fire and smoke. Flames soared up to the roof, igniting insulating material, and adding toxic fumes to the oil smoke. Within minutes the smoke and intense heat filled the 30,000-square foot (2,787 sq m) plant.

Workers in the front of the building were able to escape through the main entrance, but those in the back were trapped between a wall of toxic smoke and locked doors. Some people sought refuge from the smoke in room-size coolers, where they froze to death. Others died of smoke inhalation as they groped through the dark, looking for an unlocked or unblocked exit. In the end, 25 people died and over 40 more were injured. The fire was the final blow to a workforce that

had suffered under unpleasant working conditions for years. The owner, Emmet Roe, pleaded guilty to 25 counts of involuntary manslaughter and was sentenced to 19 years, 11 months—of which he served less than four years before being paroled.

FIRE REPORT

CAUSES
• Ruptured hydraulic line spewed cooking oil into the flames of a 26-foot (8 m) long fat fryer.

FIRE FACTS
• The worst industrial accident in the history of North Carolina.

• Smoke inhalation was the primary killer.

LOSSES
• 25 fatalities; at least 46 injuries.

MALDEN MILLS
—— METHUEN, USA, 1995 ——

A 6-ALARM FIRE
Firefighters battled 45 mile-per-hour winds that quickly spread flames over the four-building compound. In the intense cold, water hoses froze.

AT ABOUT 8:00 PM on December 11, 1995, a 6-alarm fire—one of the worst in Massachusetts history—struck the four-building Malden Mills complex in Methuen, Massachusetts, injuring more than 30 people. Miraculously, there were no fatalities. Founded in 1906, Malden

METHUEN'S HERO
Aaron Feuerstein, owner of Malden Mills, New England's last great textile mill, became a hero to his employees for his unstinting support and determination to rebuild the factory.

Mills was (and is again today), best known for Polartec®, Polarfleece®, and upholstery fabrics. At the time of the fire, the factory was worth $400 million in annual sales and employed almost 3,000 people from the local area.

The first explosion occurred in the Manomac building, which housed three boilers used in the manufacturing process. Workers escaped from the burning and collapsing walls of the building while the fire, fanned by 45-mile-per-hour (72 kmph) winds, quickly spread to nearby buildings. A series of explosions from propane tanks followed. The entire complex was outfitted with sprinklers, but the system was severely damaged by the initial blast and then by collapsing floors. Flames shot out the windows, heavy machinery and elevators were heard crashing through the burning floorboards of the factory, and a massive cloud of smoke could be seen from 10 miles (16 km) away.

MASSIVE EMERGENCY RESPONSE

The town of Methuen's Fire Department was first on the scene, but they were soon joined by nearly 300 firefighters from 36 communities, including nearby New Hampshire. Area hospitals were put on red alert status and several ambulances and medevac helicopters arrived to help transport the seriously injured to Boston and Worcester. On the ground, firefighters were hampered by near freezing cold, low water pressure, collapsing walls, and furious winds. But by daybreak the massive firefighting effort had paid off. The fire at Malden Mills, which had been described earlier as "like standing at the gates of hell," was extinguished.

The third-generation owner of Malden Mills, Aaron Feuerstein, became an overnight hero—and hailed as a saint by many—when he chose not to take $300 million dollars in insurance money and relocate. Instead, he announced that he would keep all of his 3,000 employees on the payroll with full benefits and would rebuild the company in the same location. Feuerstein kept his promises and the new Malden Mills was open for business 14 months later.

FIRE REPORT

☙ CAUSES
• Massive boiler explosion plus propane gas explosions.

☙ FIRE FACTS
• The 6-alarm blaze drew 300 firefighters, 67 engine companies, and 22 truck companies from the surrounding area, including New Hampshire and southern suburbs of Boston.

• Collapsing walls landed on firefighting equipment, such as a pumper truck from Lawrence, Massachusetts.

☙ LOSSES
• 33 injuries—8 of them critical—but no fatalities.

☙ DEVELOPMENTS
• Malden Mills was rebuilt, at enormous expense to the owner.

THE FIRE THAT DIDN'T WIN
Smoke and flames leap skyward from Malden Mills. Almost one million square feet (93,000 sq m) of factory space were destroyed, but no lives were lost and the mill reopened 14 months later for the 3,000 employees, who had been kept on the payroll in the interim.

COCOANUT GROVE

—— BOSTON, USA, 1942 ——

BY NOVEMBER 28, 1942, the U.S. had entered into World War II and hundreds of military personnel getting ready to ship out joined their dates and other revelers at Boston's most fashionable club at the time, the Cocoanut Grove. The nightspot was dangerously overcrowded that night, the Saturday after Thanksgiving. The official capacity for the two-floor building was 600 people; almost twice as many were celebrating in the club's dining room and two bars.

The Cocoanut Grove had only one main entrance on Piedmont Street—a revolving door that led into the dining room. The Melody Lounge, in the basement, was accessible by a stairway near the main entrance. A recently renovated bar area called the New Lounge was connected to the dining room, but the corridor was hidden and patrons entered from Broadway through an inward-opening door. Other doors and windows were painted over and covered with decorations or made to look like part of the walls. Some doors were locked or welded shut—ostensibly to prevent customers from running out on a tab.

Thick, poisonous smoke from the flame-retardant on the leather walls

DESPERATE RESCUE EFFORTS
Firefighters and policemen were joined by servicemen to make countless—and largely futile—efforts to save the victims of the Cocoanut Grove fire, which claimed 492 lives and sent 212 to area hospitals.

FLAMMABLE DECOR

The Melody Lounge and the dining room were trimmed with highly flammable "Polynesian" decorations—paper and tinsel coconut trees and tropical foliage, rattan furniture, rope braiding, and on the ceiling and leather walls, swaths of satin fabric. At about 10:05 PM, the deadly fire started in the Melody Lounge. The first reports that appeared in the aftermath of the blaze traced the fire's origins to a romantic couple in search of some privacy: They unscrewed a light bulb on the wall to darken their nook. A 16-year-old busboy named Stanley Tomaszewski testified at the inquest that he was sent to replace the bulb, lit a match in the darkness to find the light socket, and inadvertently set wall drapery on fire. The tinsel decorations caught fire, then the ceiling burst into flame. Other reports blame a dropped cigarette or faulty wiring

INSPECTING THE RUINS
Firefighters study the remains after the fire was extinguished and the human victims removed. The ceiling decorations hang limply and fire damage is evident in the bar area of the "New Lounge," which had been renovated shortly before the fire occurred.

in the electrical system. Finally, there was the rumored connection between the club ownership and organized crime. The actual cause has not been, and probably never will be, established.

PANIC AMID THE SMOKE

When the fire erupted, panic ensued. Patrons in the basement-level Melody Lounge died almost instantly from the toxic fumes and intense heat. As the fire reached the first floor, crowds in the dining room rushed to escape through the only clearly visible exit to the street —the revolving doors— which quickly jammed with people. Some managed to escape through one of the painted-over doors, which had been discovered and eventually forced open. As the fire raged, the air was sucked out of the room and replaced by

BUCK JONES – *CONTROVERSY*

DURING THE 1920S AND 1930S, Buck Jones was a B-Western movie cowboy, one of the most successful actors in the genre. At the height of his popularity he received more fan mail than any Hollywood actor. On November 28, 1942, Jones stopped in Boston during a cross-country bond-selling/movie promotion tour. He attended a dinner at the Cocoanut Grove, given in his honor by local movie theater owners.

Jones was seriously burned in the fire and died from his injuries two days later. The popular actor was rumored to have been led out to safety, but then went back three times to rescue people. This has never been verified, and Jones's badly burned body was found in the dining room in a seating area with the rest of his party (only four of whom survived).

A YOUNG FAN is shown with Buck Jones in one of the last pictures ever taken of the actor, in his visit to a pediatric hospital on that fateful day.

FIRE REPORT

CAUSES
• Lit match or cigarette combined with highly flammable decorations and furnishings.

FIRE FACTS
• Worst nightclub fire in American history.

• Filled to twice its capacity and with insufficient fire exits, the club was destroyed within 12 to 15 minutes.

• The Boston Fire Department, nearby in a full alarm response that turned out to be a car fire, arrived immediately.

LOSSES
• 492 people killed.

DEVELOPMENTS
• Combustible materials outlawed in decorative or building components.

• Occupancy limit requirements should be strictly enforced, with signs posted in visible area.

• All places of assembly must have plainly marked exits that are kept clear of obstructions, as well as exit lights and emergency lights.

• Wherever revolving doors are used as an exit, there must also be doors on both sides that open outward.

RELATED FIRES

• Sennichi Department Store disco, Osaka, Japan, 1972: killed 118 people.

• Happyland Social Club, the Bronx, New York, 1990: an argument with his ex-girlfriend at the Happyland prompts Julio Gonzalez to torch the club, killing 87 people. The Honduran club was unlicensed, overcrowded, and had insufficient exits and fire protection.

CHARRED RUINS
Charred tables and chairs, broken wine glasses, and other debris outside the gutted Cocoanut Grove. Some people escaped out of a second-floor dressing room and climbed down the ladder at left.

REVOLUTIONARY DOORS
As a result of the Cocoanut Grove fire, legislation was passed nationwide to require outward-opening doors to accompany any revolving doors used as exits, as seen in this modern office building.

poisonous smoke—many people died still seated at their tables. In the New Lounge, the inward-opening door also wedged shut as frantic customers pushed it closed in the frenzy to get outside.

FIRE-CODE REVISIONS
Within 15 minutes, the Cocoanut Grove was destroyed in the worst nightclub fire in American history. More than 200 victims were found in front of the revolving door, while 100 were discovered in front of the Broadway exit; 492 died in the catastrophe and more than 200 were seriously injured.

A criminal investigation followed with resulting indictments, convictions, and imprisonment for a number of Boston officials, and the club owner, Barnett Welansky, was sentenced to 12 to 15 years in prison after being convicted of manslaughter for negligence in providing enough fire doors and other exits. The use of revolving doors came under extreme, and specific, criticism. The result, across the nation, was a general fire-code requirement that any time revolving doors were used as an exit, there must also be doors on both sides that open outward. Other important legislation prompted by the Cocoanut Grove disaster includes laws requiring emergency lighting, occupancy capacity signs, and exit lights in nightclubs, restaurants, and other establishments where large groups of people assemble.

INADEQUATE EXITS
Arches show the location of the revolving doors, outside a narrow vestibule where frantic guests were crushed and smothered in their attempt to escape.

BARNETT WELANSKY – CLUB OWNER

COCOANUT GROVE BAR BOY APPEARING BEFORE GRAND JURY
Stanley Tomazewski (left) testified at the inquest in January 1943 that he had lit a match so that he could see to replace a lightbulb, thereby igniting palm-tree decorations and nearby wall drapery. He also testified that he led some patrons to safety through smoke so thick he could hardly breathe.

COCOANUT GROVE OWNER, Barnett Welansky, was convicted of involuntary manslaughter for negligence in providing enough fire doors and other exits. Not only was the club filled to twice its legal capacity, but some of the exits had been either locked or hidden to prevent patrons leaving without paying their bill. Welansky was sentenced to 12–15 years in jail. A number of Boston officials were also tried, convicted, and imprisoned for their failure to enforce fire regulations properly. There were also rumors of a connection between Welansky and organized crime.

5–7 DISCO
—— ST. LAURENT DU-PONT, FRANCE, 1970 ——

THE "5-7" DISCO opened in April 1970, in a small village outside the city of Grenoble in southeastern France. The club, built in a huge warehouse, was a magnet for young adults throughout the region, a psychedelically decorated dance hall that featured the most popular bands from Paris. The interior was constructed almost entirely with highly flammable material: a maze of intimate lounges throughout the club were decorated with polyester fabrics, foam-covered chairs, and couches designed in a new type of hardened cardboard. Above the main dance floor was a circular balcony made of plastic, suspended from the ceiling and accessible via one flimsy spiral staircase.

The evening of Saturday, October 31, 1970, was Halloween and the club had heavily advertised the holiday and the premiere of the Paris band, Storm. Around 200 people were still partying at 1:45 AM, when a young student from Canada saw flames shooting out of one of

the foam chairs—it was later determined that the blaze was caused by a malfunction in the heating system. Attempts to smother the fire failed and soon heavy smoke, laden with toxic fumes from the burning synthetic material, covered the dance floor. Panicked teenagers rushed to the emergency exits and found the doors locked to keep out gate-crashers. Turnstiles, installed to count heads, blocked escape by the main entrance.

There was no telephone or fire alarm in the club, but the local fire department, assisted by engines from nearby towns, arrived quickly. By the time they arrived, 146 young people had died. Heaps of

bodies were found against the locked fire doors and main entrance; only a few dozen had escaped over the turnstiles, which still stand as a memorial. Firemen finally extinguished the blaze at 5:00 AM.

The trial exposed a flagrant disregard of fire codes. Five people were indicted: Gilbert Bas, only surviving owner of the club; Marcel and Joseph Wimfles, who installed the heating system; Alfred Moskovits, director of the company that supplied the furnishings; and Mayor Pierre Perrin, removed from office and charged with criminal homicide and injury through gross negligence. All received only suspended sentences.

FIRE REPORT

CAUSES
• Malfunctioning heating system caused a blaze that was greatly accelerated by flammable polyester and hardened cardboard furnishings.

FIRE FACTS
• The fire doors were locked and the main exit was blocked by turnstiles, making escape almost impossible.

• The backdraft produced when two barmen escaped through a door prevented others from using that exit.

LOSSES
• 146 young people between the ages of 14 and 22.

MELTED BALCONY
Firemen sift through the debris directly below the remains of the balcony. As flames fed on the hardened cardboard and polyester fabrics, the intense heat melted the plastic second-floor balcony off its moorings and onto the dance floor below.

BEVERLY HILLS SUPPER CLUB
SOUTHGATE, USA, 1977

LOCATED IN SOUTHGATE, KENTUCKY, across the Ohio River from Cincinnati, the Beverly Hills was a glamorous casino in the 1950s—a mecca for stars like Frank Sinatra and Dean Martin. After strict federal gambling and racketeering statutes were enacted in the early 1960s, the club shut down until 1969, when it was purchased by the Schilling family. The Schillings undertook major renovations and additions such as the Cabaret Room, a dinner theater, and the Zebra Room, a smaller ground-level party room.

The sprawling, 72,000-square-foot (6,700 sq m) multilevel club reopened in 1971, and soon became a regional showcase for performers like Joey Heatherton and Frankie Valli, and the place to celebrate birthdays, anniversaries, and proms. The reopening took place despite a 1971 *Cincinnati Enquirer* report that 10 major defects, including "flaws involving stairway enclosures

and exits" had not been corrected, and that the state did not conduct a final inspection of the club. Prophetically, in January 1977, a state-ordered fire inspection reported that "in case of emergency, evacuation should be no problem with existing exits." Four months later, on the evening of Saturday, May 28, Memorial Day weekend festivities filled the club with several hundred people over its 2,300-person capacity. The Cabaret Room was severely overcrowded, with some 1,300 patrons (three times the recommended occupancy) waiting for popular singer John Davidson to start his show. Chairs blocked the aisles, chairs were set up on the stage ramps—and even more people were lined up in the hall waiting to get in.

ELECTRICAL FIRE

At approximately 8:30 PM, a wedding party in the Zebra Room dispersed, complaining of uncomfortable heat—employees thought the air-conditioning was broken, not knowing that an electrical fire had been smoldering in the walls behind the wood paneling. When the Zebra Room door was opened by a staff member at

CHARRED WOOD
An aerial view of the front façade and several outside walls—all that remained of the Beverly Hills Supper Club after burning for five hours and smoldering for another 24.

SUPPER CLUB FIRE
Newly renovated in 1971, the club burned to the ground in May 1977, due to major defects in contruction and fixtures.

8:50 PM, smoke poured out, and the entire room ignited simultaneously in a flashover. The fire department received its first call at 9:01 PM, one minute before busboy Walter Bailey ran upstairs to alert people. As he headed for the Main Bar, the fire also raced upstairs and down the corridor toward the Cabaret Room, fed by the flammable carpeting and paneling in the hall. At about 9:08, Bailey next reached the Cabaret Room, and jumped on stage to announce the fire. Hundreds of guests tried to move to the exits through the blocked aisles to the main exit, although some thought Bailey was part of a comedy act and stayed seated. Within minutes, toxic, oily, black smoke poured from the air ducts; moments later a fireball erupted, blocking the main exit after only 100 escaped. The room's two other exits were out-of-the-way and unmarked.

UNMARKED EXITS

Temperatures in the Cabaret Room—where all but two of the fatalities occurred—soon reached 2000° Fahrenheit (1100° C); firefighters later discovered dozens of

horribly burned bodies stacked near each of the unmarked exits. The total death toll was 165. Kentucky governor Julian Carroll ordered an investigative task force, who found code violations such as substandard wiring; flammable building materials and furnishings (in particular the foam seat cushions, which released deadly toxins when burned); a shortage of exits (and the existing exits were inadequately marked and too narrow); overcrowding; and lax

enforcement and oversight by the state fire marshal and insurers. A grand jury declared that no criminal negligence was involved, although Stan Chesley later won the civil suit filed on behalf of the victims. Major developments that arose from the case include the requirement for public-assembly buildings holding 300 or more people to install a sprinkler system, and laws dictating the use of fire-resistant wiring and seat cushion materials.

STAN CHESLEY - LAWYER

IN 1985, CINCINNATI LAWYER Stan Chesley (left) was the lead attorney in the civil suit. Over 1,000 defendants were sued in 250 lawsuits, including the club owners, the fire marshal, the maker of the foam seat cushions, and the local power company (for providing electricity without confirming that the club had passed inspection). Chesley was much maligned for his insistence on preserving the fire scene—unheard-of at the time— so that his team of experts could examine the ruins. They discovered, among other things, that the electrical system used hazardous old-technology aluminum wiring, which, back in 1970, was known to ignite nearby materials if not properly installed. The victims were eventually awarded settlements totaling $50 million, and Chesley's trailblazing investigative technique has become standard legal practice today.

Flames roar through the club's roof, which was melted by the intense heat

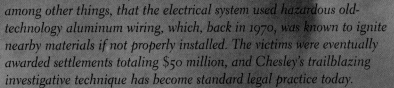

CAUSES

• Electrical fire started by hazardous aluminum wiring; was exacerbated by flammable building materials and furnishings and lack of alarm and sprinkler system.

FIRE FACTS

• The club was severely overcrowded, and the extra fire exits were unmarked, too few, and too narrow.

• The front façade and several outside walls were all that remained of the club after burning for 5 hours and smoldering for 24 more.

• The jury concluded that the victims died as a result of "panic" and not evacuating immediately, and not because of criminal negligence or structural liabilities.

• Governor Carroll accused inspection officials of accepting bribes of free food and drinks from the Schillings in return for lenient reports.

• Some experts believe that the toxic fumes accumulated in the roof deck over the Cabaret Room, where combustible roof materials would have kept the fire raging over the ceiling—defeating the purpose of sprinklers, even if they had been installed.

LOSSES

• 165 people killed.

DEVELOPMENTS

• Aluminum wiring banned.

• Advances in flame-retardant furnishings, such as cushions.

• Preservation of fire scene and legal investigation of ruins as evidence become standard practice.

• Public-assembly buildings holding 300 or more people must install a sprinkler system.

OZONE DISCO
— QUEZON CITY, PHILIPPINES, 1996 —

THE PHILIPPINES' WORST FIRE in the 20th century started as a spark in the deejay booth at a disco in the Manila suburb of Quezon City. On March 19, 1996, almost 400 teenagers celebrating the end of the school year were jammed into the 7,500-square-foot (700 sq m) Ozone Disco, a converted residential space with a licensed capacity for not more than 60 people. The dancers thought the flashing spark was part of the strobe-light show, and were unable to hear DJ Mervil Reyes as he attempted to shout "fire" over the next song he had cued. Two minutes later, the entire club was engulfed in flames. The crowd surged toward the only visible exit (the other exit was apparently blocked by construction of a building next door), a narrow inward-opening wooden door that was stuck, or as some witnesses claimed, locked. In the trampling, frantic rush to get out, the door was ripped off its hinges, creating a backdraft fireball that burned everything and everyone in its path. The ceiling melted from the heat and collapsed. The fire killed 154 teens.

The cause was thought to be either an exploding fuel tank in the kitchen, or faulty or overloaded wiring in the deejay booth, greatly accelerated by the highly combustible soundproofing material used on the walls. Public outcry focused on corrupt building officials and fire inspectors who had allowed the former residence to be turned into a club and who overlooked the club's many fire-code violations as well as the culpability of the club's owners. One patron of the club testified that the club had no exit, although the owner claimed there was one but it had been obscured by smoke. There may have been an emergency exit in the VIP room that several staff members used to escape. Although two dozen discos were closed for failing to pass fire inspections and the Ozone's owners and several local officials were indicted on charges of reckless imprudence resulting in multiple homicide, no criminal time was served—the maximum penalty in the Philippines for reckless imprudence is only four years, and all of the defendants received probation.

CHARRED RUINS
An inspector examines the remains of the Ozone Disco. The fire, started by sparks that seemed at first just a special effect of the strobe lighting in the deejay booth, quickly destroyed the ceiling. As the terrified adolescents tried to flee, a fireball ripped through when the one exit door was opened.

FIRE REPORT

⚜ CAUSES
• Kitchen fuel-tank explosion or faulty or overloaded wiring in deejay booth.

⚜ FIRE FACTS
• The club was filled to over 6 times its capacity, and had only one, inward-opening door (some witnesses claimed that it was locked).

• Furor over the corruption that led to the fire continues today, with debate over how the Philippines fire code can be revised and stricter penalties for owners and inspection officials for fire deaths.

⚜ LOSSES
• 154 teenagers killed.

DONGDU BUILDING

LUOYANG, CHINA, 2000

ONE OF THE WORST DISCO FIRES in recent history occurred in Eastern China, at the Dongdu Building, a department store in the populous city of Luoyang, Henan Province. On December 25, hundreds of people were enjoying a Christmas party at the Dongdu Disco. Although Christmas is not observed as a national holiday in China, the Chinese often spend the day by exchanging presents or getting together in the evening with friends.

The Dongdu Disco was located on the fourth floor of the low-rise shopping building, which only the previous week had failed a fire inspection because emergency exits were obstructed by boxes of merchandise. In addition, the building was breaking several fire regulations because it lacked sprinklers, fire alarms, and smoke detectors. On Christmas, the boxes had not been removed, and there was unlicensed construction work going on throughout the building. Except for the construction workers and the disco, the building was empty on Christmas day. The fire started in the basement due to sparks from welding torches; the welders fled the building without warning anyone, and by the time the disco patrons realized that smoke was filling the loud, darkened nightclub, they were trapped.

The fire department arrived quickly, but because food vendors surrounded the building, only a few trucks were able to get close enough at first to send up ladders. Many patrons could not wait to be rescued or to position themselves in front of the airbeds set up at various positions below—the heat and panic sent dozens of people jumping out of the fourth-floor windows. Most of the victims succumbed within minutes to smoke inhalation: 309 people were killed—the second-deadliest fire in the Chinese republic since its founding in 1949.

This fire was one of the first major disasters with extensive media coverage in China. Spurred by a large number of fatal accidents in 2000—including explosions in both a schoolhouse and a tin mine—and accusations of government corruption and neglect, Chinese officials succumbed to victims' families pleas to allow the trial to be open to the public. Defendants included the welders; store managers who had given

THE DONGDU DISCO TRIAL IN SESSION
Over 1,500 family members and other spectators jammed two courthouses in Beijing at the public trial. A total of 23 people from the private and public sector were tried, and sentences ranged from seven to 13 years.

shelter to the welders after they fled; the building manager for violating fire codes and failing to obtain a licence for construction; the owner for renting out the fire-escape route to a merchant whose shop blocked it; a fire inspector who falsified reports; two policemen for bribery; and the construction manager. The premier apologized on television for failing to keep the public safe and the prosecutor vowed to "mete out severe punishment for this crime, in order to ease people's anger, uphold the country's laws, and rest the souls of those wronged."

FIRE REPORT

CAUSES

• Sparks from welding torches used during unlicensed construction in unsafe building.

FIRE FACTS

• There were no sprinklers, fire alarms, or smoke detectors in the building.

• Fire extinguishers and hoses that had been purchased were never installed.

• The building's fire exits were blocked by boxes of merchandise and a shop illegally sited on the fire-escape route.

LOSSES

• 309 people killed.

DEVELOPMENTS

• One of the first major disasters in China with media coverage, the outrage of the victims' families focused the attention of the nation on the issues of corruption in the fire-safety inspection process and building malpractice, in both government and private sectors, and the need for stronger enforcement of fire-safety regulations.

DESTRUCTION IN THE DONGDU BUILDING
The Dongdu Disco fire started in the basement and ravaged the entire building, which housed a department store, specialty shops, and, on the fourth floor, the disco. Multiple violations of the fire code led to this tragedy on Christmas night. It took firefighters three hours to put out the intensely hot blaze.

HARTFORD CIRCUS FIRE

HARTFORD, USA, 1944

ON THE AFTERNOON OF JULY 6, 1944, a fire broke out on a sidewall of the big top at the Ringling Brothers and Barnum & Bailey Circus in Hartford, Connecticut. It was the afternoon performance of the Greatest Show on Earth, which had just rolled into the north end of Hartford, bringing its clowns, elephants, big cats, and high-wire acts to a crowd of seven thousand people, many of them women and children. In less than 10 minutes the blaze consumed the canvas tent, leaving 168 people—more than half of them under the age of 15—dead and hundreds more seriously injured. What started out as a light-hearted diversion from the news of war in Europe ended as the worst tragedy in American circus history, as well as a disaster of monumental proportions for the city of Hartford.

THE END OF THE BIG TOP
A Hartford police officer examines the charred remnants of the big top—76,500 square feet (7,100 sq m) were reduced to little more than tatters in 10 minutes .

CROWD ESCAPING THE BURNING TENT
Panicked circusgoers stampeded from the burning tent. Moments after this picture was taken, the center pole gave way and the burning tent collapsed onto the people still trapped beneath.

The canvas of the big top, treated with its waterproofing of paraffin and gasoline, acted as an accelerant, speeding up the progress of the fire.

The fire was so small at first that no one rushed to put it out. Others thought it was part of the show—until the flames suddenly roared up the tent's supporting structure and spread across the roof. The flames consumed the big top at an alarming speed, greedily eating the canvas, which had been treated with 6,000 gallons (23 kl) of gasoline and 18,000 pounds (8165 kg) of paraffin as waterproofing. Meanwhile, far above the grandstands, the Flying Wallendas, who were just about to start their high-wire act when the fire broke out, barely escaped by sliding down a tent pole.

Below, it was total pandemonium. The panicked crowd stampeded and surged toward the exits, toppling chairs and trampling anyone in their way. Strips of burning canvas rained down while bandmaster Merle Evans swung into "The Stars and Stripes Forever," the traditional circus disaster march. As if on cue, Ringling employees rushed onto the scene, directing people, as well as guiding animals toward the exits, some of which were blocked by animal cages. In the panic, men, women, and children injured themselves by jumping from the grandstands or were crushed underfoot in the stampede.

THE FIRE ABOVE

The heat from the burning big top was so intense it felt like a blowtorch, and flames, licking down from the canvas, burned people's hair, skin, and clothing. Just minutes after the blaze broke out, the center pole gave way and the big top collapsed directly onto the hapless crowd, trapping everyone beneath it. Almost all of the circus fire deaths were from burns, rather than suffocation or smoke

inhalation, which made it difficult to identify some victims. "Little Miss 1565"—a six-year-old child whose identity is still a mystery—was one of the most baffling cases. Even the legendary, Hartford-born detective Rick Davey devoted 10 years to the case. In the end, "Little Miss 1565" was buried as eight-year-old Eleanor Emily Cook, even though their dental records didn't match.

As firefighters arrived, they found it difficult to get close enough to the fire to put a hose line on it. They were hampered even further by the fact that the only available water hydrant was 300 yards (274 m) outside the grounds. An investigation showed that the circus had neglected to provide adequate firefighting equipment or enough personnel to operate it. The circus actually owned a number of portable extinguishers and water buckets, but had neglected to use them. In addition, the number of exits inside the big top was insufficient (the main exit had been blocked by an animal chute) and steel railings along the front of the bleachers made it difficult for the panicked crowd to reach the exits.

STILL A MYSTERY
Mildred Cook sits next to the grave of her daughter, Eleanor—who was presumed to be Little Miss 1565 although their dental records did not match. Controversy still surrounds the identity of the six-year-old girl, whose body lay unclaimed for days.

Finally, the big top itself, with its deadly coat of paraffin and gasoline, was Ringling's worst liability. In a matter of minutes the fire reduced it to smoldering ashes.

Five of Ringling Brothers' top managers were arrested on charges of manslaughter; four served sentences, including James A. Healey, the vice president. An arrangement was eventually made to funnel circus profits into an account that would pay off four million dollars in claims.

WAS THE HARTFORD CIRCUS FIRE THE WORK OF AN ARSONIST?

TO THIS DAY THE EVENTS OF JULY 6, 1944 still resonate in the public imagination, perhaps because the actual cause and origin of the Hartford circus fire, like that of the Cocoanut Grove fire, remain a mystery. At the time, the blame fell squarely on the shoulders of Ringling Brothers' top management. Four of them served jail sentences for manslaughter as a result of irresponsible practices such as the use of a flammable big top, blocked exits, and failure to provide adequate firefighting equipment and staff.

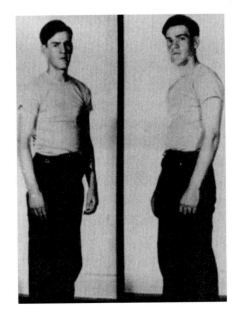

ROBERT DALE SEGEE (left) was arrested in Ohio in 1950. He confessed to starting the circus fire in Hartford, among several others, and said that a demonic fanged "Red Man" appeared in his dreams, showing him how and where to set fires. Segee, who had also confessed to four murders, served time for arson, but he later recanted, maintaining that he never killed anyone and never set a fire at any time. In 1954, after serving four years in jail, Segee was committed to Lima State Hospital for the Criminally Insane. In the end, it was never proven that Segee had anything to do with the Hartford fire or had, in fact, ever killed anyone.

DREAMLAND, CONEY ISLAND
BROOKLYN, USA, 1911

DREAMLAND, ONE OF THE GRANDEST and most expensive amusement parks of the early twentieth century, was the brainchild of a former New York State Senator, William H. Reynolds, whose ambition was to profit from the immense crowds that flocked to Luna Park, Coney Island's premier attraction. Backed by a consortium of real estate investors and political cronies, Reynolds built Dreamland for $2.5 million ($50 million today) plus the cost of land, making it bigger and far more expensive than Luna Park, which had been built for a mere $700,000 ($14 million today). From the day

LUNA PARK—THE COMPETITION
Luna Park, above, was a popular destination for New Yorkers on hot summer weekends in the final decades of the 19th century. Its success inspired the designers of Dreamland to build an even more elaborate amusement park than Luna—one that would draw bigger crowds and turn even bigger profits.

it opened, on May 15, 1904, Dreamland drew hundreds of thousands of visitors, many of them traveling by steamship from three terminals in Manhattan. Dozens of attractions included a circus, a 25,000-square-foot (2,322 sq m) ballroom, the biggest waterslide ever built, a hippodrome featuring chariot races, and "Lilliputia," a half-scale replica of a 15th-century Germany city, which housed 300 little people. Seven years later, on May 27, 1911, as they finished the last preparations for their annual summer opening on Memorial Day Weekend, a fire broke out in Hell Gate, one of Dreamland's popular boat rides, and spread to the rest of the park. Miraculously, no one died, although many thousands of workers subsequently lost their jobs, and over $5 million worth of property was destroyed. The blaze started at around 1:30 AM when workers, using hot tar to seal a leak in a water flume, noticed that overhead light bulbs were exploding, either from the heat of the tar or a short circuit. The lights suddenly went out and a panicked worker accidentally kicked over a bucket of hot tar. It was quickly ignited by stray sparks from an overhead fixture and a moment later

THE END OF A DREAM

The desolation of Dreamland was so complete—except for the park's new steel Giant Racer roller coaster, which can be seen in the distance on the right— that it was never re-opened. Today, the New York Aquarium, at Surf Avenue and West Eighth Street, occupies the site where the "white ramparts" of Dreamland once stood.

the plaster caverns of Hell Gate went up in flames. The workmen escaped with their lives. A night watchman was the first to alert a nearby fire house on West Eighth Street, only 100 yards (91 m) from Dreamland. Firefighters raced to the scene in horse-drawn engines and hook-and-ladder trucks.

INSUFFICIENT WATER PRESSURE

At the same time, a second alarm rang at a high-pressure pumping plant that had been recently constructed to help fight Coney Island's periodic fires. But it was too late. Fed by winds blowing inland, the fire had spread to the rest of the vast park and was consuming everything in its path, including Dreamland's 375-foot (114 m) Beacon Tower, a white monolith that lit up

the night sky with 100,000 electric lights. Despite the new pumping plant, which was operating at full capacity, firefighters were unable to get enough pressure in their hoses to reach the highest flames. The reason was as simple as it was disastrous: Panicked merchants in the area had illegally tapped into the high-pressure system to wet down their building facades. By daybreak, all 15 acres (6 ha) of the world-famous amusement park had been reduced to ashes.

No human lives were lost, but the park's wild animals, from antelopes to lions, were not as lucky. When the Beacon Tower collapsed in flames at 3:10 AM many of them panicked and escaped; some had to be shot. But at least one bear cub was rescued by a motorist on Surf Avenue.

FIRE REPORT

CAUSES
• Short circuit or, possibly, a burst light bulb may have ignited the blaze.

FIRE FACTS
• 33 fire companies responded to a "double-9 alarm." This meant that every fire company in Brooklyn that would usually answer a third alarm was to rush to Coney Island.

• More than 400 firemen fought the blaze.

• Teams of fire-horses pulled equipment from as far away as eight miles.

LOSSES
• More than $5,200,000 in property damage ($1 billion today)—most of it uninsured.

• More than 3,500 people lost their jobs.

• The owners of Dreamland suffered a $3,500,000 loss and decided not to rebuild.

RAJIV MARRIAGE PALACE
MANDI DABWALI, INDIA, 1995

TRAPPED BY THE WALLS
The synthetic fabric of the tent burned quickly, but here some scraps remain after the fire. The brick walls of the Rajiv Marriage Palace are visible at the back of this photograph. They were high and topped with barbed wire, and the main gate was blocked by the fire. The only escape from the compound was a single door.

THE WORST FIRE in recent Indian history, the blaze in Mandi Dabwali, at the Rajiv Marriage Palace, on December 23, 1995, claimed the lives of 441 people, most of them school children; 146 others suffered serious burns. What was to have been a festive, school prize-giving ceremony turned to tragedy when a short circuit from an electric generator sparked and ignited a synthetic cloth tent under the tin roof of the marriage hall. More than 1,200 students, and their parents and teachers, from the Dayanand Anglo Vedic (DAV) School were reportedly at the celebration when the tent caught fire and collapsed.

Surrounded by high brick walls and barbed wire on three sides and a row of rooms on the fourth, the hall was described as a "recipe for disaster" and "a virtual deathtrap" by police constable Om Prakash. According to eyewitnesses, the fire started at the main entrance shortly before 2:00 PM and quickly spread along the cables of the tent. Traveling with horrific speed over the tent, which was made from a synthetic fabric that easily catches fire and sticks to the skin when it burns, the fire effectively cut off the main exit. Within moments the fiery tent began to collapse, causing a stampede toward the only available exit—a single door in one of the high walls surrounding the tent. Hundreds died or were injured as they attempted to escape the flames, while hundreds more were incinerated under the tent. Other synthetic materials used in the dressy clothing worn by many of the celebrants also contributed to the high death toll. Coconut-fiber floor mats and chairs containing plastic netting added fuel to the conflagration. It lasted only 5 minutes, but the fire

WEDDING TENTS

ELABORATE TENTS KNOWN AS PANDALS OR SHAMIANAS are set up in India to entertain large crowds at weddings, religious ceremonies, or election rallies. Some, like the tent pictured above, are open-sided, but many are closed on all sides, with no clearly marked exits. Unauthorized, temporary constructions, they often lack the most basic fire protection. Increasingly, they are made of inflammable synthetic fiber, as was the tent in Rajiv Marriage Palace, which resulted in the death of over 400 people.

was so intense that many victims were burned beyond recognition—200 children were cremated without any identification. A town of 50,000, Mandi Dabwali had just one hospital with only 10 beds and few supplies. As hundreds of victims—many of them children—were brought in, relatives were told to go to local pharmacies to buy drugs and painkillers.

Others had to be transported in private cars, for lack of ambulances, over distances of 100 miles (161 km) or more to find an available hospital bed. Police filed a criminal negligence case against the owner and manager of the Rajiv Marriage Palace, who admitted that he had not received municipal authorization to construct the hall—nor had he made any firefighting provisions. Five years

later, a special court sentenced the owner and two electricians to two years of imprisonment for their negligence.

MASS FUNERAL PYRE
A national disaster, calamity or epidemic may result in the death of hundreds, even thousands of people in India. Whenever the bodies are not easily identifiable–such as those of the victims in Mandi Dabwali, which were charred beyond recognition–or are too numerous to cremate singly, mass funeral pyres are erected, sometimes in land adjoining the cremation grounds. Friends and relatives of the deceased gather there to mourn and pay their last respects.

A RUINED AWARDS CEREMONY
Overturned chairs were reminders of the scramble to escape. Students and parents had come to attend an awards ceremony for their school. Of the 200 children who died, most were between the ages of five and 17.

FIRE REPORT

CAUSES
• Short circuit from an electric generator materials.

OTHER CAUSES
• Highly flammable tent materials.

• Insufficient number of exits.

FIRE FACTS
• Worst fire in recent Indian history.

• No permit had been issued for the school function at the Rajiv Marriage Palace, and like so many marriage halls that had mushroomed in the area over recent years, construction of the Rajiv Palace was unauthorized.

• Owners of the hall had no firefighting provisions.

LOSSES
• Fire killed 441 people, most of them children, in about five minutes.

WORLD WAR II
—— THE BLITZ, LONDON, ENGLAND, 1940–45 ——

BOTH THE ALLIED AND THE AXIS POWERS used bombing campaigns to destroy their opponents' cities and demoralize their populations. *Blitz*, the German word for "lightning," was used in the British press to describe the heavy and frequent bombing raids carried out by the Luftwaffe (the German air force) on Great Britain— particularly over London in 1940 and 1941. The appearance of German bombers in the skies over London signaled a tactical shift in Adolf Hitler's attempt to subdue England.

During the previous months the Luftwaffe had targeted British radar stations, aircraft factories, and fighter airfields, resulting in the deaths of over 500 Royal Air Force (RAF) pilots and the destruction of 792 airplanes. Now, in an effort to destroy the morale of the population, bombing would be concentrated on London.

The Blitz began on Saturday, September 7, 1940. At 4:56 PM, London's air-raid sirens, later known as "Moaning Minnies," announced the arrival of 375 German bombers and an escort of several hundred fighter planes. Dropping a seemingly endless supply of incendiary bombs and explosives, they set the London docks ablaze. The fire service had anticipated major fires when the Germans attacked, but they were stunned by what they saw. Gerry Knight, a Station Officer, sent this message

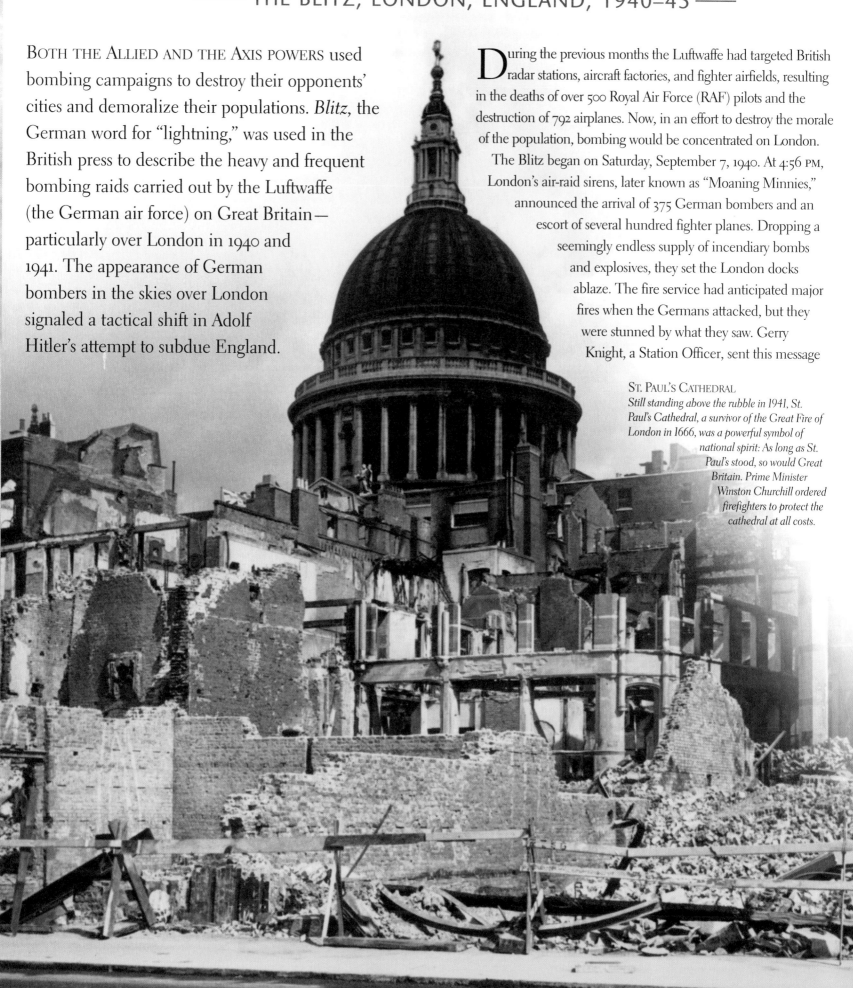

ST. PAUL'S CATHEDRAL
Still standing above the rubble in 1941, St. Paul's Cathedral, a survivor of the Great Fire of London in 1666, was a powerful symbol of national spirit: As long as St. Paul's stood, so would Great Britain. Prime Minister Winston Churchill ordered firefighters to protect the cathedral at all costs.

SIR ARTHUR HARRIS AT WORK, JULY 1943.
Arthur "Bomber" Harris was leader of the RAF Bomber Command. In 1942, he introduced massive bombing campaigns that targeted individual German cities, just as the Luftwaffe had zeroed in on London during the Blitz.

FIREMEN AT WORK NEAR ST. PAUL'S CATHEDRAL, 1940
As the blitz began, the Germans concentrated on bombing the heart of London. To fight the raging blazes that would come to be known as the Second Great Fire, fire engines were stationed every 700 feet (213 m). Approximately 2,000 pumpers and 9,000 firemen, women, and messenger boys fought the fires.

to the alarm office: "Send all the bloody pumps you've got . . . the whole bloody world's on fire!" Over 25,000 auxiliary firefighters joined the London Brigade to battle the flames. Five hundred fire pumps were dispatched to the docks. Water mains broke. Power, telephone, gas, and fire alarm service ceased. By 6:00 PM the first attack was over, but fires were still burning fiercely at 8:10 PM, when the bombing resumed. The assault lasted until 4:35 AM. By dawn, London had nine major conflagrations, huge spreading areas of flame, and nearly a thousand smaller fires.

MASSIVE CASUALTIES

After the first day of the Blitz, 430 citizens were dead and 1,600 were severely injured. German bombers returned the next day and 412 more civilians were killed. By the end of September alone, the German airforce had dropped 5,300 tons of explosives on London; 5,730 people had been killed, and nearly 10,000 were badly injured. London was bombed by day and night for 57 consecutive days; fires consumed huge sections of the city; and

residents—as many as 177,000 a night—sought refuge in the subway stations. By the end of November 1940, almost 13,000 civilians in the London area had died, about 20,000 had been seriously injured, and approximately 36,000 bombs had fallen on Britain's capital. After November, the pattern of bombing became more widespread, though no less destructive, but for the most part the strength of the Blitz had

diminished. Raids continued until May 1941, when Hitler turned his giant war machine east, toward Russia. By then between 40,000 and 60,000 British civilians had been killed and between 46,000 and 87,000 were seriously injured. Meanwhile the Luftwaffe had lost almost 2,500 aircraft without achieving Hitler's aim of crushing Great Britain or subduing the will of her people.

REFUGE IN THE UNDERGROUND STATIONS OF LONDON
London Underground stations provided shelter for thousands of people during almost two months of relentless bombing. Thousands were left homeless and took up permanent residence in the tubes, where it was not unusual to see crowds of people sleeping on station platforms piled high with their belongings.

FIRE REPORT

☙ CAUSES
• Incendiary bombs and other high explosives.

☙ FIRE FACTS
• 2 million houses (60 percent of housing stock in London) were destroyed.

• Bomb craters filled with water from rain and fire hoses, and became reservoirs for the fire service.

• Firefighters worked quickly during the day to extinguish fires so that they would not provide illumination for enemy bombers at night.

☙ LOSSES
• Between 40,000 and 60,000 people killed.

• 1,027 firemen and over 24 firewomen died in the line of duty.

• 46,000 to 87,000 were seriously injured.

☙ DEVELOPMENTS
• The Soap Box Fire Engine, carrying hand pumps, sand bags, and water buckets, was constructed out of cardboard boxes and mounted on baby-buggy wheels.

RELATED FIRES

• Washington, D.C., 1814: British forces out of Bermuda attacked the U.S. capital and set fire to the White House.

• Korea, 1950–1953: Used on a limited basis in WWII, napalm was first used widely by U.S. in Korea to attack Communist strongholds.

• Vietnam, 1963–1971: Napalm was employed with devastating effect during the Vietnam War. Beginning in 1963, the U.S. used over 335,000 tons of napalm, along with fuel air explosives, against the North Vietnamese.

WORLD WAR II
—— FIREBOMBING, HAMBURG AND DRESDEN, 1943–45 ——

RESULTS OF AREA BOMBING
Smoke pours out of a burned building in central Hamburg after a firestorm was unleashed on the city in July and August 1943. After the raids on Hamburg, most German civilians felt it was time to capitulate to the Allies before any further damage was done, but the German High Command insisted that "total war" should proceed.

HAMBURG FIRESTORM

Hamburg was the first of several German cities targeted by the Allies for area bombing (known in Germany as "terror bombing"). The main idea behind these campaigns—the annihilation of entire cities in order to "de-house" civilians and shatter morale—was carried out through the creation of firestorms.

These were achieved by dropping clusters of incendiary bombs filled with highly combustible chemicals such as magnesium, phosphorus, or jellied gasoline (napalm), on a specific target. After the bombed area caught fire, the air above it became extremely hot and rose rapidly. When cooler air rushed in at ground level, a huge suctioning force was generated, and in some cases, grew into the powerful force of a tornado, whipping up fiery winds exceeding 150 miles per hour (240 kmph).

On July 24, 1943 Air Marshal Arthur Harris ordered the firebombing of Hamburg. The dropping of incendiary bombs, alternated with 4,000-pound high-capacity bombs, made firefighting impossible: The concentration of high buildings, combined with the quantity of bombs that rained down on Hamburg from 731 RAF planes, started thousands of fires that created a huge firestorm, sucking up oxygen and generating hurricane-force winds. Thick trees were uprooted and human beings were thrown to the ground or sucked into the flames. Panic-stricken citizens—as many as 60,000 at a time—took refuge in the city's air-raid shelters, but thousands of others burned to death or were asphyxiated from carbon monoxide poisoning in basements and cellars. Dockyards and industrial installations were devastated and essential services were severely damaged; coal and coke supplies, stored for the winter in many houses, continued to burn for weeks; and a pall of smoke and dust lingered over the city for days.

THE FIREBOMBING OF DRESDEN

The air war on German civilian targets, in which area bombing and the creation of lethal firestorms were prominent, continued for about 18 months after the Hamburg conflagration. On February 13, 1945, Air Marshal Arthur Harris ordered the firebombing of Dresden. Arthur Harris considered the medieval city of Dresden—the seventh largest city in Germany—a good target for firebombing because it had not been attacked during the war and was virtually undefended by antiaircraft guns. This decision would later haunt him. Prime Minister Winston Churchill was so appalled by the destruction and loss of life in Dresden that he could no longer justify bombing German cities simply for the sake of increasing terror. The United States, however, under the leadership of Major General Curtis LeMay, decided to adopt British firebombing tactics in Japan as a final effort to force the Japanese to surrender.

RECONSTRUCTION
Dresden's ruined town hall looms in the background as the city's residents reconstruct a bomb-damaged wall. Allied bombers pummeled the city for four days in February 1945.

LIFE GOES ON
Amidst unthinkable ruin, residents of Dresden line up for a streetcar—virtually the only means of conveyance in the rubble-strewn city. The decision to bomb Dresden is still widely perceived as lacking military justification, even within the context of the area bombing policy pursued by Britain in 1942–45.

That winter, Dresden's population had increased dramatically with the influx of refugees pouring westward, in flight from the advancing Soviet army. The city was considered of little industrial or strategic importance, but it was one of Germany's greatest centers of art, architecture, and culture, famous for its museum, historic churches, and state opera house. On February 13, 773 RAF Avro Lancasters pummeled the city, first with tons of high-explosive bombs that exposed timbers within buildings, and then with incendiary bombs that set the buildings ablaze. A third volley of high explosives effectively hampered the efforts of Dresden's firefighters. The result was a terrific, self-sustaining firestorm with temperatures peaking at over 2,730°F (1,500°C). Over the course of the next two days, February 14 and 15, 800 American air force bombers dropped another 2,000 tons of bombs on Dresden, destroying the remainder of the city.

Dresden has never regained its pre-war population of about 650,000. As a result of the three-day firestorm it was impossible to count the number of dead, but recent research suggests that as many as 135,000 people were killed, and over 1,600 acres (6.5 sq km) of the city were devastated.

FIRE REPORT

CAUSES
HAMBURG:
• Area bombing: concentration of incendiary bombs and other explosives targeted on a single city.

DRESDEN
• Three days of continuous bombing with incendiaries and other explosives.

FIRE FACTS
HAMBURG:
• Thousands of smaller fires merged into a massive firestorm that swept over and burned hundreds of city blocks.

• Fires could not be prevented from flaring up again.

• Temperatures rose to 1,830°F (1,000°C).

DRESDEN:
• 3,300 tons of bombs contributed to a huge blaze.

• Continuous bombing hampered firefighters' attempts to put out the enormous fires.

LOSSES
HAMBURG:
• 40,000 deaths in a single day; 40,000 wounded; 900,000 homeless or missing.

• At least 40% of residential buildings destroyed.

DRESDEN:
• 135,000 estimated fatalities.

• 1,600 city acres were obliterated.

DEVELOPMENTS
• British high command began to question—and later abandoned—their policy of firebombing civilian centers.

WORLD WAR II
—— FIREBOMBING, TOKYO, JAPAN, 1945 ——

Allied area bombing campaigns and the deadly conflagrations they had brought to cities in Germany culminated in Japan in August 1945, when the U.S. bombers dropped atomic bombs on Hiroshima and Nagasaki. These bombings, however, were preceded by a catastrophic firestorm in Tokyo, the capital of Japan, only five months earlier. In that city, people were killed in considerably greater numbers than in Nagasaki, where 75,000 died.

Tokyo had long been a major target of the U.S. bombers during WWII. Bombing raids on the city began late in 1944 from bases in the Mariana Islands, but with the capture of Iwo Jima, in February 1945, the U.S. moved quickly to end the war in Japan by decimating its capital, a city of six million people.

On the night of March 9, 1945 nearly 600 B-29 bombers dropped 1,665 tons of napalm-filled bombs on the city's inhabitants. A survivor remembers hearing shrill air-raid sirens, then, minutes later, seeing a horrible red glow in the sky. That night 100,000 people died in the firestorm. Most of the victims were women, children, and old men. The firestorm was so powerful that the available firefighting methods could not stop the destruction.

U.S. planes continued to firebomb Tokyo and more than 60 other cities in the following months, but the campaign only stiffened the resolve of the Japanese to fight on. Eventually they would surrender, but only after their country lay in complete ruins and the hope of victory was lost.

FIREBOMBED CITYSCAPE
Twisted tree branches and in the background, radio towers, are among the few remains amid the rubble after the firebombing of Tokyo. Incendiary bombs burned over 41.5 square miles (107 sq km) of Tokyo.

SCORCHED EARTH
An Allied journalist views a a sea of debris that was once a city block and the remains of a former movie theater.

FIRE REPORT

ᨆ CAUSES

• Napalm bombs ignited the city, which was largely constructed of wood.

ᨆ FIRE FACTS

• The Tokyo firebombing received little attention, eclipsed by the atomic bombing of Hiroshima and Nagasaki—many young people today are unaware of the event, even in Japan.

ᨆ LOSSES

• 100,000 people dead after one night of bombing.

• Intensity of fire reduced 41.5 square miles (107 sq km) of Tokyo—the heart of Tokyo, 16 square miles (41 sq km) was totally incinerated.

ᨆ RELATED FIRES

• Subsequent firebomb attacks on Nagoya, Kobe, Osaka, and Yokohama left 260,00 people dead and 9.2 million homeless.

BATTLE OF NEW YORK
NEW YORK CITY, USA, 1776

CHAOS AS NEW YORK BURNS IN 1776
The fire, as depicted in an 18th-century French engraving, shows utter mayhem: slaves moving valuables, billowing flames, women in terror.

ON SEPTEMBER 21, 1776, a fire broke out near the southern tip of Manhattan Island and quickly spread north, burning a wide swath up Wall Street and consuming all of the buildings between Broadway and the Hudson River. Many of the city's early buildings went up in flames, including the original Trinity Church, although St. Paul's Chapel survived. The cause of the fire is unknown, but some suspect arson: General George Washington had just surrendered the city to the British, and military practice at the

time would have prompted the Americans to burn down the town rather than leave it intact for the British. Congress had forbidden such burnings, but it is possible that an American sympathizer was involved in setting the blaze. Another possible motive for the fire was looting. The British, for their part, executed a few suspects, either by hanging or throwing them into the flames. The British command was undoubtedly embarrassed to have won the city, only to see it burn down. In the end, no matter who set the fire, the conquering army was denied the use of the better part of the city.

GEORGE WASHINGTON AT KIPS BAY BATTLE, SEPTEMBER 15, 1776
In this 19th-century engraving Washington is shown trying to stop American troops from fleeing the Kips Bay Battle (at present-day 34th Street in Manhattan), where they were greatly outnumbered. Six days later the fire broke out.

FIRE REPORT

ᨆ CAUSES

• Unknown, but possibly arson by American patriots who did not want to leave the city intact for the British occupiers.

ᨆ FIRE FACTS

• The city burned very quickly because it was constructed of wood.

ᨆ LOSSES

• 500 houses were burned.

• Several Americans were executed for arson by the British.

RUSSIAN CAMPAIGN OF 1812

MOSCOW, RUSSIA, 1812

NAPOLEON BONAPARTE
This statue of Napoleon can be found in the Loire Valley of France. The French Emperor conquered much of Europe, but his attempt to invade Russia failed.

THE USE OF FIRE AS A WEAPON and a strategy to consume resources in order to keep them out of the grasp of others came into play in the summer of 1812, when French military leader and emperor Napoleon Bonaparte began his campaign to conquer Russia. All of continental Europe was under his control, and the invasion of Russia was an attempt to force Tsar Alexander I to submit to the terms of a treaty that Napoleon had imposed on him four years earlier.

Napoleon entered Russia leading nearly 500,000 soldiers, the largest army ever seen. The Russians, under General Mikhail Kutuzov, knew that they could not defeat Napoleon in a head-on confrontation, so they began a defensive strategic retreat, destroying the land as they fell back. When Napoleon entered Moscow on September 14, 1812, the city was virtually empty. Despite the French army's strict orders against pillage, soldiers began to plunder what remained of the city's riches. A few fires broke out in the city, and it became obvious that these were being set by the Russian army in order to prevent further looting, although looters were involved in setting fires, too. The fire grew into a conflagration that raged for three days. Most of the city burned to the ground, but the rest was saved by a sudden change in the weather when rain began to fall.

The snows came early; Napoleon's troops were decimated by cold, hunger and disease; his winter housing had burned down; and the Russian grain stores were empty. He retreated on October 19, leaving behind any hope of establishing peace with Russia.

FIRE REPORT

⚜ CAUSES
• Fires were set by Russian army to prevent Napoleon's army from looting valuables and grain stores. Looters were involved, too.

⚜ FIRE FACTS
• Conflagration lasted for three days.

• Fire made Moscow's buildings uninhabitable for remaining Russian troops, and destroyed supplies as well.

⚜ LOSSES
• Casualties from the fire were small—only 25,000 Russians were still in Moscow when the French army arrived.

• Most of Moscow—many of its buildings were wooden— burned to the ground.

THE WEALTH OF MOSCOW
An engraving shows the flames roaring behind Moscow's grand architecture, the domes of the St. Basil Cathedral in the background. Most of the riches that the Russians had not destroyed already were stolen by the French or burned to the ground.

CONFEDERACY

VIRGINIA, GEORGIA, SOUTH CAROLINA, USA 1864–65

By LATE SPRING OF 1864, the tide of the Civil War had turned decisively in favor of the North. Union troops began massive assaults against a reduced Confederate army in three Southern strongholds: Richmond, Virginia; Atlanta, Georgia; and Columbia, South Carolina. Fire, used defensively and offensively, was the campaign's most potent weapon—destroying human lives, military targets, and Southern morale.

CONFEDERATE STRATEGY

In June, 1864, General Ulysses S. Grant began a 10-month siege against Robert E. Lee's troops in Richmond. Grant's armies cut off all supplies to Richmond, and systematically attacked the city from the north and south. By April 2, 1865, Lee's troops were decimated, and he gave orders to evacuate and burn the city. Retreating Confederates torched tobacco, munitions warehouses, and factories. The resulting explosions, combined with wind and mobs of torch-carrying looters, spread fires throughout the city's waterfront and business areas. Nearly all of Richmond's dockyards and central business district were destroyed.

CONFEDERATE GENERAL ROBERT E. LEE
An 1867 lithograph of Lee and his generals. After the Union isolated Richmond, Lee evacuated the the city and had it torched.

UNION COUNTERATTACKS

Union General William T. Sherman and his troops arrived in Atlanta in May 1864. Skirmishing throughout the summer with the Confederates, Sherman was initially pushed back and lost nearly 10,000 men. He regrouped and mounted repeated counterattacks until Confederate forces evacuated the city on September 1, 1864. The legendary "burning of Atlanta" actually began with a fire started by Confederate troops when they blew up an ammunitions train. Contrary to myth, Sherman did not burn Atlanta to the ground: civilians were evacuated during his 10-week occupation; most homes were left standing. His troops did burn anything that might further the Confederate war effort: railroads, factories, storehouses, foundries, and cotton gins.

In November, Sherman and his troops traveled 250 miles (402 km) east to Savannah, Georgia. Along the way, his soldiers cut a wide swath of destruction, burning railroads, factories, farms, barns, and some homes. They took Savannah on December 21, 1864.

Sherman arrived in Columbia, South Carolina on February 17, 1865. His army set fires throughout the city, which was virtually leveled. Thousands were left homeless. The damage was so extensive that it sparks controversy to this day. Certainly, the devastation delivered a mighty blow to the South's morale. A month and a half later, the Confederacy conceded defeat.

BUSINESSES DESTROYED
A hand-painted photograph of Richmond from 1865 shows flour mills destroyed by the Confederates.

FIRE REPORT

CAUSES

• Torching, small incendiary devices, or explosives: Lee burned Richmond and Atlanta to thwart Sherman's army from using valuable supplies; Sherman burned a large area between Atlanta and Savannah, as well as burning Columbia.

• Accelerated by high winds and torch-bearing looters.

LOSSES

• Richmond: 25,000 Union troops, 12,500 Confederates.

• Atlanta: 11,000 Union troops, 10,000 Confederates.

• Georgia March and Columbia: 25,000 Union troops, 10,000 Confederates, major railway route destroyed.

• Widespread property damage in all four campaigns.

TEXAS CITY

—— TEXAS CITY, USA, 1947 ——

THERE WAS NOTHING THAT FIREFIGHTER TRAINING, modern equipment, or modern communications could have done to contain or extinguish the fires that occurred in Texas City on Wednesday, April 16 and Thursday, April 17, 1947. But many firefighters and civilians would still be alive if city and industrial safety plans had been in place. In the months following the disaster, municipal and state authorities, along with representatives of chemical and oil companies, took steps to prevent a similar tragedy from ever happening again. For one thing, the proximity of lethal ship cargoes to equally dangerous industrial plants was an issue that had to be addressed.

Early on the morning of April 16—a beautiful spring day—at about 8:00 AM, a small fire broke out in the hold of the *Grandcamp*, one of two cargo ships anchored in the harbor of Texas City. It contained 2,300 tons of ammonium nitrate fertilizer that was destined for Europe. Anchored nearby, a ship called the *High Flyer* carried another 1,000 tons of the volatile fertilizer in its hold, along with a cargo of sulfur. Although there has been much speculation over the years as to the cause of the fire aboard the *Grandcamp*, no specific cause has been determined, although a burning cigarette is the most popular theory. Attempts were made by the crew of the *Grandcamp* to control the fire by closing the hatches, but by 8:30 they had blown wide open. Observers and ships crews noted the peculiar—even beautiful—orange color of the smoke. A crowd of spectators, including many children, gathered on the dock to watch firefighters battle the blaze, unaware of the immense volatility and

INCENDIARY CARGO
The French cargo ship SS Grandcamp, moored in Texas City, was carrying small-arms ammunition and other products when it arrived in the harbor on April 11, 1947. Bound for Europe, the ship took on 2,300 tons of ammonium nitrate a fertilizer to help farmers recover from World War II. The fire in the hold, possibly caused by a carelessly tossed cigarette, quickly burned out of control and the entire ship exploded. Fertilizer containers and fragments of the ship were hurled as much as one mile (1.6 km) away by the explosion.

destructive power of ammonium nitrate fertilizer. The hold was reported to be so hot that water from the hoses vaporized before it could do any good.

In those days, dangerously burning vessels were tugged out to sea, but before a tug could come to the rescue, the *Grandcamp* suddenly exploded at about 9:00 AM, sending a giant column of black smoke 2,000 feet (610 m) into the air. The roar of the blast was heard almost 200 miles (322 km) away and pedestrians in Galveston, only ten miles (16 km) away, were knocked off their feet. Ten to fifteen minutes later—at about 9:12 AM—a second explosion rocked the *Grandcamp*, and fire quickly engulfed a Monsanto Chemical plant and a Humble oil refinery, which were located opposite the docks. Within moments, almost the entire Texas City Fire Department was killed along with scores of other adults and children who were watching the spectacle nearby. At the same time, whole boxcars and massive pieces of the *Grandcamp* were sent flying through the air and landed, in some cases, one mile (1.6 km) or more away from the site of the explosion. Huge fires were ignited in Texas City when large bails of burning hemp were propelled through the air from the hold of the *Grandcamp* and landed on the roofs of buildings, including homes

MONSANTO CHEMICAL PLANT ENGULFED BY SMOKE
The chemical plant was totally destroyed by the fire, which then traveled along the pipelines of the plant to the refineries in the area.

FIRE REPORT

⚜ CAUSES
• Unknown, possibly a cigarette.

⚜ FIRE FACTS
• The blast from the first explosion could be heard 200 miles (322 km) away.

• The iron hold of the *Grandcamp* was so hot that it vaporized water.

• Fireboats were pressed into service, as well as tugs, but they were unable either to extinguish the fires aboard the *Grandcamp* or tow the *High Flyer* out of the harbor.

• Fires burned for six days.

⚜ LOSSES
• Nearly 600 deaths, over 2,000 injured.

• Property losses of over $67 million ($540 million today).

• Most of the Texas City Terminal Railway (TCT) was destroyed.

⚜ DEVELOPMENTS
• An investigation was made into the deadly consequences of anchoring volatile ship cargoes next to stores of explosive materials on shore.

⚜ RELATED FIRES
• Cali, Colombia, 1956: seven Army ammunition trucks exploded, killing 1,100 and destroying eight city blocks.

• Piper Alpha Oil Rig, North Sea,1988: This accident led to a worldwide revolution in offshore safety and emergency response. An explosion in the gas compression module and subsequent fire killed 167.

• Trans-Siberian Railway, Russia, 1989: A gas pipeline in southeast Russia, blew apart, engulfing two passenger trains in fire. Over 500 people were killed.

and industrial facilities. As buildings collapsed, trapping people inside them, fires traveled swiftly along pipelines and spread from the Monsanto plant to the surrounding refineries in the Texas City industrial complex. This is where many of the city's 1,600 residents worked.

The devastation of Texas City continued for hours after the initial explosion aboard the *Grandcamp*, which was quickly followed by a miniature tidal wave that washed over the docks, sweeping away everything in its path as far inland as 150 feet (46 m). The water, displaced from the bay by the explosion, did little to extinguish the raging fires. The fireboats in the harbor were not powerful enough to extinguish the flames. As the day progressed, the full horror of events deepened as the deaths of more plant- and dock-workers, firefighters, bystanders, and children were reported. Police officers and firefighters from surrounding towns flocked to the area, while rescue workers and ambulances sped through the city ferrying the injured

FURTHER EXPLOSIONS
The fires at this oil refinery, like others in Texas City, were causes by flames spreading along the delivery pipelines between the refineries and the Monsanto Chemical Plant.

and dead to hospitals in Galveston and Houston. Volunteers from the city worked tirelessly around the clock to assist in rescue efforts.

As night fell, attempts to find the living among the wreckage continued, while anxiety about the *High Flyer*, which had been burning in the harbor for most of the day, mounted. Tugboats had been unable to tow the ship, loaded with ammonium nitrate and sulfur, out of the harbor. At 1:15 AM the next morning, the *High Flyer* exploded even more violently than the *Grandcamp*. In the blast another

vessel, the *Wilson B. Keene*, was destroyed, along with a concrete warehouse and a grain elevator. There was more fire, and a mist of black oil wafted over Galveston.

It was difficult to establish exactly how many people perished in what came to be known as the Texas City Disaster; it was impossible to retrieve many bodies, and others were simply unrecognizable, but in the end the figure came close to 600. Over 2,000 people were injured. The toll was so high that virtually no family was left untouched.

FIRE TRUCK SKELETON
Blasts occurred so quickly and, in some cases, spontaneously, that some equipment was not even used. This truck sits amid the wreckage of a warehouse, its hose still neatly coiled.

HALIFAX
— NOVA SCOTIA, CANADA, 1917 —

LISTING RED CROSS SHIP
The Belgian SS Imo, which had been carrying Red Cross supplies, after its collision with the munitions-bearing SS Mont Blanc. The port of Halifax was a common transit point for ships bearing soldiers and equipment for the war in Europe.

IT WAS A SUNNY, seasonally brisk Thursday morning, December 6, 1917. The war in Europe was in full swing, and the port city of Halifax, in Nova Scotia, Canada, was bustling with warships carrying munitions, relief supplies, and troops. The harbor was also open to neutral ships, one of which was the SS *Imo*, a cargo vessel carrying Red Cross supplies, and heading for Europe. On that morning, the *Imo* weighed anchor and headed for the sea. At the same time, the SS *Mont Blanc*, a French munitions ship loaded with explosives, was making her way into the harbor. Stored in the holds or simply stacked on the deck of the *Mont Blanc* were 2,300 tons of picric acid (used for making explosives such as artillery shells), 35 tons of high octane fuel, thousands of tons of TNT, 300 rounds of ammunition, and 10 tons of

guncotton (nitrocellulose explosives). At about 9:05 AM the two ships collided in the bottleneck known as "The Narrows." The blast that resulted 20 minutes after the collision was the biggest man-made explosion on record.

There has never been an explanation as to why the ships collided except for the prevailing theory that neither one correctly understood the signals from the other. Flaming debris from the explosion of the 3,000-ton *Mont Blanc* fell on a completely unprepared city. The barrel of one of her cannons landed three and a half miles (5.6 km) away; part of her anchor shank, weighing over half a ton (450 kg), flew two miles (3.2 km) in the opposite direction. Windows shattered 50 miles (80 km) away, and the shock from the explosion was felt in Sydney, Cape Breton, 270 miles (430 km)

to the northeast. Fires burned through Halifax, virtually leveling its entire north end. Houses, factories, and schools were destroyed. The number of homes that disappeared in the flames was in the thousands, perhaps as many as 3,000. The death toll has never been firmly established, although some totals have gone up as far as 3,000 and even 4,000. Serious injuries were at least twice that figure.

Halifax has the dubious honor of being the first modern city to be decimated by a fire that was not war-related, and which was completely beyond its immediate control. While waterfront fires had resulted in serious damage ashore to St. Louis (Missouri) in 1851; London (England) in 1861; and Hoboken (New Jersey) in 1900, nothing equivalent to what happened in Halifax would occur again until 30 years later in Texas City.

SHIPWRECKED CITY
Men dig through the ruins of Halifax, burned as a result of the collision between SS Mont Blanc and SS Imo, in the winter snows of 1917. Sixteen inches (41 cm) of snow fell the day after the explosion.

FIRE REPORT

CAUSES
• Collision between two ships.

FIRE FACTS
• The biggest home-front explosion of World War I.

• The largest man-made explosion until the dropping of an atomic bomb on Hiroshima, Japan in 1945.

• The Canadian government gave Halifax $18 million in relief funds.

• The British government donated almost $5 million.

LOSSES
• Over 2,000 dead and 4,000 injured.

• 325 acres (132 ha) and 1,000–3,000 homes destroyed.

DEVELOPMENTS
• Medical treatment, social welfare, public health, and hospital facilities increased and improved.

• Regulations relating to the harbor were tightened, making it as safe as human errors of judgment would permit.

• The Hydrostone development, built as relief housing, still stands, an early example of exemplary urban development.

GIFT TREE
Every year Halifax sends a Christmas tree to Boston as a token of gratitude for aid and supplies given by Massachusetts during the relief effort of 1917.

PORT CHICAGO
—— CALIFORNIA, USA, 1944 ——

As U.S. MILITARY INVOLVEMENT in the Philippines began to heat up during the latter half of World War II, munitions bases, such as the one in Port Chicago California, were built or upgraded to meet the U.S. Navy's demands. In July of 1944, African-American navy personnel were moved into the area and assigned the dangerous work of loading munitions, for which they had no previous training. On the night of July 17, 1944, the SS *Quinault Victory*, a new merchant ship, was empty and waiting for a delivery of ammunition that was to have begun at midnight. The holds of a second transport ship, the SS *E.A. Bryan*, however, had been taking on cargo around the clock for days, and were packed with over 4,000 tons of munitions, almost 2,000 tons of which were high explosives. At around 10:20 PM a massive explosion occurred at the pier. In actuality, it was two blasts—the first was relatively minor, but it set off a second, catastrophic explosion that sent a two-mile-high (3.2 km) column of fire and smoke into the night sky. The *E.A. Bryan* and *Quinault Victory* were

obliterated in the explosion, instantly killing 320 American naval personnel and injuring hundreds more. Small boats in the Sacramento River, half a mile (0.8 km) from the explosion, were reportedly hit by a 30-foot (9 m) wall of water—and an airplane, flying 9,000 feet (2,700 m) above the base, reportedly saw chunks of white metal "as big as a house" fly past. The base at Port Chicago was flattened. Barracks were blown off their foundations. Servicemen were knocked off their feet by the concussion and pelted with debris including everything from shards of wood and hot metal to broken glass. The little town of Port Chicago, located a mile and a half (2.4 km) from the site of the blast, was badly damaged.

The explosion and loss of life at Port Chicago was so horrific that it was considered the worst home-front military disaster of World War II. "Spontaneous explosion" was thought to be the cause of the calamity, even after the navy convened a special Court of Inquiry to investigate other possible causes.

FREDDIE MEEKS, one of 50 African-American sailors, was imprisoned for mutiny in October 1944 for refusing to load ammunition onto a Navy transport ship after the Port Chicago explosion took the lives of 202 black enlisted men. The sailors' trial was a catalyst for the civil rights movement. In 1946, President Franklin D. Roosevelt released the men under a general amnesty, but they were never granted veterans' benefits, and their convictions were not exonerated. In 1999, Freddy Meeks was officially pardoned by President Clinton.

FIRE REPORT

⚡ CAUSES
• Unknown. Possibly a spontaneous explosion.

⚡ OTHER CAUSES
• Insufficiently trained personnel and deviations from safety standards, due to tight loading schedules, may have been factors in the disaster.

⚡ FIRE FACTS
• Explosion was as large as a 5-kiloton bomb.

• The largest U.S. home-front military disaster of World War II.

⚡ LOSSES
• 320 American naval personnel killed instantly; 390–500 injured.

• Naval base at Port Chicago completely destroyed.

• Estimated $12 million in military and civilian property damage.

⚡ DEVELOPMENTS
• New training and safety procedures introduced for the handling of ammunition and explosives.

• In 1948 President Harry Truman called for the armed forces to be desegregated.

SINKING HULLS
The splintered hulls of the two munitions ships, the SS E.A. Bryan, which had already been packed with explosives, and the SS Quinault Victory, not yet loaded, in Port Chicago Harbor several days after the explosion occurred.

AZF FACTORY

—TOULOUSE, FRANCE, 2001—

AT 10:15 AM ON FRIDAY, September 21, 2001, a huge explosion ripped through the AZF (Azote de France) fertilizer factory on the outskirts of Toulouse. The blast, which originated in a silo containing 200–300 tons of ammonium nitrate, caused the deaths of 30 people and injured as many as 2,500 others. An electrical goods store about 1,000 feet (300 meters) from the AZF plant collapsed 45 minutes after the explosion, and the factory itself was reduced to little more than a tangle of metal and rubble. The explosion blew out windows in the city center two miles (3 km) away and left a crater 164 feet (50 m) across and 33 feet (10 m) deep. Experts said the explosion was equivalent to an earthquake measuring 3.4 on the Richter scale. In the wake of the fire and collapse of the World Trade Center in New York City just ten days earlier, many local residents thought they were under fire or being bombed as the AZF factory exploded.

More than 500 homes became uninhabitable after the blast and almost 11,000 children and adults were forced to evacuate 85 local schools and colleges because of structural damage. Immediately after the explosion, hundreds of residents ran into the streets of Toulouse, fearing that the cloud of acrid smoke hanging over their city might be toxic. Police blocked off the area, but tests later showed that there was no danger of poisoning.

The AZF plant had been built in 1924 in open, green fields, but urban sprawl from Toulouse eventually led to the construction of homes, schools, and shops that were all too close to the plant's giant chimney-stacks. An investigation was quickly launched due to a firestorm of public outrage and protest against southern France's chemical-industrial complex. The minister of the interior said that the explosion at AZF was an accident caused by an "incident in the handling of products," and French President Jacques Chirac, who visited the site, also said that the explosion appeared to be accidental. The mayor of Toulouse, Philippe Douste-Blazy, called for all potentially hazardous factories to be relocated away from areas where people live. The local population was angered by official explanations, and felt that responsibility should be acknowledged by both governmental authorities and TotalFinaElf group, the world's fourth-largest oil company and owners of AZF.

SEARCH FOR SURVIVORS
Firemen attempted to find survivors amid the tangled remains and rubble of the AZF factory on the day the plant exploded.

EXPLOSIVE FERTILIZER
Like the Texas City disaster, this accident was abetted by the explosive nature of the compound ammonium nitrate, combined with dynamite during World War II but now reserved for use as a fertilizer.

FIRE REPORT

CAUSES
• Accidental. Official theory is that workers may have inadvertently made a mistake while mixing chemicals.

FIRE FACTS
• Worst civilian disaster in France in 20 years.

• Up to 100 firefighters searched for survivors through the wreckage.

• A red cloud seen near the factory following the blast was thought to be an ammonia cloud; later tests showed there was no danger of poisoning and the alert was lifted.

LOSSES
• 30 dead, 2,500 injured, 1,400 families homeless.

• 600 homes destroyed, 10,000 homes damaged.

• 2 schools destroyed, 1 hospital badly damaged.

• Insurance costs were estimated at $73–145 million (520 million–1 billion FF).

DEVELOPMENTS
• The following measures were suggested as guidelines to prevent future disasters:

• *Control urban growth around dangerous sites.*

• *Close or relocate potentially hazardous factories and plants away from residential areas.*

• *Enhance security for workers at high-risk plants and factories.*

• *Require high-risk factories to split up their stock, seal it in double containers, and bury it.*

• *Require regular accident drills.*

• *Increase number of chemical plant inspectors from 1,020 to 2,000.*

• *Communities in potentially dangerous areas given right to be consulted and warned of risks.*

OUR LADY OF THE ANGELS

CHICAGO, USA, 1958

LIKE MOST AMERICAN SCHOOLS that were built before 1949, Chicago's Our Lady of the Angels was ill-equipped to survive the events of December 1, 1958, when a fire destroyed the north wing of the school and killed 92 children and 3 adults. In the wake of the fire a blue-ribbon panel was assembled by the county coroner in order to investigate the cause of the fire and suggest ways to prevent a similar tragedy from happening again. OLA, as the parish school was known in the surrounding community, had no smoke alarms or sprinkler system, and its antiquated internal-alarm system was not connected to the fire department.

Classrooms were dangerously overcrowded, stairwells were open, without fire doors, and there was only one fire escape. The two-story building itself, like so many of its contemporaries, contained wood, wood lathe, and plaster, which, combined with other combustible materials such as heavily varnished wood floors and trim, painted walls, and acoustic ceiling tiles added up to nothing less than a firetrap. The death toll may have been much higher at two other notorious school fires— New London, Texas, in 1937 and Collinwood, Ohio, in 1908—but it was the fire at Our Lady of the Angels School in Chicago that would finally tip the scales in favor of nationwide fire-safety reforms.

Sometime after 2:00 PM on Monday, December 1, 1958, a fire started in a trash bin at the bottom of a stairwell in the basement of Our Lady of the Angels School at 909 Avers. Incredibly, the fire had burned undetected for at least 20 minutes. After the first alarms were called in, firefighters still did not arrive for another 20 minutes because they were sent to the wrong address.

The north wing had become progressively warmer, but students and teachers attributed the heat to an over-stoked furnace and were not particularly alarmed. What they did not know was that a window near the basement stairwell had burst from the heat. Replenished by a fresh supply of air, the fire leapt up the stairs, gobbling fuel and growing to an enormous size. It bypassed the first floor, where it was blocked by a closed fire door, and flowed up the stairs into the 85-foot-long (26 m) hallway leading to the second-floor classrooms. Here, the fire quickly consumed the combustible flooring, walls, trim, and ceiling tiles, filling the corridor with black, choking smoke. At the same time, fire gases and superheated air were traveling through a shaft from the basement to a narrow loft under the roof. Another fire ignited just above the ceiling of the second-floor classrooms, which housed 329 fourth- through eighth-grade students and their six teachers. Burning debris dropped from the loft through ventilation grilles into the corridor, now an inferno, where the temperature spiked to over 1400°F (760°C).

AN ANXIOUS CROWD
News of the fire at Our Lady of the Angels traveled quickly through the close-knit community. Crowds gathered outside the school to view the scene and to help transport the injured to local hospitals.

98

INVESTIGATING THE FIRE SCENE
Firefighters pick through charred debris in a classroom on the second floor of the north wing—the scene of unimaginable pandemonium just a few hours earlier. The fire trapped the children in their classrooms, leaving them no way out, except through the windows. Many of the younger children, however, were too short to climb over the window ledges, which were over 37 inches (94 cm) off the floor. Others managed to leap to the courtyard below. Firefighters rescued 160 children from second-floor windows, passing them from hand to hand down the ladders.

MICHAEL MASON—*A SURVIVOR'S STORY*

HE WAS ONLY SEVEN YEARS OLD when the fire at Our Lady of the Angels took the lives of 92 of his schoolmates. But Michael Mason still remembers the chaos, the smoke—and the fear. Although he lived only four blocks from the school, Mason has no memory of how he got home that day. Now a firefighter, as well as an accomplished jazz flautist and recording artist, Mason's latest CD—Angels of Fire—was conceived as a living memorial to both the victims and survivors of the fire—as well as to the firefighters who responded to the devastating blaze.

MICHAEL MASON as a first grader. He was in the annex of the main school when the fire broke out and vividly recalls the chaos and the smell of the smoke.

FIVE SURVIVORS OF THE FIRE AT OUR LADY OF THE ANGELS SCHOOL became firefighters, including Lt. Jeff Pinpelksi, left, and Lt. Michael Mason, right. A member of the Downers Grove, Illinois, Fire Department, Mason is a 20-year veteran of the fire service, a paramedic and Senior Fire Instructor who teaches rescue techniques at three different fire academies.

NO WAY OUT

When glass transoms above the doors exploded from the heat and sent flames roaring over the ceiling, there was nowhere to go, except the windows.

Despite the nuns, who implored their students to stay seated, pray, and wait for help, some children took matters into their own hands and began to jump from the second-story windows to the concrete and gravel courtyard below. In the pandemonium, many children were trampled to death, or died of asphyxiation and burns. Children who jumped or were pushed from windows sustained grave injuries, as well as burns, some of which were fatal.

Not all of the children who did not jump perished. Many were saved by fast-thinking school staff, neighbors—and the firefighters, who arrived on the scene at 2:44 PM.

When the firefighters of Engine 85 pulled up to Our Lady of the Angels, they were confronted with a raging fire and utter chaos: screaming children were hanging out of smoke-filled windows or leaping from them, two and three at a time. Neighbors had brought old painting ladders to the walls, but most of the ladders were too short to reach the second story. After overcoming many obstacles, firefighters were able to get water on the blaze and ladder the building. They rescued 160 children in a matter of minutes.

But despite their courageous efforts, a large portion of the roof on the north wing succumbed to the fire, making further rescue impossible. By 3:45 PM the fire was brought under control.

LOOKING FOR ANSWERS

In the following inquest, no one was held responsible for the fatal blaze. Although arson was suspected, evidence at the time showed that the fire was accidental, and it was classified as "undetermined."

Years later, two individuals were investigated, but not prosecuted, for setting the blaze. Others theorized that a student, sneaking a cigarette in the stairwell, had started the fire by accident, but it was never proved.

CLASSROOM STILL LIFES
A statue of Jesus stands amid the jumble of overturned chairs and fallen debris. Open schoolbooks were a poignant reminder of the victims' youth, many of whom were only 10 years old. As the fire closed in, nuns encouraged their young students to stay seated and pray, but some fought their way to the windows and jumped.

MOURNING
A mass for 27 of the dead children was offered in the Illinois National Guard Northwest Armory on North Kedzie Avenue, Chicago, on the Friday after the fire. In all, 61 wakes and funerals were held privately throughout the city for the remaining children.

FIRE REPORT

⚜ CAUSES
• Undetermined.

⚜ POSSIBLE CAUSES
• Arson.

• Lit match or cigarette combined with highly flammable materials in basement trash bin.

⚜ FIRE FACTS
• Worst fire in Chicago since Iroquois Theatre fire in 1903, which killed 602 people.

• Firefighters crawled through dense smoke without air masks—which were not standard equipment in 1958—to get their hose lines to the fire.

⚜ LOSSES
• 92 children and 3 adults were killed.

⚜ DEVELOPMENTS
• Approved, automatic sprinkler systems must be provided in all school buildings.

• All vertical passageways must be enclosed with fireproof construction and provide fire doors leading into them.

• All corridors and room partition openings must have fire doors.

• All schools must provide automatic internal fire-alarm systems linked directly to the fire department.

RELATED FIRES

• Cleveland School Fire, Beulah, South Carolina, 1923: During a school play a coal lamp fell from a post beside the stage, igniting the building and killing 77 people. 47 of the victims were under the age of 18.

LAKEVIEW ELEMENTARY SCHOOL
COLLINWOOD, USA, 1908

FUNERAL PYRE
Parents could only watch in horror as the flames eventually reached the children trapped behind the blocked doors of the Lakeview School. In less than 30 minutes, 172 children and two teachers were killed.

ON MARCH 4, 1908, a fire swept through Lakeview Elementary School in Collinwood, Ohio. It was about 9:30 in the morning and the children were just settling in for the day. In less than 30 minutes, 172 of the school's 366 students would be dead. The cause was a fire that broke out in the cellar, where a dry, wooden joist had come into contact with an overheated steam pipe. The fire roared up the main stairway of the school, consuming everything in its path. The volunteer firefighters who responded to the fire lacked the training and equipment to fight a fire in a three-story building.

Almost 200 students managed to escape the fire. The others were trapped inside the first of two sets of exit doors on the first floor—the only way out of the school. Panicked children pressing against the first set of doors, which were inward-opening, were jammed up against them by the crush of other children attempting to get out. The result was a huge pileup that blocked the exit. The children never made it to the next set of exit doors. Within minutes they were overwhelmed by smoke and fire so intense that some of the children's bodies were charred beyond recognition.

The tragedy sparked numerous school inspections across the country. New legislation in Ohio and other states quickly changed school architecture from the imposing Victorian structures of the late 19th century to Neo-classical two-story buildings with firewalls and multiple exits.

FIRE REPORT

CAUSES
• Contact of overheated steam pipe with wooden joist.

FIRE FACTS
• Volunteer firefighters were unable to effectively combat the fire, due to lack of training and insufficient equipment.

LOSSES
• 172 children, two teachers die.

DEVELOPMENTS
• Exit drills are required in all public schools.

• Stricter codes required in all school construction.

• More school inspections are mandatory.

• Installed fire protections, alarms, and first-aid firefighting equipment are required.

FIRE TRAP
Built only seven years before the fire, the school was built to the construction codes of the time, but students and teachers were not trained to respond to emergencies. The tragedy resulted in sweeping changes in fire-response methods in schools across the U.S.

NEW LONDON SCHOOL
NEW LONDON, USA, 1937

CONFESSED ARSONIST
On July 18, 1961, William Estel Benson confessed that 24 years earlier he had sabotaged gas lines under the New London School causing the explosion that killed 294 students and teachers. He said he wanted to "run up a gas bill" because he had been reprimanded for smoking.

THE NEW LONDON SCHOOL FIRE and explosion, which occurred on March 18, 1937, in New London, Texas, killed 294 children and teachers instantaneously. At 3:05 PM, an instructor of manual training at the school—a modern, steel-framed building—turned on an electric sanding machine in an area that was filled with a mixture of gas and air. The instructor, however, was unaware of the danger

FRANTIC SCENE
Desperate parents, rescue workers, and oil-field employees searched through the tangled mass of wreckage and shattered brick for any signs of life after a massive blast leveled all but this corner of the school.

because unprocessed natural gas is virtually odorless. The switch ignited the mixture and carried the flame into an unventilated space beneath the building. The explosion that followed blew the school off its foundation and then slammed it to the ground. Walls collapsed and the roof fell in, burying children and teachers under mounds of debris. The blast, which could be heard four miles (6.4 km) away, was so powerful that it hurled a one-ton (900 kg) slab of concrete across the school parking lot.

Inquiries into the cause of the explosion, which began three days later, revealed that the school had been saving $300 a month by tapping into a "green" gas line (a source of gas that is not odorized)—a common money-saver for many schools and homes at the time. Investigators concluded that gas had leaked from a faulty connection and accumulated under the building. Despite dozens of lawsuits, no school officials were found liable.

Within weeks of the disaster the Texas legislature passed new regulations requiring that all utility gas must be odorized so that leaks can be more easily detected. Today, natural gas and propane are odorized with the strong scent of ethyl mercaptan.

FIRE REPORT

CAUSES
• Sabotage. A disgruntled employee tampered with natural gas lines under the school causing the lethal explosion.

FIRE FACTS
• Community residents and volunteers from the East Texas oilfields came with heavy-duty equipment to help dig victims out of the debris.

• Texas Rangers and highway patrol rushed to the scene to aid the victims.

LOSSES
• 294 fatalities.

DEVELOPMENTS
• All utility gas must be odorized so that leaks can more easily be detected; previously gas was odorless and therefore undetectable.

ALL-NIGHT SEARCH
Rescue workers at the site dug through the wreckage in an effort to uncover bodies of victims of the gas explosion.

KING'S CROSS STATION
───── LONDON, ENGLAND, 1987 ─────

KING'S CROSS UNDERGROUND STATION is one of London's busiest, serving over 100,000 passengers at peak hours. On the evening of November 18, 1987, at about 7:30 PM, smoke began to seep from under one of the wood escalators transporting passengers from the underground platform levels to the station's ticket-selling office. Within minutes a fire traveled up the escalator and erupted with catastrophic force into the hall.

RESCUE OPERATIONS
Firemen — in their protective gear of yellow helmets, black jackets, and yellow pants — as well as police and appliance crews, remained outside the King's Cross Station on standby until 6:20 PM on November 19, nearly 24 hours after the fire started.

THE ESCALATORS
More than 100,000 passengers used these escalators every day because King's Cross is not only an underground station for five different lines, it is also an overground station for train routes heading north and east from London. At the far left is the wood escalator, showing the effects of the fireball that swept up to the ticketing area. On the near left is the remains of one of the more modern escalators after the fires swept through the station.

The blaze killed 31 people, injured dozens more, and became a milestone in government policymaking, the results of which would have far-reaching implications for both public and private safety. But first, an inquiry—the longest of its kind in British history—was charged with answering the question of how the fire at King's Cross started, spread, and became a killer.

At 7:36 PM the fire department received a report that smoke was pouring through the underground station at King's Cross. Their response was swift. At 7:42 PM four fire engines and an aerial ladder arrived on the scene. Firefighters entering the ticketing area, below street level, discovered a fire burning 20 feet (6 m) down the escalator shaft. The flames were already four feet (1.2 m) high. At the same time, at various platforms on lower levels of the station, trains continued to arrive and discharge passengers. Met by thick smoke and searing heat, commuters were led to safety by a handful of police officers and station workers. Others were able to escape via stairwells and escalators that had not yet been

affected by the fire. The group of firefighters in the ticketing area had split up: several men returned to the trucks to retrieve hose and breathing apparatus, while three others stayed behind to supervise the evacuation of passengers. Two of the firefighters then descended to the platforms below, in order to prevent commuters from using the Piccadilly line escalator as an exit route. One man—Station Officer Colin Townsley of the Soho Fire Station, the first firehouse to arrive on the scene—remained in the ticketing area, at the top of the escalator shaft.

FIREBALL ERUPTS

Just moments after the first fire trucks arrived, at 7:45 PM, a fireball suddenly roared up the Piccadilly escalator shaft and exploded into the ticketing area—a flashover effect occurred and every surface immediately erupted into

flames. Thick clouds of black smoke spewed out from the station entrances, and for those still in the underground station, the smoke was both acrid and so dense that they were unable to see through it. A crowd of screaming passengers rushed into the street. The fire continued to burn for several hours, taking with it the life of Officer Colin Townsley, who was trying to save a woman just as the fire erupted in the ticketing hall and killed both of them.

The official inquiry into the King's Cross fire concluded that a carelessly discarded match had probably started the fire after it fell through the steps and into the grease track located under the escalator of the Piccadilly line. The investigation also discovered evidence that several other fires had broken out in the same area previously, but had gone unnoticed and burned out on their own. However, the grease-impregnated dirt and dust that

TICKET MACHINES STANDING SENTINEL OVER THE REMAINS OF THE TICKETING AREA
These ticket machines for the London Underground, burned and rendered useless, were pulled away from the walls and ready to be removed from the station by disposal and reconstruction crews. After all the blazes were extinguished, officials of the various departments—fire, transit, police, and others—toured the station, illuminated by temporary lights strung across the ceiling.

FIRE REPORT

CAUSES
• Match dropped between escalator steps ignited grease-impregnated dirt and dust in a track under one escalator.

OTHER CAUSES
• Arson has not been ruled out.

FIRE FACTS
• One of the worst fires in recent British history.

• Within two minutes the fire evolved from a small blaze to a serious conflagration.

LOSSES
• 31dead; 60 injured.

DEVELOPMENTS
• Smoking banned in London underground trains and stations.

• Wood escalators replaced with stainless steel.

• Escalator mechanisms are cleaned regularly.

• Smoke and fire alarms and automatic sprinklers installed in underground stations.

• UK becomes first European country to adopt a residential smoke detector standard.

RELATED FIRES

• Joelma Building, São Paulo, Brazil. Fire in 25-story building kills 179 people and injures 300 on February 1, 1974. Massive portions of exterior concrete walls literally exploded during fire. Cause unknown.

• L'Innovation Department Store, Brussels, Belgium. "Chimney Effect" blamed for killing 322 on May 22, 1967.

• Taiyo Department Store, Kumamoto, Japan. Fire killed 101 on November 29, 1973.

• Ballantyne's Department Store, Christchurch, New Zealand. January 18, 1974; 41 dead.

---

accumulated in the track under the escalator provided the perfect fuel for a fire. Flammable gases built up in the space under the escalator; the wood steps ignited; and flames spread with lightning speed toward the ticketing area, where the fire suddenly flashed.

FACIAL RECONSTRUCTIONS
In some instances in which identification of the victims from dental records or other clues was difficult or even impossible, forensic experts are still able to make reconstructions of unknown victims' faces in the hope that relatives and friends of missing people might see the mask and recognize the deceased. This mask was made for one of the victims of the King's Cross fire.

Both the severity of the King's Cross fire and the speed with which it developed were unexpected, and therefore the subject of extensive inquiry. There are various theories as to what caused the flashover conditions in the ticketing area. Fire gases may have built up and ignited, the way they would in a classic backdraft scenario. Alternatively, the escalator fire might have been pushed up the shaft by a "piston effect," if trains arriving at platforms forced air out of the tunnels and up into the ticketing hall.

However, the extensive computer simulations and mathematical modeling that were performed after the fire of King's Cross Station proposed a third and more likely scenario: rapid fire development within inclined shafts that have combustible surfaces, a theory known as the "trench effect." This caused hot gases to move along the escalator surface, creating a rapid airflow that pushed the gases up the escalator, step by step. The airflow in the trench grew in proportion with the size of the fire, which eventually shot into the ticket hall with the destructive force of a massive flamethrower. From their models, investigators concluded that once the trench effect was established, the piston effect from arriving trains would not have played an important role in the rapid spread of the fire. This computer modeling was later used to design buildings that would be better able to contain a fire.

POSSIBLE ARSON?

Investigators have not yet ruled out the idea that the fire in King's Cross was caused by an arsonist. There had been several fires in other underground stations in London that involved wood escalators. On the evening of November 18, 1987, numerous witnesses recall seeing a small fire at the base of an escalator in the Victoria line shaft just minutes before the fire in the Picadilly line shaft was reported. The smaller fire involved a rolled-up, burning piece of paper that had been tossed into the shaft from the top of the escalator, certainly more suggestive of an arson attempt than the cigarette purported to have started the fire on the Piccadilly line escalator, although no likely perpetrator was ever determined.

SOHO FIRE STATION OFFICER COLIN TOWNSLEY

"GUV" TO THE FIREMEN under his command, Officer Colin Townsley sent the men answering the King's Cross call back out of the station to retrieve their breathing apparatus and a jet spray, while he stayed in the ticketing area to rescue a victim. His directive undoubtedly saved the lives of all his men, but the fire flashed through in the few minutes they were gone, and they could only recover his body, using the jet spray to protect themselves.

HONOR GUARD, composed of hundreds of firemen all in dress uniform, line the way as the coffin, covered in flowers, is carried on a fire station truck to its final resting place.

SOHO FIRE STATION

King's Cross Station lies within the area protected by the Euston Road Fire Station, but that firehouse was out on another call. Therefore, the first team to respond to the 7:36 PM call was the Soho Fire Station, followed closely by Clerkenwell and Manchester Square. The officers and firemen who went

MAKESHIFT MEMORIAL
A few bouquets were laid out by the locked Underground doors by friends or strangers, creating a temporary memorial to the 31 people who perished in the King's Cross fire.

down into the station and tunnels, including Colin Townsley, were drawn from all three fire stations. Townsley had sent the Soho team back up for their breathing apparatus and a water jet.

The prestigious Chief Officer's Certificate of Commendation was awarded to six firemen, including Officer Townsley, who received his award posthumously. The Chief Officer's Letter of Commendation was given to 14 additional firemen for their actions during the fire.

CHANNEL TUNNEL
FRANCE AND ENGLAND, 1996

CHANNEL TUNNEL RIBS
Damage extending to the southern end of the tunnel, three days after the fire. Much of the concrete had already been removed, but extensive work remained to be done before it could reopen.

ON NOVEMBER 18, 1996, a potentially lethal fire was expertly controlled by UK and French emergency response teams. The event took place in the Channel Tunnel, 150 to 250 feet (46-76 meters) below the seabed, where fire had broken out on a 29-car Heavy Goods Vehicle (HGV) shuttle that was transporting cargo trucks. Despite very difficult conditions in a confined space, firefighters from both sides of the 31-mile (50-km) "Chunnel"—which runs between Folkestone, England and Coquelles, France—successfully rescued 33 train passengers and escaped serious injury themselves.

The fire, burning at the rear of the train, was first spotted at 8:45 PM, about 12 miles (19 km) into the tunnel from the terminal at Coquelles. Emergency response teams from both sides of the channel were

alerted and rushed to the scene through the service tunnel, a tube 16 feet (5 m) wide that runs between the north-running and south-running tunnels. The service tunnel is connected to the running tunnels by 270 cross passages located at intervals of 1,230 feet (375 m). Firefighters led passengers from the club car of the

DEVASTATION IN THE TUNNEL
Workers surveying the damage after the fire was extinguished. The heat of the fire was so great that pieces of concrete exploded from the tunnel lining, and the concrete rubble underfoot had burned right through the firemen's boots.

train, which had now stopped—and where heavy smoke had forced people to lie on the floor to breathe—into a cross passage. Here they were treated by rescue workers and put on a passenger train traveling in the opposite direction. Firefighters then connected hose lines to the service tunnel's wall hydrant and entered the running tunnel. Due to the extreme heat, crews could not advance hose lines toward the rear of the train for more than eight minutes at a time before having to retreat and be replaced by fresh crews. At 5:00 AM on the next day the fire was under control. It was extinguished at 11:15 AM and passenger service in Channel Tunnel trains resumed 15 days later.

FIRE REPORT

CAUSES
• Unknown.

FIRE FACTS
• 233 French emergency services' personnel mobilized from 31 rescue centers.

• The UK contributed 209 fire department personnel, 24 ambulance personnel and 50 police officers.

• No injuries to firefighters were reported from either the UK or France.

LOSSES
• No deaths.

• Eight HGV s and their contents, a loader, and the rear locomotive of the train completely destroyed.

KAPRUN TUNNEL
— KITZSTEINHORN, AUSTRIA, 2000 —

ON SUNDAY, NOVEMBER 12, 2000, 155 people, mainly skiers and snowboarders in their teens, were trapped inside a burning cable train in an alpine tunnel in Kaprun, Austria. The victims were trapped inside the smoke-filled tunnel while the train burned for more than three hours. The inferno, which reached temperatures of more than 1800°F (1000°C), virtually vaporized the train. A survivor told the Austrian Press Association that a door had jammed, sealing many passengers in the train. Some people managed to escape the burning car, only to be killed by acrid smoke as they attempted to flee up the steps out of the tunnel. Those who survived ran in the opposite direction and successfully evaded most of the smoke blowing upward through the narrow, steep tunnel, which had been transformed into a giant chimney, sucking in air to fuel the flames.

The cause of the fire is still unknown, although some speculate that the blaze may have resulted from an electrical fault or a cable snapping near the front section of the train. An engineer who had inspected the train in the past stated that it was equipped with a safety system designed to bring the vehicle to an immediate halt if one of the cables snapped. He added that materials used in the construction of the train were fire resistant. But how would that explain the fury with which it was engulfed by flames in the middle of the tunnel, or why poisonous fumes quickly overcame the trapped skiers? Accounts from eyewitnesses suggest that the blaze had started before the train entered the tunnel and began its long ascent up the 10,500-foot (3,000 m) Kitzsteinhorn Mountain. Attempts by firefighters and rescue workers to recover bodies deep inside the mountain were hampered by fears that the cable pulling the train might break, allowing wreckage to plummet down the mountain.

FUNICULAR HEARSE
The wreckage of the funicular, covered out of respect to the remains of the victims still within, was escorted out of the tunnel by rescue workers. The only bodies recovered were of those who died at the top of the tunnel from smoke inhalation.

TWISTED METAL
The fire was so fierce that rescuers found virtually nothing remaining intact. The metal base of the train, thoroughly twisted out of shape, bears grim and silent witness to the funicular's fiery demise.

FIRE REPORT

CAUSES
• Unknown. May have been the result of an electrical fire or a snapped cable that started a fire under the train.

FIRE FACTS
• Austria's worst peacetime tragedy.

• Recovery efforts were difficult due to fears that train cable might break, sending wreckage down the mountain.

LOSSES
• 155 dead, mostly teenagers.

DEVELOPMENTS
• Raised serious questions about fire safety in Europe's tunnels. In 1999, 40 people died in an inferno in the Mont Blanc road tunnel between France and Italy that started when a truck caught fire. Again, the ferocity of the fire was blamed on the tunnel's ventilation.

LIMA HISTORIC DISTRICT
LIMA, PERU, 2001

SETTING OFF FIREWORKS to celebrate Christmas and New Year's Eve is a popular tradition in many Latin American countries, despite the tremendously high number of accidents and fatalities that occur every year. In 1990, 1991, and 1993 alone, fires caused by exploding fireworks ripped through the historical Central Market district of Lima, Peru, destroying property and taking lives. Nevertheless, in each subsequent year, a fresh supply of illegal fireworks and other explosives—an estimated 1,000 tons or more—has flowed into the crowded markets and narrow streets of downtown Lima, just in time for the holidays.

On Saturday, December 29, 2001, around 8:00 PM in the evening, a wall

WOULD-BE REVELERS FLEE HISTORIC DISTRICT
These youths ran ahead of the wall of fire, which was ignited by exploding fireworks and fueled by the many other fireworks offered for sale, consuming the historic district of Lima.

of fire, propelled by exploding fireworks at dozens of sidewalk stands, swept across four blocks of Lima's historic downtown, killing at least 280 people and injuring about 150 others. Firefighters eventually brought the blaze under control, despite a shortage of water and crowds of onlookers. Firefighters and rescue teams, digging through the charred rubble, had little hope of finding survivors inside the burned-out buildings, where temperatures had exceeded 1,100°F (600°C) at the height of the fire. Emergency workers, using infrared cameras to locate bodies, worked under constant threat of being buried by damaged buildings on the verge of collapse. Lima

City fire chief Tulio Nicolini described the fire as the worst he had seen in his 40-year career. As authorities began the grim work of identifying bodies and remains at the city morgue, condolences poured in from peope around the world, including Pope John Paul II and British prime minister Tony Blair.

At first, officials blamed the fire on an explosion at a local warehouse where fireworks were stored. But a growing number of reports from witnesses claimed that a shopkeeper, demonstrating his wares to a prospective buyer, was responsible for the blaze. To date, no one has been held responsible for the tragedy, and plans have been made to implement Peruvian president Alejandro Toledo's promise to ban the production and sale of fireworks in Lima.

CATACLYSMIC EXPLOSIONS
In the words of volunteer fire department chief of Lima, Carlos Malpica, who was an emergency medical doctor as well as a firefighter on the scene, the disaster was similar to an "airplane having fallen in the middle of the city." A row of taxis stood in front of Block 8 of the Junior Cusco shopping center, some deserted or overturned, others with driver and passengers still within, but overcome by the heat and smoke of the fire.

FIRE REPORT

CAUSES
• Explosion caused by illegal fireworks.

FIRE FACTS
• Four city blocks of Lima's densely inhabited historic district completely destroyed.

• 500 firefighters and 50 ambulances were brought to the scene.

• Firefighters extinguished the massive blaze in three hours.

LOSSES
• 280 to 300 fatalities; 150 people injured.

DEVELOPMENT
• Anticrime task force organized to reduce corruption, including the manufacture, sale, and usage of illegal fireworks.

KUWAITI OIL FIELDS

—— GULF WAR, KUWAIT, 1991 ——

ON MARCH 16, 1991, shortly after the withdrawal of the last Iraqi forces from Kuwait, a massive firefighting effort began when firefighters started to tackle hundreds of oil-well fires. Experts predicted that at least four years would pass before the last oil well would be extinguished. An estimated 6 million barrels of oil per day were being lost at 1991 oil prices of $40 per barrel ($318 million per day in today's terms). The operation was named *Al-Awada* (The Return), and actually took only eight months—at an estimated total cost of over $12 billion.

On January 16, 1991, after the start of the Gulf War, Iraqi leader Saddam Hussein ordered the destruction of the Kuwaiti oil fields as well as the release of crude oil into the Persian Gulf. What he set off was the world's largest and worst man-made ecological disaster—exacerbated by Coalition (the U.S. and allies arrayed against Iraq) bombing of Iraqi targets in Kuwait. Warnings were made of massive, worldwide flooding, global cooling, crop failure, and environmental collapse. It was difficult to predict what effect the Kuwait oil fires would have, not only locally where lakes of oil still exist, but globally, where results can take years to emerge.

KUWAIT'S INFERNO
An aerial view of the Kuwaiti oil fields. By the end, over 10,000 workers from 37 countries had created 361 one-million-gallon (3,785 kl) water lagoons, 280 miles (450 km) of water piping, and used over 5,000 pieces of heavy equipment at a total cost of approximately $1.5 billion. Efforts began on March 16, 1991 and finished November 8, 1991—four years ahead of the predicted time.

What is certain is the amazing bravery and ingenuity exhibited by firefighting teams from all over the world in putting out over 750 oil-well fires in only eight months.

A GEYSER OF FLAME

When fighting a land-based, oil-well fire, the usual method is to first remove as much as possible of the remaining oil-well equipment. Next, the surrounding area is cooled down using massive quantities of water. It's imperative that any remaining metal be cooled below the ignition point of the geysering crude to stop the oil reigniting. Once the temperature has been lowered, an explosive charge in a 55-gallon (208 liters) steel drum mounted on a long boom is carefully positioned in the center of the flames, just above the remains of the well. The charge is then exploded and the blast momentarily consumes all of the oxygen, snuffing out the flames. The oil, however, will still be rocketing upward and so the well must immediately be capped. Any delay increases the risk of the well reigniting from hot metal or, in Kuwait, other, nearby flaming oil wells.

INVENTIVE MEASURES

Faced with such a huge number of petroleum blazes, firefighters pushed their ingenuity to the limits. One method inserted a hollow tube 40-feet (12 m) high to raise the plume of the fire above the wellhead. Liquid nitrogen or water was then injected into the tube, removing the oxygen supply. A more dramatic method was used by Hungarian firefighters, involving an old, Soviet T-62 tank with MiG-21 jet engines mounted on it. The jets produced a blast of air, into which water was injected, creating a horizontal geyser.

PILLARS OF FIRE
A Kuwaiti prays while, in the background, flames roar toward the heavens. Some of the pillars reached over 250 feet (76 meters) in height.

FOLLOWING PAGES: FEBRUARY 1, 2002
Kuwaiti firefighters are pictured on the scene at the Raudhatain oilfield in Kuwait. Four were killed in this enormous fuel blast caused by a leaking pipeline that spread to a power station and a gas-booster facility.

RED ADAIR- *HELLFIGHTER*

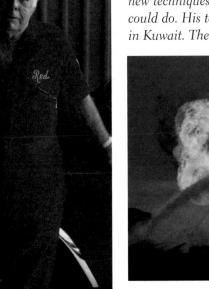

PAUL "RED" ADAIR *in 1986, wearing his trademark jumpsuit. Adair has been a leading firefighting innovator.*

FOUNDER OF *the most famous oil-well firefighting company, Paul "Red" Adair started the Red Adair Company in 1956 after training for 14 years with the legendary Myron Kinley, the grandfather of oil-field firefighting. Red pioneered new techniques in extinguishing oil-well fires, often taking the jobs no one else could do. His team alone capped 117 of the approximately 750 damaged oil wells in Kuwait. The 1968 John Wayne movie Hellfighters was loosely based on his life.*

A RED ADAIR CO. FIREFIGHTER utilizes protective heat shielding to direct water onto an oil-well fire in Wyoming, 1973. Because of the presence of so much combustible fuel, the superheated metal must first be cooled down to below the oil's ignition point before the fire is "blown out" with an explosive charge. Otherwise, the hot metal would simply reignite the ample quantities of oil present.

FIRE REPORT

⚜ CAUSES
• Purposely set by the Iraqi military.

• Up to one-third of the fires caused by Coalition bombing of Iraqi positions within the oil fields.

⚜ FIRE FACTS
• Involved over 10,000 firefighters from 37 countries.

• Took only eight months to extinguish instead of the predicted four years.

⚜ LOSSES
• One firefighter killed, a member of the Chinese team at the Ahmadi Field.

• Estimated total cost in lost production, firefighting, and rebuilding was $15 billion, or $20 billion in today's terms.

⚜ DEVELOPMENTS
• Recommendations to oil drillers to equip all fields with subsurface-control valves for each well. They allow the oil flow to be shut down even in the event of a blowout.

• Mass use of oil-eating bacteria to clean up "oil lakes." Depending on the bacteria, their byproducts are water and carbon dioxide.

RELATED FIRES

• There are a total of approximately 20 oil-well fires a year worldwide, both onshore and offshore, wherever drilling for oil takes place. Fighting these is considered one of the most hazardous firefighting duties in part due to the combustibility and toxicity of the materials involved.

COAL FIRES
—UNITED STATES, CHINA, INDIA—

MOST COAL FIRES START UNDERGROUND in coal seams—unmined beds of coal deposits that lie just below the earth's surface. Some have been burning for thousands of years. Fires in coal seams can be ignited through self-combustion (just a small amount of oxygen is needed to heat coal, which then begins to smolder and finally to burn); or by forest fires, lightning, burning refuse, carelessness, and vandalism.

CENTRALIA, PENNSYLVANIA, U.S.
In the early 1960s, burning trash dumped on a coal seam started an underground coal fire in Centralia, Pennsylvania. Sometimes called "the granddaddy of mine blazes," and certainly the most publicized, the Centralia coal fire steadily spread underground through abandoned mine tunnels, defeating all firefighting efforts to control it. It burned steadily for 40 years.

KENTUCKY, UNITED STATES
In the U.S., accumulated costs for damages by and containment of long-burning underground coal fires—like this one in Kentucky—are nearly $1 billion. Coal fires also burn in Colorado, Pennsylvania, Utah, West Virginia, and Wyoming.

By 1983 the fire was widespread and threatened the small community of 1,100 residents, 500 homes, and 22 businesses. Fire assessment engineers concluded that the two most viable options for dealing with the fire were either evacuating the town and letting the fire burn itself out, which might take upwards of 100 years, or totally excavating 195 acres (79 ha) that were burning at dangerously high temperatures—at a cost of $600 million. The government opted to let the fire burn and bought out the citizens of Centralia—and their homes and businesses—for $43 million.

Today Centralia is still burning and much of the town is a polluted wasteland. Plumes of steam and thick smoke rise from pitted and collapsed streets, the coal beneath the town continues to smolder, and the odor of sulfur punctuates the air.

BIHAR, INDIA
The coal fires of the Jharia Coalfield in Bihar, India, rage both above and underground, and they have been burning since 1916. The cost of the damages from these fires amounts to hundreds of millions of dollars. Even more staggering to the nation's economy is the fact that 1,500 million tons of coal in Jharia cannot be mined because of the fires. The land is so damaged and strafed that it is clearly visible from space. Open fires, heavy smoke, scalding steam, and polluted air seriously threaten the health, safety, and quality of life of Jharia's 1.1 million residents and more than 150,000 mine workers, who have learned to labor around the flames and smoke. In 1995, the bank of a river weakened by fire collapsed. Water flooded underground mine shafts, and

JHARIA COALFIELD, INDIA
The 150,000 workers at the Jharia Coalfield in Bihar, India, have learned to work around the coalfield's many open fires. The million residents of the area have learned to adapt, too, often moving their homes when the fires grow too large or too close.

78 workers drowned. Residents of Jharia who live close to spreading, open fires often have to relocate their homes, and deal with damaged land, poor air, and ill health on a daily basis.

The fires of Jharia are so large and widespread that it is financially impossible for India to put them out. The most effective way of extinguishing such fires is to excavate them completely. But this would cost India more than $2.4 billion. Some fire containment may be achieved by dealing with the situation on a fire-by-fire basis using conventional measures, such as filling old workings and digging isolation ditches around the fires.

NORTHERN CHINA

The effects on a small town—however costly on a personal level—of one self-limiting coal fire cannot begin to compare to the human and environmental impact of China's underground coal fires.

China is the world's largest producer and consumer of coal. It has also been home to one of the most extensive and damaging networks of long-burning coal fires. Hundreds of underground fires burn unchecked across a stretch of landscape

STANLEY MICHALSKI

NORTHERN CHINA
Stanley Michalski, Senior Staff Geologist at GAI Consultants—who has worked with the federal government's Office of Surface Mining on many major coal fires, including the one in Centralia—stands on a large, burning coal refuse pile near Pingdingshan, China. Thermal heat-tracking satellites monitor the earth's surface around China's mines, pinpointing hot spots that can be contained by firefighters before they grow into full-scale blazes.

3,100 miles (5,000 km) long and 430 miles (700 km) wide. Some of the individual fires are as big as 13 miles (20 km) across. These fires burn 200 million tons of coal annually and release as much carbon dioxide into the air in one year as do all the cars and small trucks in the U.S. And carbon dioxide is the major contributing factor to global warming. The land and vegetation around many of these fires have been permanently destroyed, and whole areas have been rendered uninhabitable.

Since conventional methods for dealing with China's coal fires—cooling down with water or liquid nitrogen; excavating burning coal beds; or cutting-off air supplies by covering or filling cracks—are either ineffective or not economically feasible, coal-fire experts are looking into long-term prevention measures. One such measure involves using satellites with thermal-mapping capabilities to pinpoint hot spots so that firefighters can contain a fire before it spreads.

SUNKEN STREETS IN CENTRALIA

SEPTEMBER 11
—NEW YORK CITY, USA 2001—

ON THE MORNING of Tuesday, September 11, 2001, the Fire Department of New York City (FDNY) was ready for a normal working day. Approximately half of its some 11,500 members were on duty, assigned to the department's 212 fire houses, and other numerous special duties, offices and bureaus. There is no question that the FDNY, called with good reason "New York's Bravest," is one of the largest, best-equipped, and best-trained fire departments in the world.

All ranks undergo continuous training for their levels and assignments. The basic course of 13 weeks is a rigorous one, held at the department's modern academy on Randalls Island in the East River. It is a very large organization, not only in people and responsiblities, but in area covered and equipment that is maintained. The FDNY has 203 engine companies, 143 ladder companies, 10 foam apparatus units, and other assorted specialized and support units. The department responds to fire and related emergencies in all five boroughs that constitute the city, an area of 321.8 square miles (833 sq km). It operates at least three fire boats that cover the city's hundreds of miles of shoreline.

On this particular day, when most of New York had gone to work, the shift was changing at the normal time of 9:00 AM. The fact that a new shift was reporting for duty citywide as the old one was going off was to have a tragic and, in the case of 343 firefighters, a fatal result.

TWIN TOWERS ARE HIT

At 8:46 am, the first of two passenger planes hijacked by members of Al Qaeda—a terrorist group linked to Saudi dissident Osama bin Laden—hit the World Trade Center (WTC) complex, slamming into the north face of the center's north tower at the 96th floor. The Boeing 767, weighing 350,000 pounds (158,760 kg), struck the 110-story building at an estimated speed of 410 miles an hour (660 kmph). It had taken off from Boston at 7:59 am and was loaded with 15,000 gallons of jet fuel. The crash ignited the fuel as the plane roared into the building's core, tearing away steel support columns and trusses; the impact also blew the fire-retardent foam off of the steel, making it vulnerable to heat stress. The tower's inner core, which contained the emergency stairwells and elevators, was surrounded by fire-resistant dry-wall. This too was blown away at the point of impact, leaving the escape routes exposed to heat and flame.

Only seconds after the plane hit the tower, the first call was received by the FDNY's communications center; within a few more seconds, the switchboard was overwhelmed.

Some of the telephone calls were received from people in the tower, many of whom would soon perish.

The initial official fire department notification was sent in by Engine 10, located on Greenwich Street near the WTC. Its report was that there had been an explosion. The radio frequencies operated by the city's emergency services were quickly flooded. The first fire units to respond, including Engine 10, were those located close to what soon became known around the world as Ground Zero. Firefighters from the outgoing and incoming shifts responded as the alarms were sounded, including a signal 1060, the major emergency response signal. Sixty of the just off-duty firefighters bravely joined their comrades and doubled up on the engines (although within the hour they would be technically on duty, when the commissioner ordered a recall). There was no time to enter their names on engine riding lists, and many were not carrying radios. Battalion leaders trying to keep track of personnel at the horrifying scene organized firefighters into ad hoc companies, but it was difficult to monitor them amid the chaos.

While en route to the north tower, Chief of Department Peter J. Ganci authorized a second alarm that was then increased to five, followed by a full department recall

CHRONOLOGY OF DISASTER
Top: Flames and smoke pour from the stricken towers; the thick black smoke was produced by burning jet fuel. Hundreds of people tragically died jumping from the top floors. Bottom left: Huge gray dust clouds erupted as the towers collapsed, formed when the concrete floors were pulverized in the fall. Bottom right: Pedestrians on Church Street run as the south tower fell.

of off-duty personnel. Firefighters from New York and other states responded within hours to provide assistance. The rest of the city remained protected through mutual aid provided by departments on its borders as well as by its own resources. As an illustration of the FDNY's effectiveness and organization, a multiple-alarm fire in Brooklyn unrelated to the WTC disaster was fought and brought under control at the same time.

As firefighters, along with police and other emergency personnel reached the north tower in a valiant rescue attempt, another Boeing 767 hit the south tower of the complex at 9:03 am. The impact caused even more damage to the targeted structure than the earlier attack on the north tower. The aircraft hit the building's southeast corner at the 80th floor. This plane went through the building, ripping a gaping hole into the structure. Flaming jet fuel poured into the building's core.

TWIN TOWERS COLLAPSE
The impact of the crashes destroyed portions of the towers' lightweight steel perimeter columns and floor trusses, which were further weakened by intense heat, and failed.

FOLLOWING PAGES: INFERNO
A firefighter from Engine Company 212 of Brooklyn points his hose at a raging inferno. Temperatures reached as high as 2000°F (1093°C).

Raymond M. Downey, Chief of Rescue Operations and an internationally recognized rescue expert, recommended another five alarm authorization, which Chief Ganci approved. Firefighters valiantly climbed up thousands of stairs, as thousands of people who had been in offices below the impacts climbed down to evacuate. Police and other rescue personnel assisted those in distress.

THE TOWERS FALL

The destructive forces that had been unleashed proved far too great to handle. As temperatures reached 2000°F (1093°C), the exposed steel trusses supporting the floors nearest the fire began to distort, weaken, and buckle from the intense heat. At 9:55 AM the south tower began to implode with a domino effect toward the weakened southeast corner at a rate of 200 miles per hour (321 kmph). The entire building collapsed in 10 seconds, after burning for 56 minutes. A huge cloud of smoke and dust exploded like a mushroom cloud over lower Manhattan. Although the tower weighed 500,000 tons, it was 95 percent air—the mass of rubble left was only five stories tall.

Shortly before the south tower collapsed, a third hijacked plane—a Boeing 757—crashed into the Pentagon, in Washington, D.C., killing 189 people. The siege continued with a fourth hijacked plane crashing outside of Pittsburgh, Pennsylvania, at 10:10 AM when several passengers attempted to overcome the hijackers. Forty-four people died.

Meanwhile, in New York the north tower was still burning, but it too collapsed, at 10:28 AM. As the fire burned, fireground communications—radio transmissions between units—continued. Many calls for assistance from trapped firefighters ended

FIREFIGHTERS HOSE DOWN SMOLDERING FIRE
Fires smoldered above and below ground for three months. This facade remnant, all that remained of the north tower, came down on December 15; it has been saved for a memorial.

RUDOLPH GIULIANI – "RUDY THE ROCK"

CANDLELIGHT VIGIL,
Manhattan residents hold a candlelight vigil several blocks from the WTC on September 14, 2001. Thousands of people joined in candlelight vigils the week after the disaster, not only in New York but around the world.

ON THE SCENE
Mayor Giuliani at Ground Zero, October 16, 2001.

RUDY GIULIANI, the outspoken and often controversial former mayor of New York, became a national hero and internationally famous after September 11. His stalwart and compassionate leadership of the city during the crisis reassured and inspired not only New Yorkers, but all Americans, earning him the monikers "Mayor of America," and "Rudy the Rock." On September 11, Giuliani got to the WTC as the second plane hit the south tower. He set up a command post at the site, but he had to escape from it when the towers fell; then led his staff, journalists, and others through the dust and soot to a second makeshift headquarters in a nearby firehouse, where he gave the first of many press conferences to inform and calm citizens. Over the next few weeks Giuliani was seemingly everywhere at once—on television, at Ground Zero, visiting hospitals and search centers, attending funerals—with a grace, composure, and resilience that literally kept New Yorkers going. He was named Time magazine's 2001 Person of the Year, and received an honorary knighthood from Queen Elizabeth II. Giuliani briefly considered rerunning for mayor after his term ended on the wave of his enormous popularity, but changing term limits would have required state legislation and he decided against it. He formed a management consulting firm in February 2002.

in silence, creating an eerie atmosphere matched by the beeping of PASS monitors sounding from beneath the rubble. The monitors did not assist rescuers in their efforts to reach trapped firefighters because the devices were separated from them along with their airpacks when the collapses occurred. Firefighters were hampered not only by the collapse and the choking clouds of dust, but by the loss of water supplies as mains broke. Several fireboats were used to increase the water supply.

THE WORLD MOURNS

As the Twin Towers collapsed, thousands of people died: 343 firefighters, 23 New York City police officers, 37 Port Authority police officers, and more than 2,800 civilians were brave victims of the disaster. The fire department toll included Chief Ganci, First Deputy

SEARCH FOR SURVIVORS
This photograph of Ground Zero was taken on September 18, as hopes grew dim that more survivors would be found. The last survivor was pulled from the wreckage on September 12.

Fire Commissioner William M. Feehan, Chief Downey, Fire Chaplain Mychal Judge, 18 battalion chiefs, and 77 lieutenants. Some responding units were particularly hard hit: Rescue Company 1 lost 11 firefighters and its truck was crushed. Engine 22 lost four firefighters and its engine. At the time of the collapse, five FDNY rescue companies had personnel in the buildings. The city-wide response affected stations in every borough, including Squad 288 and Hazardous Materials Company 1 from Queens, which lost 19 firefighters. From Brooklyn, Squad 1 lost 12 members. Ladder Company 7 of Manhattan lost six—they had also suffered the loss of 12 members during the 1966 23rd Street fire which, until now, had claimed the most deaths in a single incident in the city's history.

The cost of replacing equipment lost by the FDNY is estimated at $48 million. Many other buildings partially collapsed or suffered major damage. The cost in reconstruction and property lost is measured in the billions with much higher estimates of long-term economic or consequential damage. Fires deep inside the remains of the buildings smoldered for 12 weeks, and recovery of victims continued for months. Within days

AERIAL VIEWS OF GROUND ZERO: UNTOUCHED AND 3-D HEAT SENSITIVE IMAGES
The top photograph was taken on September 17. The bottom one, taken a day later, was done with infrared thermal imaging sensors; the hot spots (in red) show where lingering underground fires were located.

of September 11, the FDNY began a study to determine what could be done differently, if anything, in handling such a catastrophic disaster in the future. There will always be some incidents that no level of training, expertise, or resources can overcome. The events of September 11 surely will remain an example of such a disaster.

FIRE REPORT

CAUSES
• Two hijacked Boeing 767s carrying a total 30,000 gallons of jet fuel crashed into the WTC Twin Towers; the jet fuel ignited upon impact.

• Force of crashes blew fire-proofing off steel perimeter tubes and trusses, exposing them to intense heat and weakening them to the point of total structural failure.

• Collisions also destroyed fire-resistant drywall surrounding towers' inner core, exposing elevators and stairwells to heat and flame.

FIRE FACTS
• Each tower collapsed in only 10 seconds.

• Attacks took place as fire-fighters were changing shifts; when off-duty members joined on-duty teams they were not entered on riding lists.

• Fires smoldered for 12 weeks.

LOSSES
• 343 firefighters, 23 NYPD police officers, 37 Port Authority police officers, and over 2,800 civilians were killed; hundreds more injured.

• $48 million in FDNY equipment; billions in property and long-term economic costs.

DEVELOPMENTS
• $16 million federal probe into towers' collapse.

• Many building code changes considered: emergency lighting better fire-proofing, extra exits, energy-absorbing materials.

• Federal and local agencies working to enhance fire service support and training for terrorism response and preparedness.

RELATED FIRES

• Chicago, 1910: 21 firefighters killed at a cold storage warehouse.

• Waldbaum Fire, Brooklyn, NY 1988: six firefighters died and 34 injured when super-market roof caved in.

• Storm King Mountain, Colorado, 1994: 14 smoke-jumpers died when a wind-storm notification was not relayed, trapping them in a blowup.

23rd Street
—— NEW YORK CITY, USA, 1966 ——

At 9:36 PM ON THE EVENING of October 17, 1966, as the men of Engine 24 were finishing their evening meal at 227 Avenue of the Americas, a box call came in. It was followed at 9:58 PM by an "all hands" —which meant that the companies that had responded to the first alarm were on the job. Engine Co. 24 was scheduled to respond on the second alarm and to go on the fourth. The second and third alarms came in at 10:06 PM and 10:37 PM. By now, the men at Engine 24, who had previously been calm, switched into another mode

altogether, as they prepared for "a really big one." By the time the fourth alarm came in the company was ready. All their gear was on the rig and the men were dressed for the weather.

A Tale of Two Buildings
The location of the fire was a cellar in a four-story brick brownstone at 7 East 22nd Street, which extended for about 35 feet (11 m) under the first floor of a five-story brick commercial building at 6 East 23rd Street occupied by the Wonder Drug Store. A two-story extension of

7 East 22nd Street also abutted the rear of 6 East 23rd Street. When firefighters from Engine 24 were directed to 7 East 22nd Street, they didn't know that the fire, which originated in the cellar of the building, had spread to 6 East 23rd Street and had been burning under both buildings for some time. At the moment, the blaze was feeding on large stores of wooden picture frames (and their combustible finish), lacquer, and paint from an art dealer's shop on the first floor and in the cellar at 7 East 22nd Street.

The Fire Below
Firefighters with Ladder 7 and Engine 18 responded to the fire at the Wonder Drug Store at 6 East 23rd Street. Initially, the 5-inch-thick (13 cm) concrete terrazzo floor in this building acted as an insulator, concealing the severity of the fire and heat below the firefighters. The underlying floor beams, meanwhile, were being eaten away by the fire in the cellar. A weakened 15 x 35-foot (5 x 10 m) section of the floor suddenly collapsed at around 10:39 PM, plunging 10 firefighters into the burning

cellar below them. Two more firefighters were killed by the resulting blast of flame and heat on the first floor.

Engine 24 arrived at 7 East 22nd unaware of the tragedy that already had occurred on the other side of the building. As the men of Engine 24 fought the flames around them, an inferno was still burning directly under their feet. When the floorboards got too soft to walk on, the firefighters evacuated the building, which collapsed moments later, engulfing them in smoke and barraging them with debris. Only once the fire was out did the exhausted firefighters of Engine 24 learn of the other firefighters' deaths. Until September 11, 2001, the 23rd Street fire was the greatest single loss of New York City firefighters since the Metropolitan Fire Department was created in 1865.

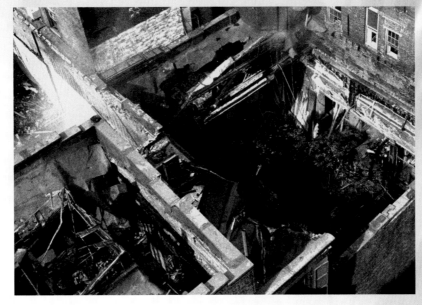

ROOFTOP VIEW
Firemen peer down into the 5-story crater that was 6 East 23rd Street, where 12 city firemen were killed in a 5-alarm blaze.

FIRE REPORT

⚜ CAUSES
• Unknown, accelerated by combustible materials in an art gallery.

⚜ FIRE FACTS
• Greatest single loss of New York City firemen in the line of duty before September 11, 2001.

• The concrete floor temporarily concealed the dangerous fire burning underlying floor beams in the basement.

• When they arrived at the scene, the firefighters in Engine Company 24 were unaware that the floor had collapsed, killing men from Engine 18 and Ladder 7 who had arrived earlier.

⚜ LOSSES
• 12 firefighters killed, including two fire chiefs and two lieutenants.

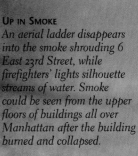

UP IN SMOKE
An aerial ladder disappears into the smoke shrouding 6 East 23rd Street, while firefighters' lights silhouette streams of water. Smoke could be seen from the upper floors of buildings all over Manhattan after the building burned and collapsed.

WORCESTER WAREHOUSE FIRE
WORCESTER, USA, 1999

ON COLD NEW ENGAND nights some of the homeless of Worcester, Massachusetts, seek shelter in one of the many abandoned brick warehouses in this former industrial center, 40 miles (64 km) west of Boston. One young homeless couple, Julie Barnes and Thomas Levesque, had been living with their cat and dog for several months in the former Worcester Cold Storage and Warehouse Company building, on Franklin Street.

One Friday evening, on December 3, 1999, they accidentally started a fire on the second floor. As the blaze started, the couple fled the warehouse, leaving their pets behind. They never called in the fire, nor did they tell anyone that they had escaped safely.

INTO THE BLAZE
When firefighters arrived on the scene shortly after 6:00 PM, they were told that two homeless people had been living in the warehouse and might be inside. Two firefighters entered the five-story, 80-year-old burning building to search for the couple and for the source of the fire. Once inside, they were faced with a dark, slightly smoky maze of poorly ventilated rooms once used to keep meat cold (there were no windows on the upper floors). As they penetrated the building, the low visibility magnified as a petroleum insulation layer beneath the 18-inch-thick (46 cm) cork walls ignited, filling the warehouse with black smoke. The building's brick construction acted as an oven, intensifying the flames and heat. Soon disoriented and running out of air—their tanks contained 30 minutes' worth—the two firefighters sent a "Mayday" signal to their comrades outside. Four more firefighters went inside the warehouse to search for their friends. All six men died in the six-alarm blaze.

PLANNING MAY HAVE SAVED LIVES
The building burned for 24 hours. The homeless couple was charged with manslaughter. They were acquitted in September 2000, but as of March 2002

the charges were reinstated and a new trial scheduled. When the National Institute for Occupational Safety & Health (NIOSH) investigated the fire, they issued 12 recommendations—many of which involved preplanning—for similar firefighting situations. NIOSH also

stated that had these measures been in place, the risk to the Worcester fire- fighters would have been less. Many of these recommendations are now standard practice.

VOLCANIC FLAMES
Ladder crews attack the 1999 Worcester warehouse blaze from the exterior.

HACKENSACK FORD DEALERSHIP
HACKENSACK, USA, 1988

THE DANGERS TO FIREFIGHTERS of wooden truss roofs were brought home tragically in the Hackensack, New Jersey, auto dealership fire of 1988. On July 1, the Hackensack Fire Department began receiving calls about a fire in the roof of a Hackensack Ford dealership. The first alarm response included a battalion chief, two engines, and a ladder company. Heavy smoke was observed coming from the roof, where auto parts and cleaning supplies improperly stored in the unsprinklered attic had caught fire (the building had not been recently inspected for violations). The dealership was evacuated, and the six-man engine crew entered the building to conduct a search and suppression effort from the interior. The ladder crew tried to gain access to the blaze from the roof, hoping both to ventilate and to attack the fire from the top of the building. As the ladder crew moved along the roof's surface, there was no obvious sign of structural weakness.

INADEQUATE SUPPORT

The dealership's roof was constructed of trusses—a series of wooden triangles laid out in a horizontal row along the interior of the roof. The triangle is the most stable structure in building construction, and the truss has several advantages over wood beams or columns: it covers larger areas and longer distances more efficiently; it does not require vertical supports; and lightweight material, such as wood, can be used to support large areas and greater weights. However, the disadvantages of the wooden truss—from a firefighting perspective—are significant. During a fire, more of the truss's surface is exposed to flames than the surface of

a wood column or beam, and because the material used in a truss is lighter, it burns more rapidly and weakens more quickly. Additionally, the steel plates (called gusset plates) holding the truss together heat up quickly and burn into the wood, further weakening the construction. Any extra weight on a roof—for example, the weight of a firefighting crew—increases structural stress.

TOWNSPEOPLE VIEW THE WRECKAGE
Bystanders watch crews clearing debris from the remains of the Hackensack Ford Dealership. The city's fire-prevention bureau failed to inspect the dealership, which had been storing hazardous waste in the attic.

THE ROOF COLLAPSES

As the fire grew larger and more alarms sounded, the battalion chief called his two crews back from their positions to fight the fire from the ground. The ladder crew cleared the roof safely. But before the engine crew inside the dealership could evacuate, the truss roof partially collapsed, trapping them inside. One firefighter escaped; the remaining five died. In 1978, a similar collapse of a wood truss roof in a Brooklyn, New York, supermarket fire had killed six firefighters. Today, many states require truss-roofed buildings to be marked as such on the exterior to warn firefighters. New Jersey, which has the most stringent fire inspection codes in the U.S., is still reevaluating ways to improve inspections.

BATTALION CHIEF IS COMFORTED
A friend consoles the Hackensack battalion chief who lost five firefighters in the dealership fire. Before the interior suppression crew could follow his orders to "back your lines out," or evacuate, the roof caved in and trapped them in the flames.

PART TWO

FIRE SCIENCE
AND
TECHNOLOGY

PHYSICS OF FIRE

THROUGHOUT MOST OF HISTORY, firefighting has been based primarily on reducing the heat of the fire by dousing combustibles with water and moving potential fuel away from the flames. As technology advanced, techniques were expanded to include reducing and eliminating the only other then-known component of a fire: oxygen. Today's modern extinguishers usually work by removing oxygen, such as displacing it with carbon dioxide, or by spraying a fine powder, similar to baking soda, and smothering the fuel; separating it from the air. Today, a better understanding of fire incorporates a fourth element: self-sustaining chemical reactions. This is the actual ignition of an item, meaning that the heat, oxygen, and fuel must all combine in a rapid combustion, which, in turn, leads to the same combustion of surrounding fuel. Without this fourth component, the chain reaction occurs too slowly and there is no ignition—and thus no fire.

TETRAHEDRON
The four components of a fire: oxidizing agent (any of various gases that support combustion), reducing agent (any material that is reducible to combustible materials, becoming fuel), heat from within or without the material, and a self-sustaining chemical chain reaction (the action of the first three).

FUEL OXYGEN HEAT

FIRE TRIANGLE
The old diagram of a fire comprised three components: fuel, oxygen, and heat. Remove any one of the three, and the fire would die. However, research has led to the addition of an equally important fourth component: a self-sustaining chemical reaction.

Represents the reducing agent: the material is reduceable through heat action (pyrolysis) into component parts such as carbon monoxide, hydrogen, alcohol, etc. These are the fuels of a fire.

REDUCING AGENT (FUEL)

OXIDIZING AGENT

CHEMICAL CHAIN REACTION

HEAT

Represents one of the necessary components of fire, an oxidizing agent (typically oxygen).

Represents the self-sustaining chemical chain reaction: the interaction of the other three ingredients. The reaction will continue until one of the components is no longer present either because it has been consumed in the reaction or removed to stop the fire.

Represents heat, which could be from any source (electrical, chemical, nuclear, or mechanical, in the form of friction).

ALMOST A FIRE
The presence of any two components, such as oxygen and fuel (oil-soaked rags in a poorly ventilated storeroom), may well create a dangerous situation, but not a fire. However, add heat to this mix (a spark), and a disaster may be born if one of the ingredients is not removed from the equation rapidly enough. For example, the pyrolytic fumes—flammable gases emitted by a material due to heat action—dispersing through an opening before temperatures rise past their ignition point.

OXIDIZING AGENT REDUCING AGENT (FUEL)

TETRAHEDRON

Why a tetrahedron and not a triangle anymore? All fire is essentially the rapid oxidation of a material. Oxidation can take many forms, such as the rusting of steel or the yellowing of paper. A byproduct of oxidation is heat, which will ignite the material if and when the temperature reaches the substance's ignition point. The ignition point relates to the material's surface area relative to its mass. Large, uncompacted objects are easier to burn than small, dense ones. In order for a fire to start from this process, those initial three ingredients must continue to act in a chain reaction: oxidation producing heat, which causes the material to undergo pyrolysis (the release of any combustible gases within the item due to heat action), which produces the fuel that feeds the fire. If this chemical chain reaction is interrupted by the failure of any of the three ingredients, the fire dies. These components must act within a short enough time span of one another to be self-sustaining: An old, rusting vehicle, the books on a shelf, the flame of an oven, and an explosion are all undergoing the same process of pyrolysis. The difference is that the flame and explosion occur over a very short time period, while the rust and page-yellowing take place over a long time period.

ROLLOVER

This technical fire term describes the point at which gases produced by pyrolysis ignite. It is not to be confused with a flashover (when other combustible objects in an area, not just gases, ignite). Rollover strictly involves only any combustible gases and is typified by a brief, sudden ignition in the overhead air. If the volatile gases around the ceiling have been disturbed through improper cooling with water, but not vented, then ignition may occur at lower room heights—a danger for firefighters. To avoid mixing these thermal layers, the base of a fire must first be tackled before cooling the upper levels. Creating ventilation at ceiling heights will also help by allowing these hot, combustible gases to escape.

A vivid example of a rollover. Fortunately, there have been no disturbances to the thermal layers, so the volatile gases can burn relatively harmlessly above these firefighters' heads as they undergo coursework at a firefighting-training center.

ROLLOVER
As combustibles burn, pyrolysis occurs, releasing combustible gases. These gases will rise to occupy the highest enclosed space, where they will continue to gather until the temperature rises to their ignition point. At that time, a spectacular sheet of fire may be seen "rolling" across the ceiling. This does not mean that the ceiling is on fire—only the gases that have gathered there. A rollover does raise the ambient temperature of an area, however, and so cause other potential combustibles to ignite.

FLASHOVER

A flashover is defined as the point in a fire at which other combustibles within the area ignite, changing the fire from, essentially, one object on fire to many objects on fire. In simple terms, this is similar to the inital ignition of the fire in the original object, but on a much larger scale: For example, a chair is burning in a room and therefore undergoing pyrolysis. These combustible gases then collect at the ceiling as in the above description of a rollover. Eventually, these gases ignite, sending a sheet of flame across the ceiling and raising the overall temperature of the room as the gases are consumed. This rise in temperature results in the coffee table, bookshelf and books, and drapes to all exceed their ignition points (remember, the more surface area to density, the easier an object is to ignite). It is at this point that a flashover has occurred: when those other objects have caught fire. This may or may not be preceded by something as dramatic as a rollover.

When a flashover occurs, firefighters have only two seconds to escape the room before the temperatures rise so drastically that they will suffer heat-related injury or death. The flashover will send temperatures into the 1000°F (538°C)–1500°F (816°C) range, which is fatal within seconds with or without protective clothing.

FLASHOVER
This photo from a training facility depicts a fire starting on the center, lower object, meant to represent a bed. As pyrolysis occurred, the gases gathered above, which then resulted in a rollover. This rapid increase in temperature has ignited other objects in the room (flashover) and now their heat adds to the mix, continuing the cycle.

BACKDRAFT

Backdraft is the rapid ignition of combustible gases because of the sudden introduction of air and is also known as a "smoke explosion." As seen in the fire tetrahedron, all the components of a fire must be present for a flame to start. If all but one are present and allowed to build up, then the introduction of that final ingredient, often oxygen or carbon dioxide, can have explosive consequences.

For example, in an enclosed space within a larger, burning structure, pyrolysis is occurring, releasing hot, combustible gases such as carbon monoxide, which is usually visible as smoke. However, the surrounding fire already has consumed the oxygen in this space. So even though there is ample fuel and the temperature is quite high—approximately 1200°F (649°C)—there can be no fire until an oxidizing agent is introduced. This occurs when someone opens a door or a window, allowing air to sweep in. The collected carbon monoxide mixes with the oxidizing agent, especially carbon dioxide, and combined with the heat, ignites instantaneously, creating an explosion or backdraft.

To avoid this hazardous situation in a burning building, firefighters first try to open ventilation holes at the top so that the gases, which are hot and therefore rise, will escape and disperse into the open air. This is also why buildings are required to have vent holes in the roof; to release hot, pyrolytic gases before they build up to dangerous levels and result in an explosion. Venting a burning structure is an important firefighting technique that has saved countless lives, and is a necessary, valuable, and basic part of any firefighter's repertoire.

FIRESTORM

The word "firestorm" was coined in 1945 to describe the horrific fires that raged through the cities of Tokyo, Dresden, and Hamburg as a result of massive incendiary bombing. The mechanics of a firestorm follow the same basic pattern as all fires: oxidation, mixed with fuel and heat, creating a self-sustaining chemical reaction. What sets a firestorm apart is the size of the conflagration. During World War II, artificial firestorms were created by the rapid buildup of heat from the very hot incendiaries and the resulting fires. As the temperature rises, the hot air and gases also rise. This causes a vacuum beneath that the surrounding air rushes into, replacing the rising air. This rotation of air is called "convection." In a firestorm, the large quantity of air that rises creates the suction of an equally large volume of air to replace it. This "new" air rushes in, feeding the fire oxygen that, in turn, raises the temperature, continuing the convection process. Firestorms may create intake winds in excess of 150 mph (241 kmph) and temperatures over 2500°F (1371°C). This hurricane-force wind is strong enough to collapse buildings and pull people into the fire. Even someone in a "safe" area can suffocate as the oxygen is ripped away to feed the inferno.

Not all firestorms are artificial, though. In 1871, a forest fire in Peshtigo, Wisconsin, created a "fire tornado," or firestorm, with convection winds of over 80 mph (128 kph) that pulled everything into the fire. Trees far from the blaze burst into flame as the temperature exceeded their ignition levels.

DEVELOPMENT OF A FIRESTORM

An example of the convection currents formed as hot air rises from a burning building, drawing in fresh air at the bottom to replace it. This replenishment of air feeds the fire and temperatures rise, igniting even more of the surrounding structures.

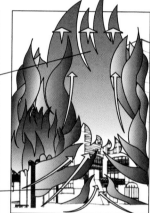

Air rushing in at the base of a firestorm, filling the vacuum created by the rising hot air.

INCENDIARY BOMBING OF DRESDEN, GERMANY, FEBRUARY 13, 1945
A firestorm of over 2500°F (1371°C) created an intake that literally swept people off of their feet and into the flames. People farther away suffocated as oxygen was torn from their lungs. As many as 135,000 people may have died.

FORENSICS

GOOD FIREFIGHTING also means preventing fires in the first place. A crucial part of that prevention training is learning about the causes of a fire and how it behaved; this is called forensics. The word "forensic" is most-often applied to the use of science as a legal tool to determine the cause or liability of an event. Beyond the courtroom application, however, forensics examines the causes of a fire to determine how it began. Having this information helps to prevent future fires that would be due to the same or similar causes.

There are three things that are first looked at by every fire investigator: the fuel, the heat's source and form, and the act or lack of action that brought those two elements together. To determine the fuel, investigators will look at the type of burning and what temperatures were achieved as well as any telltale chemical signs. For example, propane is heavier than air and will accumulate in the lowest portion of a room. The investigators will also look at the most-burned part of a structure to see what is in that area. They are specifically looking for a source of heat such as a gas pilot, stored combustibles, or even a plant—an incendiary substance that an arsonist would use. Finally, investigators consider the circumstances under which the fire occurred, for example: season (was the furnace or air conditioner on?), time of day (was something left alone? were people around?), weather (was it snowing? windy?), location (in a store? a home?), age (old electrical wiring? old pipes?). These and other conditions are considered as the investigators trace each element of the fire tetrahedron in an effort to determine how the various parts came together. Fire investigation is an ever-evolving field in which newer, more precise knowledge is constantly supplanting the old.

THERMAL PATTERNS

One of the easiest thermal patterns to recognize is the classic V-pattern (shown to right). It is the result of single-source, low-elevation fires. Because of the rising hot air (convection), flames tend first to spread upward in a dispersing pattern: narrow at the base and wider toward the top. The point at the bottom of the V will usually be the initial burn point. It is here that an investigator would first go to determine the cause and source of the blaze.

Not all fires, unfortunately, are V-pattern burns. However, a typical starting point in a thermal-pattern analysis is the location at which the burning has been most severe. In the case of a "grounder," when a structure has been totally leveled by fire, trying to spot the thermal pattern can be fruitless as the destruction is so complete. The investigator may have to rely on witnesses of the fire, including firefighters, and records of the contents or makeup of the structure to determine the cause. In the end, the source of such a fire will most likely be labeled "unknown." In regards to arson, most states' laws mandate that clear and convincing evidence of incendiary (intentional burning) must be found, which is often a difficult task.

CLASSIC V-PATTERN
Though it's not quite "X marks the spot," examining the burn marks can lead to some obvious conclusions. In this instance, at the center-bottom of the burn is the gas main (see detail below). In the end, it was determined that freezing caused contraction of the metal and a resultant gas leak. The gas was pulled into the house as the warmed air within the home escaped normally. Eventually, enough gas accumulated in the house for a probable ignition by the nearby water heater.

CHARRING AT POINT OF ORIGIN
This detail shows severe charring and melted metal, indicative of very high temperatures and/or a long burn time. The burning here was more severe than in the rest of the structure, so this was the likely source of the initial fuel.

SAFETY IMPLEMENTATION

FROM ANCIENT ROMAN TIMES to well into the 19th century, fire prevention and safety were elusive goals. An early fire safety plan was developed immediately after the Great Fire of London in 1666. When a fire broke out, citizens would be alerted by ringing church bells or hand-held noisemakers. A bucket brigade would assemble, transporting water to the site in leather buckets distributed around the city. Today, technology has become more advanced—fire extinguishers may contain water, dry chemicals, foam, or wet chemicals—but an alarm system and accessible fire extinguisher are still top priorities. They are valuable tools that, with instruction, can be used by anyone.

FIRE BUCKET, *usually made of leather*

FIRE GRENADE, *filled with carbonic acid*

POWDER EXTINGUISHER, *poured on fire to suffocate flames*

COPPER SODA-ACID EXTINGUISHER

COPPER SODA-ACID EXTINGUISHER

LANTERNS & LAMPS

Lights are used to illuminate the exterior of a building and expose hazards hidden in dark interiors. Early hand-held lanterns ran off of whale oil or kerosene; as fire trucks were converted to gasoline engines, they also provided power for portable and fixed spotlights. In the 1980s, quartz bulbs replaced incandescent bulbs, which burst when struck by water.

HAND-PAINTED SIGNAL LAMP POLE CARRIER, C. EARLY 1800S

DIETZ KEROSENE LAMP, C. 1921, *mounted on the truck and removed to be carried into the fire*

SEARCHLAMP, C. 1880, *mounted on top of steam engines*

SEARCHLAMP, C. 1950S, *mounted on trucks and powered by generators onboard*

EXTINGUISHERS

Buckets, filled with sand or water, were the earliest fire extinguishers. Fire grenades and powder were used in the 1800s. Soda-acid extinguishers, developed in the mid-1800s, used the reaction of soda and acid to propel water from the tank.

WATER HAND-PUMP FIRE
EXTINGUISHER

CO2 FUEL/ELECTRICAL FIRE
EXTINGUISHER

POWDER FUEL/ELECTRICAL
FIRE EXTINGUISHER

WATER WOOD/PAPER
FIRE EXTINGUISHER

WARNING SYSTEMS

Alarms are important for warning occupants and alerting the fire department. Church bells were commonly used since the Dark Ages, but other older devices, such as clackers and trumpets, were effective only within a limited range. In the 19th century, alarm boxes were placed on city sidewalks and telegraph wires connected firehouses, allowing more accurate communication.

LIGHT AND TRAFFIC
BOX, C. 1900, *designed
to match cast iron
streetlamps.*

*A door protects the
activation lever, which
is pulled to contact
the fire department.*

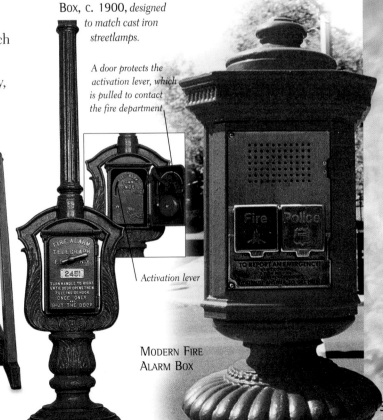

CLACKER, C. 1800S,
hand-held noisemaker

MUFFIN BELL,
C. 1800S,
*hand-held
noisemaker*

TRUMPET, *they were
outlawed in 1865, after
which they were used in
parades or given as gifts.*

WATCHTOWER BELL,
C. 1850–1870

Activation lever

MODERN FIRE
ALARM BOX

FIREFIGHTING GEAR

FIREFIGHTERS' GEAR protects against heat, smoke, and flames from the fire, and any other dangers they may encounter. Turnout gear (fire-resistant coat and pants) keeps the firefighter cool in the fire, warm in the winter, and dry in wet conditions. Helmets, boots, and gloves also provide protection from impact and sharp objects. In addition to the protective clothing they wear, firefighters carry devices that assist firefighting and rescue efforts. This gear prevents injury to firefighters, and improves their safety and firefighting success.

HATS & HELMETS

As early firefighters rarely entered burning buildings, felt fire hats were sufficient protection. Improvements in helmet design were necessary before firefighters could venture into the flames. Rigid materials protect the head from collapsing building materials and the wide brim at the back prevents sparks and water from touching the firefighter's neck.

STOVEPIPE HAT, *c. 1800, the felt material did not protect against flames, but the wide brim blocked sprays of water.*

FRENCH FIRE HELMET, *c. 1900, metal shells were dangerous because they conduct heat and electricity.*

GRATACAP, *c. 1830, developed by a volunteer firefighter, this is the forerunner of modern helmets.*

MODERN HELMET, *has a face shield that is heat and flame resistant.*

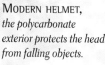

MODERN HELMET, *the number on the front indicates the wearer's rank and engine company.*

MODERN HELMET, *the polycarbonate exterior protects the head from falling objects.*

ACCESSORIES

The accessories a firefighter carries on site can be responsible for saving his or her life. By ensuring the firefighter's personal safety, they provide greater flexibility in suppression and rescue efforts. The Personal Alert Safety System (PASS) alerts rescuers to the presence of a downed firefighter, who may be obscured by smoke or darkness. The device contains a motion sensor and beeps if the wearer has not moved in 45 seconds. Breathing apparatus eliminates the devastating problems of reduced oxygen and smoke inhalation. A firefighter wearing the Self-Contained Breathing Apparatus (SCBA) is supplied with fresh oxygen and can penetrate deeper into the fire.

LADDER BELT, *worn by firefighter and fastened to the ladder.*

FLAME-RETARDANT LEATHER GLOVES, *to protect hands from flames and sharp material.*

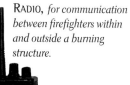

RADIO, *for communication between firefighters within and outside a burning structure.*

FLASHLIGHT, *for illuminating dark areas to search for survivors and obstacles.*

PERSONAL ALERT SAFETY SYSTEM (PASS) MONITOR, *to indicate fallen firefighters.*

SELF-CONTAINED BREATHING APPARATUS (SCBA), *has a 30-pound (14 kg) tank that supplies enough oxygen to last up to an hour.*

FULL BODY PROTECTION
Covered from head to toe in protective gear, a firefighter can go further into a fire to rescue survivors and property.

PASS monitor

SCBA gear

Reflective stripes

Heavy leather gloves

Pockets carry small accessories

UNIFORM

A firefighter's first line of defense is his turnout gear, made of synthetic, fire-resistant materials. Reflective stripes provide visibility through thick smoke and extra pockets store essential tools. The coat is long enough to overlap the pants even when the firefighter bends over. Suspenders hold up the pants and an "anti-flash" hood covers the neck area exposed between the coat or helmet. National standards ensure that clothing withstands a certain amount of heat and moisture. The gear is extremely heavy and expensive, but essential.

The external yellow layer is made of heat-resistant Nomex®.

The pale yellow vapor barrier protects against steam burns from the firefighter's own body heat.

The blue waterproof lining keeps the firefighter dry.

MULTI-LAYERED GARMENTS
Each layer of material used in turnout gear serves a specific purpose, providing protection from heat, cold, flames, and water.

READY TO GO
At the fire station, boots are left tucked into pants, so that firefighters can use one motion to put on both items.

Suspenders make the pants easy to put on and comfortable to wear.

Today's short, leather boots are more comfortable than the old rubber ones. Steel plates on the bottom provide additional protection.

FARNAM-STYLE HAND PUMPER, C. 1790
Two firefighters stood on either side of the pump, moving the arms like a see-saw to force water through the hoses.

OLD ENGINES

EARLY ENGINES were hand-drawn carts used to get water from cisterns or other sources. Later, coal-burning boilers created the steam that pumped water through the hoses. Originally, these pumpers were pulled by the firemen, but as equipment became heavier, horses were needed to pull the carts. In addition to the pumper, specialized vehicles transported the ladders and hoses. Even once horse-drawn engines were in use, firemen continued to run alongside the vehicles. This effort left the firemen so exhausted by the time they reached the fire that running boards and seating were added to the trucks. By World War I, most of the larger fire departments were beginning to motorize and by the mid-1920s, the process was virtually complete.

During parades, an ornate metal cover replaced the hose around the center spool.

Large wheels made it easier to travel over bumps and curbs.

HAND-DRAWN HOSE REEL FROM THE STEINWAY HOSE COMPANY, NO. 7, LONG ISLAND CITY FIRE DEPARTMENT
Volunteer firefighters took great pride in their apparatus and went to great lengths and expense to decorate them. Special efforts were made for the frequent parades, such as placing plumes of colored feathers in the polished brass nozzles.

METROPOLITAN STEAMER
Around 1910, fire departments were beginning to transition to gasoline engines. Although a gasoline tractor powered this vehicle, a coal-burning boiler still created steam to pump the water.

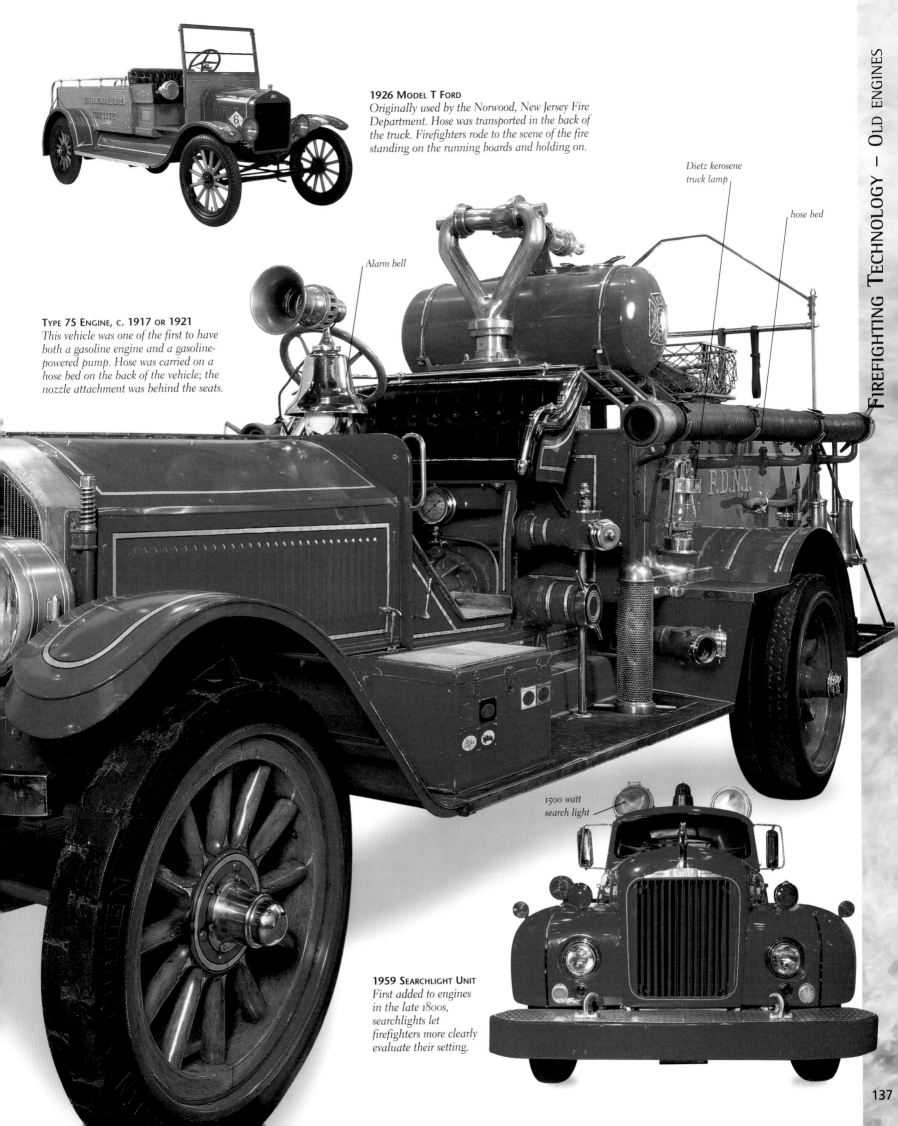

1926 MODEL T FORD
Originally used by the Norwood, New Jersey Fire Department. Hose was transported in the back of the truck. Firefighters rode to the scene of the fire standing on the running boards and holding on.

Dietz kerosene truck lamp

hose bed

Alarm bell

TYPE 75 ENGINE, c. 1917 OR 1921
This vehicle was one of the first to have both a gasoline engine and a gasoline-powered pump. Hose was carried on a hose bed on the back of the vehicle; the nozzle attachment was behind the seats.

1500 watt search light

1959 SEARCHLIGHT UNIT
First added to engines in the late 1800s, searchlights let firefighters more clearly evaluate their setting.

PUMPERS

AS THE DEMANDS ON FIRE DEPARTMENTS increase, equipment has become more and more specialized, but the pumper, or engine, is still the most versatile and the most common. Originally, pumpers were hand-drawn, but as the equipment became heavier, horses were needed to pull them. Firefighters developed a true bond of affection with their horses, that was shared by the public. Fire horses were often so well trained that, at the sound of a fire signal, they would come out of their stalls and stand under special harnesses that were automatically lowered onto them. The unit then pulled away from the station as the boiler was ignited to provide steam. Equipped with a tank, a pump, and lengths of hose, modern pumpers serve the same function today as they did in the days of horses and steam.

TODAY'S ENGINES

Pumpers carry hose and can pump thousand of gallons per minute (GPM). In 1965, the superpumper, capable of delivering over 80,000 GPM was introduced; it has the capability of pumping from several hydrants at the same time. Large Diameter Hose (LDH), made of rubber-lined plastic, is used today because—unlike earlier hoses of leather or rubber-lined cotton—it does not rot or break. LDH comes in different diameters. The pressurized streams of water create enough force to knock the firefighter down, so several people may be needed to hold the hose. Pumpers carry additional equipment—including a variety of ladders, tools, and rescue equipment—that prepares the crew to respond to most fire emergencies.

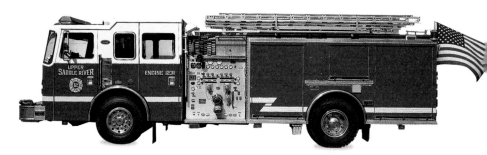

STORING EQUIPMENT
Lockers along the side of the truck provide storage space for all of the firefighters' tools. Each piece of equipment has its own location, allowing quick access at the site of the fire.

SAFETY ON THE ROAD
The enclosed cab of the fire truck provides increased room and safety for firefighters. Regulations introduced in 1991 ensure that each firefighter has his own seat and seatbelt.

Siren

NOZZLES AND HOSE EQUIPMENT

The nature of a fire determines what type of attachment, or branch, is used to direct the spray of water from the hose. Different nozzles have been developed to control the spray pattern, pressure, and flow rate. Protective valves allow the firefighter to diminish or shut off the flow of water, which can prevent the hose from bursting and minimize water damage to property. Fog nozzles disperse the water into fine droplets, absorbing heat more quickly, while other nozzles have greater reach and can extinguish fires from further away.

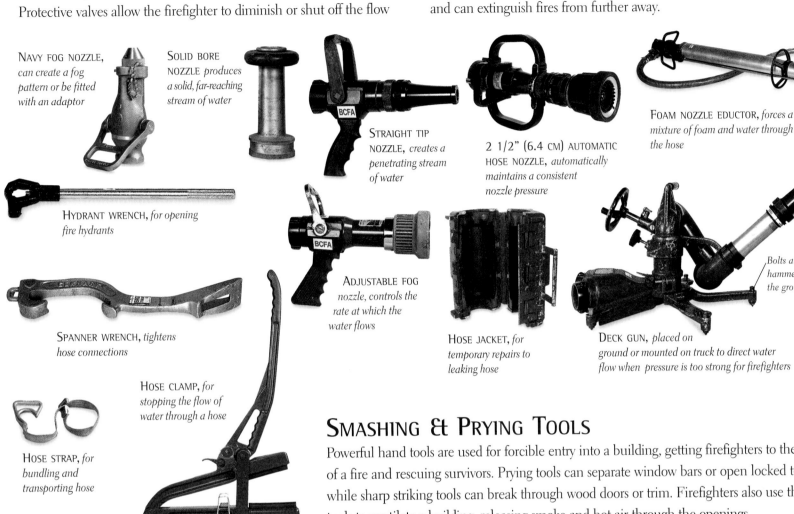

NAVY FOG NOZZLE, *can create a fog pattern or be fitted with an adaptor*

SOLID BORE NOZZLE *produces a solid, far-reaching stream of water*

STRAIGHT TIP NOZZLE, *creates a penetrating stream of water*

2 1/2" (6.4 CM) AUTOMATIC HOSE NOZZLE, *automatically maintains a consistent nozzle pressure*

FOAM NOZZLE EDUCTOR, *forces a mixture of foam and water through the hose*

HYDRANT WRENCH, *for opening fire hydrants*

ADJUSTABLE FOG *nozzle, controls the rate at which the water flows*

Bolts are hammered into the ground

SPANNER WRENCH, *tightens hose connections*

HOSE JACKET, *for temporary repairs to leaking hose*

DECK GUN, *placed on ground or mounted on truck to direct water flow when pressure is too strong for firefighters*

HOSE CLAMP, *for stopping the flow of water through a hose*

HOSE STRAP, *for bundling and transporting hose*

SMASHING & PRYING TOOLS

Powerful hand tools are used for forcible entry into a building, getting firefighters to the site of a fire and rescuing survivors. Prying tools can separate window bars or open locked tools, while sharp striking tools can break through wood doors or trim. Firefighters also use these tools to ventilate a building, releasing smoke and hot air through the openings.

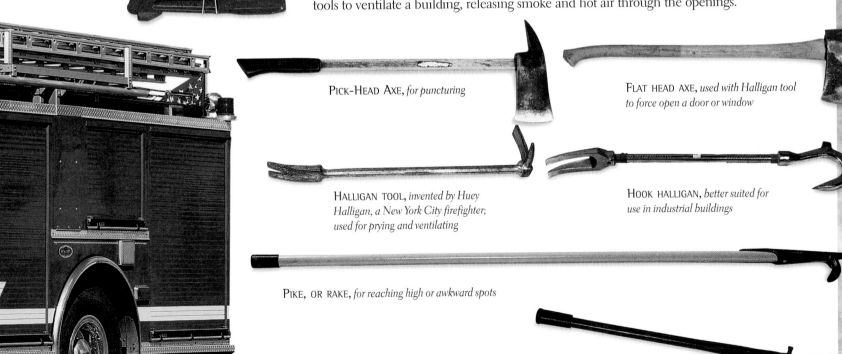

PICK-HEAD AXE, *for puncturing*

FLAT HEAD AXE, *used with Halligan tool to force open a door or window*

HALLIGAN TOOL, *invented by Huey Halligan, a New York City firefighter, used for prying and ventilating*

HOOK HALLIGAN, *better suited for use in industrial buildings*

PIKE, OR RAKE, *for reaching high or awkward spots*

BATTERING RAM, *for breaking through locked doors*

BOLT CUTTERS, *for cutting through wire*

LADDER TRUCKS

Like pumpers, ladder trucks are an indispensable resource. The long reach and flexible maneuvering of an aerial ladder can be crucial in firefighting and rescue situations. From a ladder, firefighters can reach survivors in a high building, or combat a fire in a low building by dousing the flames from above. They perform many of the same operations that they would on the ground, such as forcible entry, ventilation, and fire suppression.

SPECIALTY TOOLS

Over the years, the fire industry observes the same problems over and over, and, in response, develops tools to meet these needs. Fans, run on gasoline or electric power, are used to ventilate buildings, removing smoke and gases and forcing in fresh air. The method of operation—positive or negative pressure ventilation—depends on the structure of the building and the type of fire. Lighter weight electric fans can be hung in a window. Thermal imaging devices help firefighters locate survivors and fallen firefighters. Infrared radiation detects areas with different amounts of heat, revealing bodies hidden by thick smoke or flame. Battery-powered electric saws can cut through metal supports, but have not replaced hand saws and chain saws, used for cutting through trees or building materials. Large tarpaulins cover areas in or near the fire, protecting them from water damage from the hoses.

THERMAL IMAGING DEVICE
The white area in the view finder indicates the presence of a person who would otherwise be hidden in the darkness or smoke.

TARPAULIN, *directs water out of a building and protects personal property*

SAW, *used for cutting through roofs and other materials*

FAN, *directs smoke out of the building*

FAN HANGER, *is wedged into the door frame to suspend a fan in the opening*

BOOM UNEXTENDED

BOOM HALF-EXTENDED

MAHWAH FIRE DEPARTMENT 100-FOOT (30-METER) TOWER LADDER
Ladder trucks are equipped to fight fires independently of pumpers. They have a large tank, a pump, hose, tools, and numerous ladders. The trucks carry ladders, range from 14 to 40 feet (4 to 12 meters) long, in addition to the aerial ladder, which may be 85 to 115 feet (26 to 35 meters) long.

LADDERS

Early hook and ladder trucks were developed in the 19th century to transport aerial ladders through narrow streets. Their unique construction consisted of a front section that was originally connected to a horse team (and later housed a motor) and the rear section containing the steering apparatus. They used heavy, wooden ladders that required more work of the firefighters, who had to turn a hand crank to raise them. In the 1920s and 1930s, improvements led to lightweight metal ladders that were raised by motorized cranks. Some trucks are mounted with an articulating boom ladder; joints separate the boom into about four sections, allowing for more precise placement of the basket. Although the truck's jointed boom is difficult to use in restricted areas, firefighters can by raised to high levels and positioned in tight spots. Today, due to staffing and financial constraints, and to extend the life of ladder trucks, sometimes smaller ladder trucks called "tenders" are used to respond to medical calls. These vehicles carry enough equipment to attend to a fire if needed, but are more cost efficient.

THE BOOM
A cage mounted at the end of the hydraulic boom raises the firefighter high enough to combat the fire and rescue survivors. The boom raises a firefighter up to meet people trapped by the fire, who are then assisted into the cage and lowered to safety. A hose mounted in the cage allows firefighters to spray water down on the fire from above.

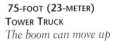

75-FOOT (23-METER) TOWER TRUCK
The boom can move up and down and swivel 360 degrees to position the firefighter as close to the target as possible.

BOOM EXTENDED TO THE BACK

BOOM EXTENDED TO THE FRONT

RESCUE

In disastrous situations where fires may endanger human life, the fire department sends a rescue vehicle to the scene. These vehicles are staffed by specially trained firefighters and rescue workers like Emergency Medical Technicians (EMT). Rescue units respond to fires and vehicle accidents, as well as situations in water, mine pits, scaffolding, or elevators. They carry more tools and first aid supplies than pumpers or ladder trucks; in addition to fighting fires, they must be prepared to rescue and tend to the medical needs of accident victims.

JAWS OF LIFE ®, *a hydraulic rescue tool, forces open a car's doors, allowing firefighters to treat or remove a trapped passenger.*

EAR PROTECTORS, *are necessary when using noisy tools such as a chain saw.*

GOGGLES, *prevent debris from entering the eyes, without restricting vision.*

WHEN FIREFIGHTERS ARRIVE AT A CAR ACCIDENT, *their first priority is to rescue people injured in the crash. A tool called the Jaws of Life ® pries the door off a car by breaking its hinges, freeing passengers without causing further harm.*

A HYDRAULIC CUTTING TOOL *slices through the metal support between the windshield and a side window. The firefighter can then remove the roof and extricate the passengers through the top of the car.*

IN A COLLISION *the hood of a car can be crushed, pinning down a passenger's leg. A rescue worker in training uses a door jack to push the car's steering column toward the front, away from the passenger. Once firefighters have rescued the car's passengers, they spray foam and water around the vehicle to prevent the ignition of fuel leaked from damaged fuel lines.*

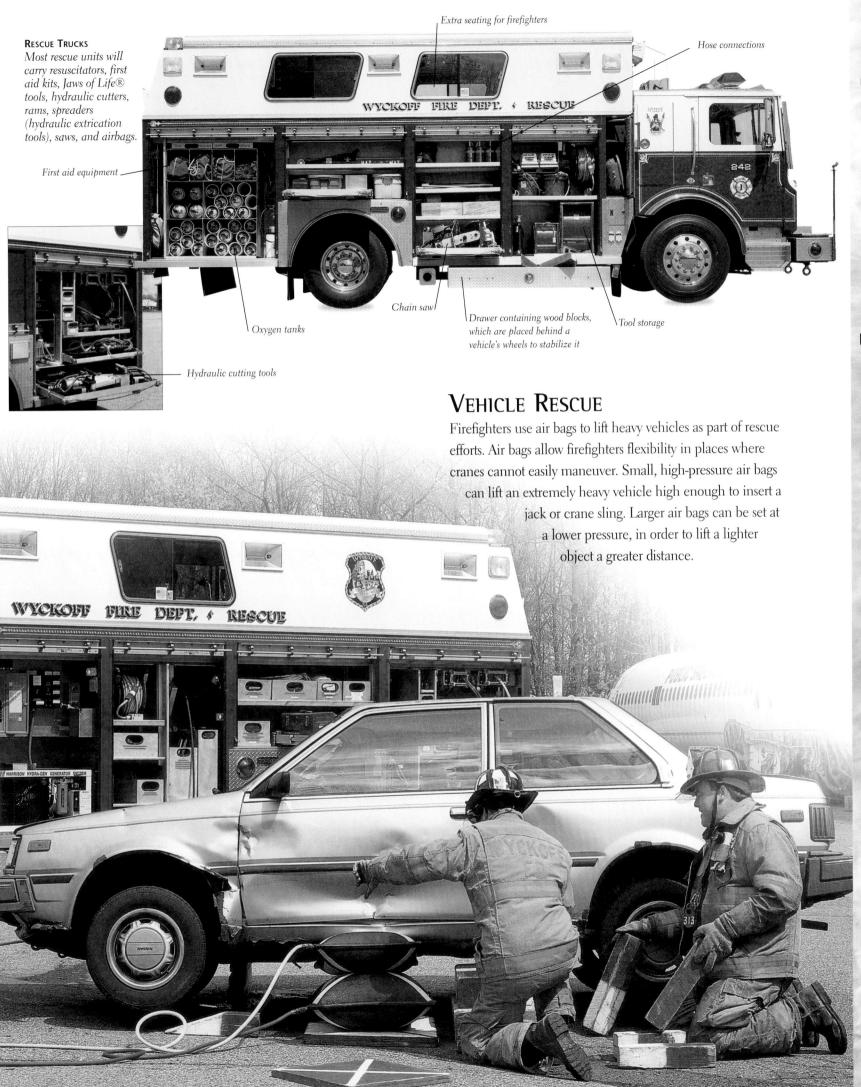

RESCUE TRUCKS
Most rescue units will carry resuscitators, first aid kits, Jaws of Life® tools, hydraulic cutters, rams, spreaders (hydraulic extrication tools), saws, and airbags.

Extra seating for firefighters

Hose connections

First aid equipment

WYCKOFF FIRE DEPT. ⬥ RESCUE

242

Chain saw

Oxygen tanks

Drawer containing wood blocks, which are placed behind a vehicle's wheels to stabilize it

Tool storage

Hydraulic cutting tools

VEHICLE RESCUE

Firefighters use air bags to lift heavy vehicles as part of rescue efforts. Air bags allow firefighters flexibility in places where cranes cannot easily maneuver. Small, high-pressure air bags can lift an extremely heavy vehicle high enough to insert a jack or crane sling. Larger air bags can be set at a lower pressure, in order to lift a lighter object a greater distance.

WYCKOFF FIRE DEPT. ⬥ RESCUE

AIR AND SEA

CHERRY PICKER
Marine and air fire crews support the efforts of pumpers and ladder trucks, like this Cherry Picker.

TODAY, THE AREA a fire department covers is increasingly large and varied. Specialized fire crews are needed to fight fires in locations where traditional firefighting methods are insufficient. Experienced firefighters receive intensive training to learn to combat fires from the air or sea. Airports have their own fire departments, specially equipped to handle the aircraft fires. Located on site, this fire crew can respond quickly to an accident when notified by the air traffic control. When a fuel fire ignites on the runway, firefighters extinguish the flames around the aircraft. In addition, crash trucks used by airport firefighters are mounted with a device that can punch through the plane's fuselage to extinguish a fire inside the plane. Just as firefighters use airbags to lift damaged vehicles at a car crash, airport units carry airbags capable of lifting part of an airplane.

DOUSING THE FLAMES
A helicopter pours water onto a wildfire burning near a suburb of Athens, Greece. Helicopter tanks can carry over 300 gallons of water.

HELICOPTERS

In departments with a large geographic area of responsibility, helicopters are used to access remote areas and transport personnel rapidly. Able to make versatile movements, helicopters may be used as airborne observation platforms for fire-spotting and tactical operations. In the event of a wildfire, helicopters carry groups of firefighters, known as helitack crews, and their supplies to the heart of the fire. Like airplanes, helicopters fly over wildland fires, dropping water or chemicals. Some helicopters are equipped with helitorches, which ignite fires for a prescribed burn. Helicopters also are used for rescue and transport in medical emergencies.

SPECIALIZED CRASH TRUCK
Airport crash trucks are equipped and staffed by airport authorities. These massive trucks are roughly 40 feet (12 m) long and 12 feet (4 m) high, with an enclosed cab that seats five or six firefighters.

FIREBOAT
The Seattle Fire Department acquired the Chief Seattle in 1984 to respond to emergencies along the 153 mile (246 km) coastline. This fireboat is equipped with an Emergency Medical Services (EMS) room, high-tech communication tools, and equipment for handling hazardous materials.

AIRPLANES

Like helicopters, fixed-wing planes are used to drop water and fire-suppressing chemicals onto forest fires. Unlike trucks, airplanes cannot pump water from a fire hydrant at the scene of the fire. These aircraft fly low over lakes or the ocean, forcing water directly into their large tanks. After World War II, pilots began to fly planes over wildland fires, dropping "smoke jumpers" down to the source of the flames. Smoke jumpers are highly skilled individuals who receive rigorous and expensive training to supplement their years of experience as ground firefighters. Smoke jumpers fly over the forest in an airplane, then parachute down near the heart of the forest fire. They remove debris around the fire, hoping to isolate the flames and prevent it from spreading. Because smokejumpers can get to a fire more easily than firefighters traveling over land, they reach the fire when it is smaller and more easily extinguished, preventing larger and more destructive forestfires.

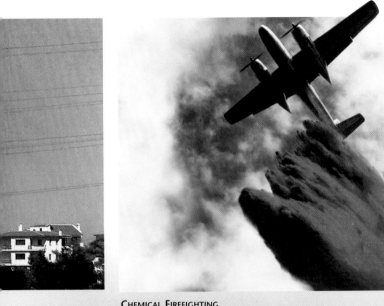

CHEMICAL FIREFIGHTING
Chemicals added to the plane's water supply prevent the water from changing into mist and direct it toward the fire more accurately. The chemicals tint the water so that the pilot can tell which areas have been doused.

FIREBOATS

On major bodies of water, fireboats are essential equipment for fighting fires and responding to other emergencies. A long stretch of waterfront may include industrial and recreational areas, bordering an urban environment. Fireboats fight fires on passenger and commercial boats, in harbors, and on land, within several blocks of the waterfront. They have a significant advantage over fire engines—located on their water source, they can pump five times as much water from numerous deck pipes onto a fire. Fireboats also can respond to oil and hazardous material spills; in the event of an oil-based fire, the firefighters use foam stored in tanks on the boat. In some events, the fire department may use fireboats to collaborate with the United States Coast Guard. Fireboats may be used to help after boat collisions, EMS calls, drownings, or search and rescue. In addition to hoses, axes, and poles, fireboats carry tools for cutting through ship hulls, diving equipment, and first aid and rescue equipment; larger fireboats may carry inflatable rafts with outboard motors. Marine firefighters are generally already experienced firefighters, and they receive additional training to prepare for the challenges of marine fires.

OUTDOOR TRAINING TECHNIQUES

FIREFIGHTERS are not fully prepared until they can make critical decisions and carry out orders effectively. Although firefighters used to learn on the job, today most receive rigorous training before they ever go out on a call. American firefighters may attend an academy for many months, learning the basics of fire behavior, safety, building construction and building collapse, hazardous materials, forcible entry, ventilation, rescue operations, and the proper use of equipment. Much of the experience is hands-on firefighting, but supplemental instruction is provided by lectures, films, and videotapes. In some states, training standards are developed and mandated by the U.S. Fire Administration (USFA), the National Fire Protection Agency (NFPA), and the fire insurance industry, which monitors and evaluates community fire response.

THE CONTROL ROOM
An instructor looks out at the fire-resistant building and the simulated runway fire. Symtron Systems is one of the companies that design the structures and computer programs on which instructors monitor and control conditions in the facility.

FIRE ON THE RUNWAY
A propane tank generates flames to simulate a fuel spill from an aircraft. When fuel leaks out onto the runway and ignites, firefighters are called to combat the blaze and rescue the airplane passengers. At the training facility, instructors control the height of the flames.

HIGH-RISK TRAINING
Aircraft Rescue Fire Fighters (ARFF) train for aircraft emergencies. Like airports, industrial facilities such as chemical companies and oil refineries often have their own training programs to meet their specific safety needs.

CLEAN FUEL
This situation simulates the ignition of fuel leaked by a 747 jumbo jet. Unlike actual diesel and jet fuels, the propane used in simulations releases no pollutants, allowing the training facility to be located near urban communities.

FIRE TRAINING CENTERS

At the Bergen County, New Jersey, Law and Public Safety Institute, a multimillion dollar complex provides the most realistic firefighting training possible. Paid and volunteer firefighters, as well as firefighters for private, industrial companies, enroll in a course designed to meet NFPA and New Jersey state standards. The centerpiece is a fire-resistant structure that has three floors of various occupancies. Within this building, trainees practice firefighting techniques in realistic scenarios. Virtually any kind of horrendous scene that a firefighter might encounter can be recreated here. A half-buried concrete pipe is used to provide training in how to rescue someone trapped in an enclosed or confined space, such as a pipeline, sewer, vault, grain elevator, or excavation. Aircraft fuselage, motor vehicles, and various pipes and pits are set up to provide other firefighting and rescue experiences. A tower on site houses a communications room where instructors monitor activities throughout the complex to ensure the students' safety.

The instructors can extinguish or increase the amount of smoke and fire and control the building's sprinkler system. The tower also houses a first aid station, eye-wash fountains, restrooms, and showers. Training does not stop once the trainee has joined the force. Like the military, firefighting has ranks which require a certain level of skill, education, and experience. In order to join a specialized team, such as helicopter, rescue, or airport fire crews, firefighters must understand that kind of fire and master the new equipment. Although the Law and Public Safety Institute exemplifies hands-on training, it is not the only such program; similar training prepares both private and community firefighters in other areas and at military facilities, major airports, and industrial facilities.

LEAKING PROPANE
A leaking pipe on the bottom of this 500-gallon propane tank catches on fire, heating up the entire tank. The heat forces the relief valve on top of the tank to blow, sending up more flames. To extinguish the fire, the firefighter first must cool down the water tank by spraying water on it. This causes the fire to subside enough that the firefighter can access and shut off a valve at the base of the tank, stopping the fuel leak and extinguishing the fire.

Chemical powder smothers the fire by preventing oxygen from reaching the flames.

PRACTICE DRILLS
A firefighter uses a fire extinguisher to attack the flames from a burning car. Car fires can break out in the engine, the interior, the trunk, or the fuel tank, all of which can be replicated on this trainer car.

INDOOR TRAINING TECHNIQUES

ENTERING A BURNING BUILDING will test a firefighter's knowledge and skills. When this happens in real life, the firefighter will be protected by technologically advanced gear and equipment. While training in simulated situations, the trainees are accompanied by instructors who teach them how to extinguish the fire, rescue survivors, and protect themselves. At the Law and Public Safety Institute, there is a three-story building containing rooms with many different scenarios that a firefighter might encounter during an interior fire.

FLASHOVER EFFECT
When smoke accumulates in an enclosed room, the increased heat can cause particles in the smoke to ignite, setting the whole room aflame. It is very important that firefighters understand the importance of cooling down the ceiling to avoid this flashover effect. When firefighters enter a room, they must spray water on the ceiling to cool it down before they attack the main fire.

The facility's fire-resistant structure houses a faux retail store, beauty salon, and garage and body shop on the ground floor; a restaurant, bank, luncheonette, and office on the second floor; and a hotel-room suite and theater on the third floor. In each of these fire-hazard areas, propane gas is used to generate flames and a computer provides artificial smoke. The artificial smoke—a non-toxic aerosol fog—is so dense that firefighters cannot see their own hands, but it does not limit a firefighter's oxygen intake, so a breathing apparatus is not necessary. Students must negotiate a hose up a spiral staircase and access the elevator as if to remove trapped people. Training is realistic; if a firefighter does not use the proper techniques, instructors in the control room make the fire blaze up, or otherwise respond as it would in a real situation. However, if firefighters still cannot control the flames, the instructors also use the computer to extinguish the fire completely.

ELECTRICAL FIRE
When an electrical panel catches on fire, water cannot be used to extinguish the flames, for fear of electrocution. The firefighter must use CO_2, or another nonconductive extinguisher. If power to the site can be shut off, the fire will subside, leaving only minor flames on flammable wires.

BEDROOM FIRE
Flames from a metal bed replicate a fire lit by a candle or cigarette. The metal does not burn, so the set up can be used repeatedly for training exercises.

Going Inside

Upon entering a burning structure, firefighters evaluate their surroundings in order to anticipate the fire's behavior and develop a plan of attack. Firefighters always carry radios, which allow them to communicate and coordinate their efforts. Of the five recognized building construction classifications, each one responds differently in a fire. For instance, although the thick wood and heavy masonry of mill-type buildings are quite fire resistant, the open spaces and vertical shafts can create a massive blaze. A building's contents are also important; industrial plants may contain large quantities of flammable material. Although firefighters in the role of first responders are not meant to be arson investigators, they are expected to look for signs that the fire was set deliberately. Clues such as the sprinklers being shut off or an odor of gasoline can alert experienced firefighters. Hazardous materials are another possible threat. Firefighters receive HAZMAT (Hazardous Materials) training that is both intensive and frightening. When working in confined spaces, firefighters must remain aware of acceptable time limits for exposures to hazardous materials.

As firefighters enter a building, ventilation is a primary concern. They must break open doors and windows and tear up the roof in order to prevent an excessive buildup of heat and gases. When this buildup occurs, it can cause an explosion that sends flames and debris flying. The firefighter must remain wary of other fire reactions, such as flashover, rollover, and backdraft, which can cause serious harm to the firefighter and make the fire far less manageable. Rollover and flashover can be prevented by cooling the ceiling with water. If monitors at the training facility note that trainees have failed to spray water on the ceiling, they can use the computer to create a propane-fueled rollover on the ceiling. Although actions that prevent such incidents—ventilating the building and using water to cool the temperature—cause significant property damage, they save lives and prevent the demolition of the entire structure.

SIMULATED FIRE IN AIRPLANE ANTERIOR
Firefighters battle the flames in a simulation of a fire inside an airplane. The structure can replicate fire in the cockpit, cabin, lavatory, galley, or cargo areas.

FIRE SAFETY TIPS

⚜ FIRE SAFETY IN THE HOME

- Install a smoke alarm on every level of your house. In addition, install a smoke alarm in any room where someone sleeps.

- Check the smoke alarm once a month; change its batteries once a year. Replace it once every ten years.

- If you have a fire extinguisher in your home, contact the fire department to learn how to use it properly. In the event of a fire, there is no time to read the instructions on the extinguisher.

- Sleep with your bedroom door closed. A closed door slows the spread of smoke and fire.

- Some fires you can try to put out, others will require that you immediately evacuate everyone in the house, then call 911 in the USA (999 for UK).
  If the fire is confined to a small area, such as one burner of the stove, you may try to extinguish it yourself. Do not try to extinguish the fire unless you are familiar with the treatment of different types of fires. If a small fire begins to spread, as when a stove fire spreads to curtains, evacuate immediately. Fires spread very quickly!

YOUR FAMILY'S EVACUATION PLAN

- Hold a family conference to establish an evacuation plan. Determine 2 escape routes from every room and an outside location where you can meet up. Practice this fire-evacuation plan.

- Make sure your children recognize the sound of the fire alarm and understand the fire-evacuation plan.

- If your household contains children too young to follow the family's evacuation plan, the parent should collect the children before exiting the house.

- AFTER you have evacuated the premises, call 911 in the USA (999 for UK).

AROUND THE HOUSE

- Always remember to turn off appliances.

- Space heaters should be kept 3 feet (1 m) from flammable materials.

- Do not overload electrical outlets or extension cords.

- Never throw water on an electrical fire. If an appliance is sparking, see if you can unplug it safely. Fire extinguishers labeled for class-C fires, or those labeled all-purpose for A, B, or C fires, can be used on electrical fires.

- Baking soda can also be used to extinguish small electrical fires. If possible, first unplug the appliance, then throw handfuls of baking soda at the base of the fire. Call the fire department so that they can make sure the fire is out.

IN THE KITCHEN

- Never leave a burner unattended.

- Turn pot handles toward the center of the stove, so that the pots are not easily knocked off.

- If the oil or grease in a pan catches on fire, place a lid on the pan, turn off the burner, and allow the pan to cool with the lid on. Fire extinguishers labeled for class-B fires, or those labeled all-purpose for A, B, or C fires, can be used on grease fires.

- For small cooking fires, baking soda can be used to extinguish the flames. Turn off the burner and throw handfuls of baking soda onto the base of the fire. Do not get too close. Call the fire department, who can ensure that the fire has been put out.

In Public Places

- As you enter any public place, such as a theater, stadium, or shopping mall, locate the fire exits and alarm-system boxes.

- Respond immediately if you hear an alarm. Do not assume it is a mistake or drill.

- If you spot a fire, activate the building's alarm system.

Exiting a Building

- Before opening a door, feel the door handle for heat. Then feel the door, starting at the bottom. If the door is not hot, exit through the door and close it behind you.

- If passing through a smoky area, stay low. Heat and smoke rise, so you will be able to breathe better lower down.

- NEVER use the elevator. Always exit via the stairwell. An elevator, responding to heat, may automatically stop at the floor of the fire.

- If all escape routes are blocked, you may be forced to return to your bedroom, hotel room, or office. In this event, close the door and seal any cracks with wet towels or other cloth. Hang a bright cloth or sheet in the window or from the balcony to alert rescue workers to your presence.

- If your clothes catch fire, **STOP** walking, **DROP** to the ground, cover your face, and **ROLL** to extinguish the flames.

- Once you have safely evacuated the building, call 911 in the USA (999 for UK).

At the Office

- Become familiar with your office's fire-evacuation plan.

- Locate the fire alarms and all emergency exits and stairwells.

- Know the office fire warden.

At a Hotel

- Consider requesting a room on a lower floor so that evacuation is faster and easier.

- Read the fire-evacuation plan that should be posted in your room.

- Locate the fire exits and run a fire drill.

- Count the number of doors between your room and the fire exit. Should you need to evacuate through thick smoke, you will still know which door is the exit.

- Bring a flashlight with you.

- If you exit your room, remember to take your key. If you cannot exit the building, you may need to return to your room.

Wildfire Safety

- Create a safety zone around your home: remove all flammable vegetation, leaves, and debris within 30–50 feet (10–12 m) of your house.

- As you exit your home, cover your body with cotton or wool clothing. Use a handkerchief to protect your face.

- Close any doors and windows to your house.

- Wet down your roof and any shrubs near your house.

GLOSSARY

AIR BAGS Inflatable sacks used in rescue efforts to raise and support damaged vehicles

ALARM BOX A street-level iron structure containing a button or lever to alert the fire department to a fire at that location.

ARSON The purposeful setting of a fire with criminal intent.

ASBESTOS Fireproof insulation material. No longer used because its airborne fibers are cancerous.

BACKDRAFT A smoke explosion caused by the sudden introduction of oxygen into an enclosed space.

BALLOON CONSTRUCTION A wood-building construction style containing no fire-stops that would prevent the vertical spread of fire.

BUCKET BRIGADE A group organized to extinguish fires by passing buckets of water between a water source and the fire.

CAUSE The reason for a fire such as an accident, a natural event, or an incendiary, namely arson.

CLACKER A 19th-century handheld noisemaker used as a fire alarm.

CONFLAGRATION An extremely large fire that effectively destroys a municipality's ability to function.

DECK GUN A metal device either placed on the ground or mounted on a vehicle. It directs the flow of water as its water pressure is too great for firefighters to manhandle.

ETHYL MERCAPTAN A strong, chemical odor added to natural gas and propane, which are otherwise odorless and therefore virtually undetectable.

FIREBREAK A planned or naturally existing open area that impedes the spread of fire.

FIRE CURTAIN A barrier to prevent the spread of smoke and flames between the stage and the audience's seating in a theater.

FIRE GRENADE A fist-size glass object filled with carbonic acid (a chemical extinguisher) that is tossed onto a fire to suppress the flames.

FIRELOAD Flammable materials.

FIRE MARK A metal sign placed on the front of buildings in the 18th century to identify the name of the insurance company that provided fire coverage for the structure.

FIRE PLUG A term from when water was held in hollowed-out logs and drained through holes kept blocked by plugs. Synonymous with "fire hydrant."

FIRE-STOP A piece of masonry, wood, or other material inserted between studs or joists to impede the spread of fire.

FIRE TRIANGLE The three basic, essential elements needed for fire to exist: heat, fuel, and oxygen.

FIRESTORM An intense conflagration during which rising, heated air creates a vacuum beneath that surrounding air rushes to fill, forming extremely strong winds.

FIRE TETRAHEDRON The modern fire "triangle" that depicts the basic components necessary to a fire's existence: oxidizing agent, heat source, and reducing agent.

FIRE WALL A fire-resistant wall built to impede the spread of fire through a building.

FIRST-WATER In the mid-19th century, a claim would be made on a water source by insurance-company firefighters to prevent other firefighters from using the same source; bonus payments were made to the company arriving first.

FLASHOVER The moment when temperatures in an area exceed the ignition points of nearby objects, setting them ablaze.

FLAT-HEAD AXE A sharp tool for smashing walls and roofs and used in forcible entry and ventilation.

HALLIGAN TOOL A steel tool used for prying.

HAZMAT The abbreviated term for hazardous materials, including flammable, toxic, explosive, or otherwise dangerous items.

HELITACK CREW A firefighting team that uses helicopters.

HOOK A firefighting tool used to break through materials for forcible entry or ventilation.

HOOK AND LADDER A two-part truck mounted with an aerial ladder for fire suppression and rescue. The front houses the engine and the rear has an operator for turning the back set of wheels so that the very long vehicle can negotiate heavy traffic and tight corners.

HOSE JACKET A metal fitting around a hose to temporarily repair a leak.

HOSE REEL A cart used to transport hoses to the scene of a fire.

INCENDIARY See ARSON.

INCIDENT-COMMAND SYSTEM A hierarchy created in an emergency situation to which various agencies or departments are responding.

JAWS OF LIFE® A hydraulic rescue tool used to remove the doors from a damaged vehicle, allowing access to passengers trapped inside.

JOKER The initial signal received from a box alarm.

JUMP-NET A large net into which people trapped at upper heights can jump. Stretched amongst a dozen or so people to support the weight of the jumper. Similar devices today use large air bags, but are reserved for last resort.

LADDER BELT A belt worn by a firefighter with loops or connections to secure the wearer to a ladder.

LIFE NET See JUMP-NET.

MUFFIN BELL A brass, handheld instrument used as a fire alarm in the 18th and 19th centuries.

NOMEX® The fire-resistant, synthetic, outer layer of firefighters' turnout jackets and pants.

NOZZLE A fixture at the end of a hose that controls and directs the dispersion of water or foam.

ORIGIN Where a fire starts.

OXIDIZING AGENT Any gas that supports combustion. See also FIRE TETRAHEDRON.

PASS Personal Alert Safety System. A firefighter's monitor containing a motion sensor and that chirps to indicate the wearer's immobility.

PLANT A mechanical, electrical, or chemical device used by an arsonist to start an incendiary fire; e.g., a can of flammable liquid with a TRAILER of paper or cloth.

PLENUM An air-filled space in a structure, especially as part of a ventilation system, through which fire can travel quickly.

PROPANE A clean-burning fuel, often used to simulate various fire situations at fire-training facilities.

PYROLYSIS The release of combustible gases from an object due to heat action. See also REDUCING AGENT and FIRE TETRAHEDRON.

QUAD A combination pumper and ladder truck. See also QUINT.

QUINT A later version of the QUAD equipped with hose, deck gun, aerial ladder, some ground ladders, and light rescue equipment.

REDUCING AGENT Any substance that, through heat action, can be broken down into its constituent, flammable parts—usually gases such as hydrogen and carbon monoxide. See also PYROLYSIS and FIRE TETRAHEDRON.

ROLLOVER An eruption of flames following the ignition of gas that has collected at the top of an enclosed space.

SCALING LADDER A now-rarely used ladder for climbing up walls.

SELF-CONTAINED BREATHING APPARATUS (SCBA) An oxygen tank, face mask, and regulator that provides fresh oxygen to the wearer.

SMOKE JUMPERS Highly skilled firefighters who parachute from planes in order to fight the flames at the heart of a wildfire.

STILL ALARM A fire alarm received from a telephone, as opposed to one received from a firebox.

SUPER PUMPER A unit that pumps water from several fire hydrants simultaneously at a rate of 8,000 GPM (gallons per minute) or more.

THERMAL IMAGER A handheld device that displays different thermal levels on a screen. Used to detect bodies obscured by smoke, flames, or darkness.

THERMAL PATTERNS The burn marks that fire investigators examine for clues as to how a fire started and burned.

TOWER LADDER A truck mounted with an aerial platform used in rescue and fire-suppression efforts.

TRAILER Arson materials such as cloth or paper to increase the spread of a fire. See also PLANT.

TURNOUT GEAR A firefighter's basic clothing ensemble, which provides protection from heat, flames, smoke, and moisture.

WATER TOWER A steel tower with a hose nozzle on top that can be elevated and used in fighting a fire.

INDEX

PICTURE CREDITS

t=top, b=bottom, l=left, r=right, c=centre, b/g=background

4–160 All Side Panels: Richard Leeney/© DK Media Library
1 © Hulton/Archive
2–3 © Paul A. Souders/CORBIS
4–5 Richard Leeney/© DK Media Library
6tl Richard Leeney/© DK Media Library/Courtesy Bergen County, NJ, Law and Public Safety Institute
6tc Richard Leeney/© DK Media Library/Courtesy New York City Fire Museum
6b © The Granger Collection
7tl © Araldo de Luca/CORBIS
7tr John Heseltine/© DK Media Library
8l © The Granger Collection
8tr Richard Leeney/© DK Media Library/Courtesy New York City Fire Museum
9tc © London Fire Brigade
9bc © Frank Serrano
9r Richard Leeney/© DK Media Library/Courtesy New York City Fire Museum
10tr © The Granger Collection
10bl © DK Media Library/Courtesy New York City Fire Museum
11tr Richard Leeney/© DK Media Library/Courtesy Bergen County, NJ, Law and Public Safety Institute
11b Richard Leeney/© DK Media Library/Courtesy Seattle Fire Department
12tl Richard Leeney/© DK Media Library/Courtesy Logan Airport, East Boston, Massachusetts

12bl Richard Leeney/© DK Media Library/Courtesy Bergen County, NJ, Law and Public Safety Institute
12cr Richard Leeney/© DK Media Library/Courtesy Bergen County, NJ, Law and Public Safety Institute
13bl © Jim Zuckerman/CORBIS
13tr © Paul Colangelo/CORBIS
14–15 © Lowell Georgia/CORBIS
16 © The Granger Collection
16–17 © Historical Picture Archive/CORBIS
18tl © The Granger Collection
18tr © City of Westminster Archive Centre, London, UK/Bridgeman Art Library
18bl Richard Leeney/© DK Media Library/Courtesy New York City Fire Museum
18–19 © DK Media Library
19cl © Michael Nicholson/CORBIS
19tc © Historical Picture Archive/CORBIS
19cr © The Art Archive/London Museum/Eileen Tweedy
20t © The Granger Collection
20b © North Wind Picture Archives
21t © The Art Archive/Museo Correr Venice/Dagli Orti
21b © Bettmann/CORBIS
22–23 © The Granger Collection
23t © North Wind Picture Archives
23b © Bettmann/CORBIS
24–25 © Chicago Historical Society
25t © North Wind Picture Archives
26–27 © Museum of the City of New York/CORBIS
27t © CORBIS
28 © Missouri Historical Society
29top Courtesy of The Bostonian Society/Old State House
29b © The Granger Collection
30l © Chicago Historical Society
30r Courtesy Eastland Memorial Society
31tc Chicago Historical Society

31b Courtesy Eastland Memorial Society
31br © Bettmann/CORBIS
32top © AP Photo
32b © Chicago Historical Society
33t,c © Guildhall Library
33b © Angelo Hornak/CORBIS
34l © Bettmann/CORBIS
34r © Brooklyn Historical Society
35l © Private Collection /Bridgeman Art Library
35r © The Granger Collection
36t © AP Photo/Las Vegas Sun
36b © Bettmann/CORBIS
36–37 © AP Photo/Las Vegas Sun
37ri © AP Photo/Saxon
38 © Bettmann/CORBIS
38 inset © AP Photo
39 © Garry Williams/AP Photo
40–41 © Bettmann/CORBIS
41 © The Illustrated London News Picture Library London, UK/Bridgeman Art Library
42 © The Mariner's Museum, Newport News, VA
42–43 © The Mariner's Museum, Newport News, VA
43 © Museum of the City of New York
44–45 © Leslie's Illustrated
46t Courtesy Bayonne Police Department
46b © AP Photo/Asbury Park Press
47 inset © AP Photo
47b/g © AFP/CORBIS
48–49 © San Francisco Historical Society
49 © CORBIS
50t © Bettmann/CORBIS
50b © Kansas State Historical Society
51t © CORBIS
51b © The Granger Collection
52–53 © Bettmann/CORBIS
53t © CORBIS
53br © Reuters NewMedia Inc./CORBIS
54t © Ken Barnedt/Missoulian
54b © Historical Photographs, University of Idaho Library

55l © Historical Photographs, University of Idaho Library
55c © DK Media Library
55r Courtesy Forest History Service
56bl © Joseph Sohm; ChromoSohm Inc./CORBIS
56tc © CORBIS
56br © Historical Photographs, University of Idaho Library
57cl © Raymond Gehman/ CORBIS
57 inset © Jonathan Blair/CORBIS
57b/g © Raymond Gehman/ CORBIS
58–59 © Raymond Gehman/ CORBIS
60 inset © Eric Risberg/AP Photo
60b/g © David J. Cross/TimePix
61b/g © Charles O'Rear/CORBIS
61cl © AFP/CORBIS
61bc © AFP/CORBIS
61br Geoff Brightling/© DK Media Library
62top © Museum of the City of New York/CORBIS
62b © Underwood & Underwood/CORBIS
63 © Underwood & Underwood/CORBIS
64tl © UNITE Archives, Kheel Center, Cornell University
64tr © The Granger Collection
64b © Collection of the New York Historical Society
65 © The Granger Collection
66 © Collection of the New York Historical Society
67tl,bl Museum of the City of New York
67tr,br © Collection of the New York Historical Society
68top Museum of the City of New York
68b © AP Photo/ Susan Vera of The News & Observer
69tl © AP Photo/John Cetrino
69cl © AP Photo/Steven Senne
69b/g © AP Photo/Matt York
70 © AP Photo
71t © AP Photo

ACKNOWLEDGMENTS

AUTHOR'S ACKNOWLEDGMENTS

A great deal of information was collected when putting this book together. Some of the material came from individuals and some from people in organizations. In all cases, however, it was sincerely appreciated.

The people and organizations are listed here in alphabetical order: Prof. Asla Aydintasbas; Bergen County, NJ Fire Academy; Bostonian Society; Center for Maine History; Cleveland, OH Public Library; Roger Conant; Connecticut Historical Society; Gerald J. DeBenedette; Chief Craig Dufford, Livingston, NJ Fire Department; Glenn L. Floyd; Forest History Society; James W. Hanson; Historical Society of Western Pennsylvania; Illinois Historical Society; Chief Joseph F. Mauro, Jr., (Ret.), Park Ridge, NJ Fire Department; Ms. Hollis Mershon; Minnesota Historical Society; Missouri Historical Society; Museum of the City of New York; National Archives of Canada; New Brunswick, Canada Provincial Archives; New Jersey Historical Society; New Orleans, LA Public Library; New York City Fire Museum; New York City Fire Department Press Office; Paris, Texas Public Library; James R. Pfafflin, Ph.D.; Philadelphia Historical Society; Richmond, VA Historical Society; San Francisco, CA Historical Center; Gerald P. Scala, Esq.; Seattle. WA Public Library; South Carolina Historical Society; Southgate, KY Public Library; Symtron Systems Inc.; US Fire Administration and National Fire Academy; US Forest Service; John West; Westchester County, NY Public Library; and Janice Wilson, Esq.

And, not to be forgotten, there was a great working relationship with the people at DK Publishing, to include Barbara Berger, a dedicated workaholic who supervised the entire project, edited and wrote a great deal of text, and (somehow) deciphered the copy I submitted on computer disks; Michelle Baxter, design editor, whose creativity and efforts resulted in a terrific visual presentation; Jennifer Williams who showed her excellent writing and editing skills; Tina Vaughan, Valerie Buckingham, and Dirk Kaufman for overseeing book design and production; and LaVonne Carlson and Chuck Wills for their ultimately successful labors in turning an idea into reality.

PUBLISHER'S ACKNOWLEDGMENTS

DK Publishing would like to thank the following people for their invaluable help:

Jack Gottschalk, for bringing this important project to DK, and for sharing his knowledge of fire history; Tracy Armstead, for her constant enthusiasm and endless days and nights of picture research; Richard Leeney for his tireless efforts behind the camera that produced such beautiful work in such a short space of time; Josephine and Katherine Yam and all the team at Colourscan for the breathtaking speed in which they reproduced this book; Larry Rauch and his staff at the Bergen County, New Jersey, Law and Public Safety Institute, for their kindness, cooperation, and so graciously opening their facilities to us; B.B. Baker, Charlie Steinel, Brett "Spooge" Paladino, and Scott Paladino and the Wyckoff Fire Department, for their generosity of time and knowledge; we are deeply grateful to Louis Orotelli, marketing manager, and his staff at Symtron Systems Inc., for their time, information, and stunning training images; at the New York City Fire Museum, Curator Peter Rothenberg, for his explications and seemingly endless wisdom on the museum collection and firefighting history, and Director Joann Kay and her staff, for opening the museum to us; Ira Pande, Kajori Aikat, Kiran Mohan, at DK India for their fleet assistance with the Mandi Dabwali fire photographs and text; Rhiannon Cackett, at the Bruce Castle Museum; Andy Davies and his team for their constant support; Jason Kalua, Tishman Speyer Properties, for explaining many fine points on firefighting techniques and equipment; Stanley Michalski at GAI Consultants, for sharing his photographs and personal expertise on coal fires; Bill Batzkall and Michael Mason for photographs, CDs, and kind cooperation; and Corine Lesnes, at Le Monde, for her time and efforts in supplying hard-to-find information on the 5–7 Disco fire and Victoria Williams for translating it. We are also deeply grateful to the following individuals and organizations for providing additional photography: Chrissy McIntyre and David Hans Plotkin, at Corbis; Cynthia Sanford, of the Brooklyn Historical Society; Karl Sup, President and Cofounder, Eastland Memorial Society; Erika Kuhlman, of the University of Idaho Special Collections and Archives; Michael Shulman of Magnum Photos; Ed Whitley and Caroline Jennings, of The Bridgeman Art Library; Margie Steinmann, at the Art Archive; Angela Troisi, of Daily News Pix, and Chris Coulter, of Pier3.org.